WAHL
History of Wahl Clipper Corp

History of Wahl Clipper Corporation
Copyright © January 2005
ISBN: 0-9765885-0-1 Hardbound
ISBN: 0-9765885-1-X Perfectbound

John F. Wahl
P.O. Box 723
Sterling, Illinois 61081

Cover Photo: Sue Wahl

Printed in the United States of America

I want to dedicate this book to the following:

To my Father, who taught me to enjoy hard work, to have an open mind and use it creatively. If only he had lived a few more years.

To my Mother, whose love, patience, strength and endurance came through in raising four distinctly different sons and one daughter.

To my late wife, Margaret, whose sense of humor made life so special, and my children—Rosemary, Greg, Joan, Ellen, Laurie, and Mark. You are one of the reasons I worked so hard to make the company as successful as it is today.

To my wife, Sue, without her encouragement, support and work on this project, I would have never completed this time consuming undertaking.

Thank you to Roger Johnson who dedicated so much of his time in helping me write this book.

Thank you to Collin and Christina Paule Canright of Canright & Paule, Inc. for your organizational help.

Jack Wahl

CONTENTS

THE INTRODUCTION

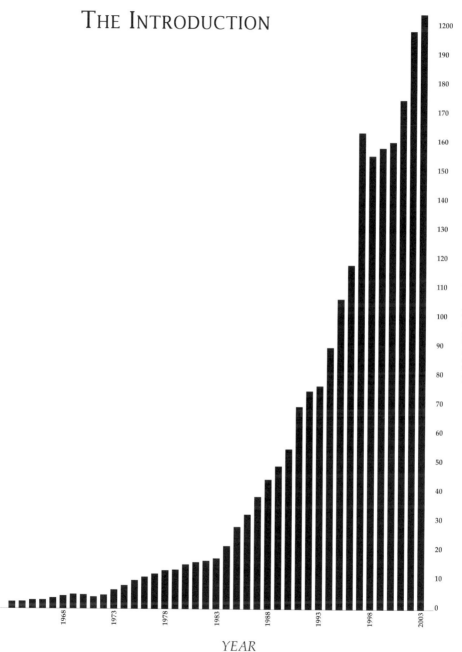

YEAR

SALES HISTORY

Throughout my career, as with any career, I have been faced with choices. If company results are any indication, I made some pretty good choices, as my father made good choices in founding the company, and as our ancestors made good choices when they decided to immigrate to Sterling, Illinois, from Oppenweiler, Germany, in the middle of the 19th century.

In German, our family name means "choice" and a derivative means "well, justly, rightly." I believe that that's the way to run a business: good, just choices. I have striven to make good choices, and if our company's performance these past 25, years is any guide, I have succeeded on more than a few occasions. Since my father, Leo J. Wahl, founded the company in 1919, Wahl Clipper Corporation has:

- Remained privately owned and operated
- Increased sales for each of the past 25 years
- Earned a profit in each of the 85 years of our existence
- Found a way to work with nepotism
- Operated U.S. plant for more than 25 years without a layoff
- Enjoyed good labor relations after decertifying to a non-union operation in the 1970s and surviving a 26 week strike
- Instituted pension, profit sharing, 401k, executive SARS and perfect attendance plans
- Embraced globalization to become an international corporation with manufacturing bases on three continents
- Outperformed the U.S. economy during several recessions and downturns

This book is my personal account of Wahl Clipper Corporation and how we have grown into the World's Largest Manufacture of Electric Hair Clippers. It's also my personal account of the people who make any business work: employees, suppliers, vendors, and, most important, customers. Wahl Clipper is and has always been a people business. Our products are designed to solve people problems, and it takes teams of hard working people to get the job done.

Finally, this book is my account of how we did it all. The Wahl Clipper Ship, as I often referred to the company, is propelled by sails on two main masts:

1. Vision and Invention
2. Family and Community

With the energy harnessed by those masts, Wahl Clipper Corporation has succeeded as a manufacturer in a market, the Midwestern United States, in which others have failed and using means that others have abandoned. In 2004, we operate a state-of-the-art facility in Sterling, Illinois, and count it's employees, our people, as our greatest asset, and we are still a vertically integrated manufacturer that makes almost every component we use in our products. We have become a global manufacturer and in 2005 will celebrate our 10th year manufacturing a portion of our product line in our own facility in China, well ahead of the current investment boom.

Vision and Invention

My father, company founder Leo J. Wahl, was an inventor and a businessman. Invention is the art of seeing something—a vision—and making it real, making it live. My father played with electro magnetic motors and saw a possible application that people would buy and he patented it. He saw the clunky and cumbersome clippers used by barbers in the first decades of the 20th century, and he saw a use for the motors he had been playing with for years: hand-held electric hair clippers.

From that vision came the invention that has driven the company's growth ever since. Making another very wise choice my father licensed a competitor who had copied his product. These Royalty payments gave funding to Wahl Clipper Corporation as they built our factory. My Father built the company from his first patented invention on the premise that we make products people will buy, products people use to make themselves feel good and look good. Wahl Clipper may be a manufacturer but, at root, it's a people business.

I, too, had a vision for the company and the people who work for it. When I took over as president in 1977, I saw the opportunities to increase our sales, markets, and product lines. I generated, and the board approved, a three-pronged short- and long-term expansion plan:

1. Expand and improve product line
2. Expand and improve sales people
3. Expand and improve sales territory

Then I went about selling the company on my vision, first to our board of directors and then to our managers and workers. It worked, and it worked because, if we did anything, we worked harder and longer than the others. Our success in making a vision live rested in large part on our willingness to do the last 10% of the work. It was in completing that last 10% where we beat the odds, our competition, and often both.

Innovation is a corollary to invention. Wahl Clipper has had to innovate throughout its history to overcome the trials that every business faces. During the labor unrest we faced in the late 60s, we bucked the trend and became a non-union shop. We did the same as globalization began to stress domestic manufacturing. Becoming an international company was our only real answer, which we realized at a time when smaller companies seldom looked beyond their borders.

The ultimate strength of the company, I believe, lies in its ability to survive beyond its founders. It's said that many family-owned businesses either do not survive beyond the third generation or do not remain family companies. As Chairman of the Board, I am retired from active operations within the corporation. My son, Gregory S. Wahl, has taken over the reins of the corporation as president and CEO and is doing an excellent job.

Indeed, it's a testament to our current success and leadership that the company has progressed beyond my own vision. Five years ago,

I could not have and did not envision the company as it is today. At our Sterling, Illinois plant, we have undergone a transformation through automation and gained an increase in productivity that is nothing short of revolutionary.

You can stay competitive for a while by outsourcing components and by providing quicker delivery of higher quality products sold under strong brand names. Made in USA still has some sales appeal but you need to bring out new and better designed products. If not covered by patents, beware of quick knock offs.

These are some of the ways for American companies to have an opportunity to stay relatively competitive with China and India, where the inexpensive labor costs are the competitive advantage, and will continue to be important as overseas manufacturers become increasingly more efficient.

Family and Community

Good Choices is a story of a family and an invention but, at the same time, it's a story of economic development in the communities of the Midwestern United States. The Wahl family has been tied to Northwestern Illinois since 1856 and has made choices to move, stay in place, or move forward with the times. Some of the choices were fortuitous, such as my brother Warren walking away from the crash of a military plane he was flying, and me doing dangerous duty on a Guinea Pig mine sweeper in the Inland Sea of Japan at the close of World War II and surviving. Others...

Wahl Clipper is family owned and family operated. At times it has been difficult but we have navigated nepotism through innovative incentive and compensation plans based on an individual's performance.

I started the job of president and CEO mindful of my responsibility to my stockholders and family members. As I grew into the job, however, I realized that I had a responsibility not only to pursue a profit but also to try to create a community in which employees can achieve their best potential. I worked hard to try to provide compensation incentives and bonuses for individual senior managers, company mid level management, and factory employees alike. Some of the individuals I see and greet as I walk through the factory today are those I have known for more than 30 years. Something here has worked.

One thing that we had to make work was teamwork. Although Wahl Clipper is a family business, built around the invention of a talented founder and extended through the efforts of his sons and grandsons, the success of the company goes far beyond the Wahl family. The story of Wahl Clipper is also a story of successful teamwork.

When we first put my growth plan into action, I realized it would take highly skilled individuals working together as teams to reach our goals. During that period of rapid growth, I hired numerous other strong managers to get the team right. It was a thrill—the thrill of victory of participating in a team effort to sell and service better than anyone in the world. We maintained high productivity with our short chain of command, with owner operators. With a good administrative assistant I was able to stay current and driving all of our entrepreneurial activities.

Sometimes teamwork took a back seat to natural competition between the Consumer and Professional division of the company, and that helped motivate everyone to work harder. At the same time, the competition between divisions had its costs. Cooperation could have been better in a number of instances.

As the company grew with its community in Sterling, it became apparent to me and the Board that its continuous growth depended on broadening our community to the world at large. As a result, Wahl Clipper was a pioneer in exporting and overseas production, especially for a company of its size. When other companies were experiencing the first ravaging of manufacturing in the Midwest, during the 1980s, when the term Rust Belt became a household media label, we were starting to look overseas both for product sales growth and manufacturing cost efficiencies.

By 1991, Wahl Clipper Corporation had been awarded the prestigious President's E Award for success in exporting by the U.S. Department of Commerce. Wahl was only the eighth Illinois Corporation to receive the award since its inception in 1961. By the early 1990s, the company realized more than 25% of its growing revenue through exports and was exporting to more than 70 countries. We had our share of failures, with a difficult start in Europe and deals that never came to pass in East Germany and Russia. But we saw our competition sourcing all of their products in the Far East and knew we had to do some of the same. However we wanted full control and ownership of any company we would consider for sourcing of our core product line. With ownership we could hold the quality to Wahl specifications. We wanted full control of the manufacturing technology and processes. Without control there is no way we could prevent transfer of intellectual property. In short, we would have eventually trained our competitor. Our Final goal in China is to be the #1 manufacturer of China-made products sold to 1.2 billion Chinese that need haircuts.

As we have since the beginning, we simply worked harder and focused on doing the last 10% well.

John F. Wahl
August 2004
Sterling, Illinois

CHAPTER 1
FOUNDING FATHERS

The road which led to Wahl Clipper Corporation becoming the World's largest manufacturer of electric hair clippers began when a Sterling High School junior, Leo J. Wahl, experimented with an electro-magnetic motor.

1. And a Young Man Shall Lead Them

In his lively history of the Wahl family, In the Beginning, Michael, Msgr Raymond J. Wahl notes that the family name means "choice." The German word wahl goes back to the Old High German word, wellan, welen, meaning "to choose." Interestingly, the English adverb, well, has its origins in the Old English word, wyllan, meaning "to wish" and in the Old High German, wela, meaning "well, justly, rightly." And so it is, the story of Leo Wahl is the story of a family that has lived up to its name and from generation to generation has shown a remarkable capacity for choosing justly, rightly, and well.

When Leo Wahl's grandfather Frederick came to America in the 1850's, he established a pattern that the American branch of the Wahl family has followed ever since: individual initiative and family cooperation. With their old world heritage of industry on the farm and in the shop, the Wahl's recognized that the New World was a good place for families that worked hard and well. In their century and a half in America, the Wahl's have prospered through an adroit mix of persistence, patience, and planning, punctuated by bold, bodacious moves.

Msgr Wahl's history suggests that Frederick was simply doing what Wahl's had always done, except now he was doing it in the New World and not in Oppenweiler, Germany. This village in the state of Baden-Wurtenberg stands on a line between Brussels and Munich, about 270 miles southeast of the former, and 100 miles northwest of the latter. A medieval castle stands on a hill overlooking it. Hot water springs, well known for their restorative powers, are nearby, and so too are the forests, which have long been useful as well as beautiful. Centuries ago, villagers burned their wood to produce coke and sold it for fuel. The Wahl family and Oppenweiler went back a long way, to 1747 at least. It was then, according to church records, that Michael and Magdalena Wahl had a son, named him Jacob, and had him baptized a Lutheran—standard practice in Oppenweiler since 1600 when the townspeople ended their part in the religious wars by voting to become Evangelicals. For the Wahl's, Catholicism was to be a New World, twentieth century innovation.

Three generations and ninety years later, Frederick was born on February 8, 1835, the first of six children that Matthias and Rosina Wahl were to have. Matthias (1809-1888) was a farmer whose family, like the Carnegies in Scotland, also worked in the cottage weaving industry. In 1848, when Frederick left school and went to work for his father weaving linen, Andrew Carnegie was on his way to America to make his fortune, or at least survive a little better than in Scotland, where the family business had been crushed beneath the weight of mechanization and superior economic combination. The Wahls were not ready to relocate just yet, but their time was coming. When Frederick turned 16, his father hired him out as a hand on a local farm for about $10 a year. Perhaps, Frederick's brother or one of his sisters was ready to take his seat at the loom, or maybe the industrial revolution had found its way to the forests and rolling hills of Baden-Wurtenberg. Certainly, the castle in Oppenweiler, once a refuge against enemy soldiers, now could not protect villagers from the invasion of modernity—the industrial revolution and the economic and political upheaval that went with it.

Times were hard. Though the Wahls were a large family, there were not enough hands to make ends meet. Germany had spent a long time recovering from the Napoleonic Wars and now the revolutions of 1848 convulsed it. Work and food were both scarce, and enterprising young men like Frederick chafed for new opportunities. The forests of Germany were not so black that he and his compatriots could not find a way out. The whole village stirred with glowing reports of opportunities in the New World. After three years as a farm hand, the 19-year old Frederick got permission from his parents to go to America and build his future. The Wahls themselves already had family there. Matthias had a sister who was married and living in Warren, Ohio and there were cousins living in Ohio and New York.

And so Frederick would make his way to America, get a start there, and then bring his family after him.

Borrowing money from his father and another friend, Frederick left Oppenweiler on April 22, 1853 for America. He had company; seventeen other local people were also going. They traveled by wagon to Dirrleich, where they took a train across the Rhine to Strasbourg and then on to Paris and LeHavre. There, in May, they sailed for America. The voyage to New York took forty days, and young Wahl battled sea-sickness the first six days and suffered another bout a few weeks later when a storm pummeled their ship and hurled three of the crew overboard. In New York, a cousin named Smith bought him a $25 train ticket that took him to his aunt in Warren, Ohio, a town about 50 miles southeast of Cleveland. When he arrived there in late June 1853, Frederick found work as a farm hand, making 75 cents a day including room and board. Even after the fall harvest, he was able to find work and soon he had made enough to pay back those who had financed his emigration.

His letters from the New World made believers of his family. Shortly after he had gotten a farm job that paid him $96 a year including board, he received a letter from his parents telling him that they would like to come over with his brother and sisters, but they had no money. Getting an advance from his boss and borrowing from his cousins in New York and Ohio, Frederick was able to get just enough money together to bring his family to America. They landed in New York in July 1854, with just enough money for railroad tickets to Cleveland, where the Wahl's arrived with only $1 to their name. Leaving his family there, Matthias journeyed the rest of the way to Warren to meet his first-born and be re-united with his sister. Borrowing some more money from his uncle, Frederick brought the family to Warren, where they rented a log cabin, Mathias and his three oldest children found jobs, and the Wahl's went to work building a new life in a new land.

2. If Hugh Builds It, They'll Come

Matthias Wahl and family remained in Ohio two years; then Frederick again led them west. By then, he had paid off all but $40 of the money he had borrowed to bring his family from Germany. In the spring of 1856, he and a friend set out for Whiteside County in Illinois, where the two young men took the most direct way west and traveled overland, probably passing through Cleveland, where John D. Rockefeller had graduated from high school the year before and was working as a bookkeeper-clerk in a brokerage firm. We have an idea of what the trip was like from James Overholser, who in 1920, when he was the mayor of Sterling, recalled the journey he and his family made to Illinois 66 years earlier. In three Conestoga wagons and one Pennsylvania buggy, the Overholsers left eastern Ohio on March 31, 1854, and schooned across the prairie at a clip of 20 miles a day. A 40-mile stretch of swamp west of Chicago slowed them down a bit but not much. They slogged through it in three days and arrived in Sterling on May 4, 1854. They found a frontier village with a downtown consisting of the post office, a blacksmith shop, and two stores, one for hardware and one for groceries.

Overholser noticed Sterling's business district, or lack of it, but other settlers were less mercantile in their view of the hamlet. Indeed it was the view itself that decided Hezekiah Brink, Sterling's founder, to settle here in the first place. When he came west in 1834, he had all of northern Illinois to pick from and went almost to the Mississippi scouting land. Evidently, he still had not made up his mind when he and his two companions journeyed back from Prophetstown to Dixon along the same river route that Lincoln and his Kaskaskian irregulars took two years before when they went off to fight in the Black Hawk War. With twelve or fifteen miles left to go, they stopped for a rest on some high ground above a river that the Indians called Sinnissippi, and the white man translated as Rock River. Just west of where Riverside Cemetery now stands, Brink stood on a bluff overlooking the river and miles and miles of land that stretched east and south and west. He looked, and that was when he knew, "the man who could not be content to spend his days in a spot like this would not be happy in any locality this side of paradise." He went back to Dixon, staked his claim, and returned to the area to build a cabin and spend his winter. In the spring, he went back to Indiana and brought his family to their new home. It was not long before they had neighbors, families, like his, Yankees from the northeast, educated and industrious and, on this point at least, inclined to agree with Brink.

Sixteen years later, another settler echoed Brink's sentiments. After her family arrived in Sterling from Lancaster County, Pennsylvania, young Ann Landis wrote in her diary, "This is a beautiful country to behold. Sterling is situated on a high bank of Rock River, impossible to overflow." Ann and her friends loved to "walk to the river," and there, where Sinnissippi Park now stands, they "saw the beautiful crab apple trees in bloom, which made a sweet perfume along the river. We also saw the sloughs, cliffs, bluffs, caves, island, and Indian Mounds." Eight decades later, another early settler, Emma Wilson Edwards, whose father was a longtime friend of Lincoln, also remembered Sterling's natural splendor.

> The river was clear as crystal, and we could see the big flat stones on the bottom…All this beauty of nature was entrancing. With such extremely productive soil added to the charm of the place, it is not any wonder that there developed here such a set of great pioneers. Those early settlers appreciated nature. There was a wealth of beauty in the trees and water and flowers and sky. There was such a sense of safety in the care of nature, a part of the blessedness of those times. Life was sweet and simple and well worth living. Its restfulness lingers with us still.

A memoir of W. W. Davis, local historian and man of letters, offers a little craggier view of the pioneer village that he and his father first visited in 1851. Writes Davis,

> Sterling stood high and dry on its limestone hills along the river, with a population of 200, in houses scattered over the prairie and west of the courthouse (on Broadway Avenue). It was a 'green country town,' as William Penn wrote of Philadelphia in its infant days.

Very likely, Frederick Wahl had the craggiest view of all, for when he reached Sterling, he had only two more dollars in his pocket than his father did when he reached Cleveland two years earlier. Survival, not scenery, was on his mind. He had to find work. Like Mr. John D. Rockefeller, his Baptist counterpart in Cleveland, the young Lutheran from Germany also kept careful accounts. "When I started West," he recalled a half century later, I had $25.00 saved, but when I reached Sterling, I only had $3.00 left." I went and boarded at a hotel for $4.00 a week, but I only stayed here 3 days." In other times and other places, Frederick's situation would have been dire, but in the spring of 1856 Sterling was a worker's market. "I went out in the country," wrote Frederick, "and was hired for 1 year at $190." Sixteen dollars a month kept the wolves away, but Frederick did not have to settle for that. "I only stayed here 3 days when I came back to town and worked for Doctor Pennington for $20.00 a month from April until Fall."

This Sterling was not the sleepy little hamlet that had greeted Ann Landis or James Overholser just a few years before. It was a booming little burg, and Frederick Wahl was too shrewd to have happened on it just by accident. More than likely he had read an advertisement about Sterling in a Cleveland or some other eastern newspaper, or he had heard about the little town from people who had read the paper. Sterling in 1856 was coming off its booming year and was beginning to capitalize on its many advantages.

Sterling not only stood on high ground. That ground and all the land around it contained some of the blackest, richest, most fruitful earth in the world. It was making Doctor Pennington, who hired Frederick, a very wealthy man. He owned several hundred acres of land north of Sterling, where he had a nursery, orchard, and fields of wheat and corn. Farmers who came to the region with a little cash found great opportunities. When the Overholsers arrived, the price of most farmland was between $2.50 and $5.00 an acre; however, improved land with timber could go for as much as $10 an acre. Mayor Overholser's father, Martin, was one of the early arrivals, and he wasted little time buying the better acreage.

Sterling also had waterpower and raw materials for industry. It was situated on the Rock River, where the river fell not once but twice. Rock River Rapids, as they were called, were a hazard for river travel, but a haven for manufacturing, which for much of the 19th century depended on using falling water to turn mill wheels. The accessibility of raw materials would make Sterling a good place to set up a shop or factory. Abundant forestland would provide wood for furniture, buggies, wagons, and caskets. Local shops would produce leather for boots and harnesses. Grain for Local distilleries and mills would be right outside the city limits.

What the town and countryside could not produce, the railroad would deliver, for Sterling also had location. It was 120 miles due west of Chicago. Of course, this geographical fact did not mean that much in 1834 when Hezekiah Brink stood on the brink and was stirred with a sterling revelation. Within two decades Chicago would begin its enormous growth and the iron horse would connect it with the rest of the continent.

The man who enabled Sterling to industrialize and connect with Chicago was Hugh Wallace (1812-1864), the area's first lawyer and the architect of Sterling's Booming Year. When Wallace moved his wife and family from Lancaster County, Pennsylvania to northern Illinois in 1837, Hezekiah Brink welcomed him to his little settlement of six families. Where Brink and, his community was situated, on the scenic land above the falls, Wallace shrewdly staked a claim to land a mile or so to the west, along the second falls. He built his cabin near the river on what is now First Avenue and the railroad viaduct. The lawyer from the Keystone state began his life on the frontier as a farmer, but in time the land that he tilled would become Sterling's new downtown. As more people settled in Whiteside County, Wallace returned to his law practice and got elected to the state legislature in the late 1840s. There, he secured passage of an act that authorized the Sterling Hydraulic Company, a group that he had helped organize, to build a dam and millrace on the lower falls.

Wallace's vision was 20-20; his timing impeccable. In the late 1840s, Chicago developer, William Butler Ogden had started the Galena and Chicago Union Railroad and was slowly extending it westward. When W. W. Davis and his father visited Sterling in 1851, they stayed with their old friend from Lancaster County, Hugh Wallace. At one point, their host stretched out a map on the dining room table, noted that Sterling was situated on a straight line due west of Chicago and declared that there was no other place for the railroad to come but right through Sterling.

Of course, Hugh Wallace was not one to leave anything to chance. By the time the Hydraulic Company had gotten the financing and had begun building the dam, the railroad stretched halfway across northern Illinois, but shaky finances and uncertainty about the rest of the route, left the line stalled in Dixon, 15 miles to the east of Sterling. Wallace and his fellow boosters brought in a newspaperman and started Sterling's first newspaper, whose mission was to campaign for extending the railroad through Sterling to the Mississippi. To persuade the railroad to run its tracks through Sterling rather than north of it, Wallace donated the site for the depot and got an agreement from the railroad to make Sterling one of its daily stops. The deal was done. Mr. Ogden's railroad went through Sterling and in a year reached the Father of Waters. In July 1855, with the dam and millrace almost completed, the town celebrated the arrival of *The Pioneer*, the first locomotive to come to Sterling. Among the dignitaries at the celebration was U. S. Senator, Stephen Douglas, who cut a gallant figure dancing with the local beauties at the ball that evening.

Wallace was a staunch Democrat who made his political connections work for him, his family, and his community. When Wallace left the state legislature in 1852, he secured an appointment from President Pierce to run the Federal land office in Dixon. In this post, he transformed his farm into Sterling's first real estate development. He parceled it up into lots, and sold it to industrious pioneers who wanted to get in on the ground floor of Sterling's prosperity. If the canal, millrace, railroad, and a brand new downtown were not enough, Wallace had one more gift for Sterling. In 1855, he and the Galt clan in Sterling persuaded Thomas A. Galt, his wife's nephew, to leave his prosperous dry goods store in Lancaster County and seek his fortune in the northwest. When Galt (1828-1912) relocated that summer, he came by way of Springfield and brought a letter of introduction that gained him an audience with Abraham Lincoln. Young Galt, who became an inventor, industrialist, banker, and builder of a hotel and theater, would be Sterling's leading citizen for over a half century.

With the canal and millrace, railroad and a newspaper to trumpet the march of progress, Sterling advertised itself in the Eastern newspapers as a booming new manufacturing center in the Northwest. Frederick Wahl was not the only one taking notice, Sterling's population climbed from 250 in 1850 to 614 in 1855 and then soared to almost 3000 in 1859.

When Lincoln came to Sterling in July 1856 to stump for John C. Fremont, he met with Wallace, Thomas A. Galt (who had called on Lincoln with a letter of introduction the previous summer in Springfield) and other local leaders.

3. Like Son, Like Father

Soon, Frederick was not the only Wahl contributing to the Sterling boom. In 1855, he had made $100 working for Pennington. When his father expressed a wish and a *wyllan* to move to Sterling, his eldest son sent him his earnings to pay for a wagon and a team of horses to bring the family west. In September 1856, Matthias Wahl and his family arrived in town and joined Frederick at a house he was renting from Dr. Pennington. It was good that Frederick had his family with him. He had come down with malarial fever in September and suffered from the ague all winter, not recovering until the warm days of spring. It was a hard winter for this intrepid family. They had little money and there were no jobs.

With warm weather, the Wahl's went to work. Farmers needed hands, and the wealthy ones needed tenants to work their holdings. Matthias and Frederick farmed for Pennington and saved as much as they could. Leo Wahl's forbearers were patient, persistent men who had the courage of their calculated risks. Matthias knew that he had found his new home and set about to become a property holder himself. Slowly, steadily bettering himself, Matthias worked for Pennington for a few years and then moved to Genesee Township, about four miles northwest of Sterling. He paid off his debts, withstood the rigors of pioneer life, and found a way to thrive. His wife, Rosina, was not so resilient and died in 1862 at the age of 52, another proof of the adage about frontier Sterling: "It was a great land for horses, but hard on women."

The land was not kind to widowers either, and Matthias remarried the following year. His second wife, Catherine Kirges, also happened to be his son, Frederick's mother-in-law. On February 22, 1858, 24 year-old Frederick had married Anna Kirges, who had emigrated from Germany with her parents in 1855. Five months after their wedding, Anna's father, George Kirges had drowned. After Matthias lost his wife four years later, widow and widower were soon drawn together. They already had the connection of children and grandchildren, and now grief and loneliness forged an unbreakable bond. They were married on August 16, 1863.

With his new helpmate, Matthias persevered, working, saving and planning. In 1867, all his work was rewarded. In two transactions that year, he paid $3560 for 240 acres of farmland northwest of Sterling. He farmed for another 12 years. When he retired at the age of 70, he sold the farm to his son William and moved to Sterling where he had purchased four lots and built a home. There he lived until his death in 1888.

His will shows how well the elder Wahl had prospered in America. Thirty-four years after he arrived in Cleveland with one dollar in his pocket, he left an estate worth a few thousand dollars. His will provided $1500 for his second wife, another $1000 for one daughter, and the balance of the estate to be divided up among his sons Frederick, and William, and two other daughters. (A fourth daughter must have been the black sheep, for she received all of $5 from Matthias.)

4. Going Home Again

Like his father, Frederick Wahl, also did very well in the Sterling area but, before he did, his restless, adventuring spirit took him further west. In the first four years of their marriage, Frederick and Anna had two daughters and they managed to get by although not to Frederick's liking. Low farm prices only allowed him to pay off his debts and save $100. Seeing greener pastures on the other side of the Mississippi, he moved his young family to Osceola, Iowa, where land was cheaper—$ 3 an acre. On the far edge of the frontier, where the economy was more rudimentary, Frederick found farming even more hazardous than in Illinois. He recalled later,

> The times were hard. All the banks went broke, and the war broke out. Money was hard to get, crops were at low prices corn 10 cents, hay 2 cents, and wheat 35 cents. Butter and eggs, you could give away. The little money I had was no good. I couldn't even buy a loaf of bread with it. I went to teaming to make a living.

Frederick did well enough to support his family, which now numbered five with the birth of William on December 7, 1862. As the North's economy boomed to meet the demands of war, conditions improved, even out in Iowa. In 1863, when the war finally turned the North's way, Wahl fenced in his forty acres and built a small house there. The next year, he was a farmer as well as a teamster and brought in a small crop. In 1865, when Frederick took his family back to Sterling to see the grandparents, he heeded their advice and decided to move back. With the birth of Frederick that January, he now had four young mouths to feed. Sterling looked more hospitable than Osceola, and it had grown, too, and would grow even more. True, the millrace was still largely unoccupied, but it did have a couple of flour mills and the railroad station was but a hundred yards away. And, thanks to Hugh Wallace who died the year before, (God rest his soul), passenger trains and freight trains still stopped there, to unload and load and would do so for another century.

Fortunately for the Frederick Wahl family, Iowa had done a little prospering itself and was beginning to grow. When Frederick and the family returned to Osceola, they only needed two weeks to sell their farm, and they received a rather handsome price too—$ 600.

The Iowa years show Frederick to be a good farmer and a shrewd businessman. He worked hard, got a fruitful yield, and like any good farmer was tight-lipped about any trace of prosperity—in his memoirs he sounds like any Illinois or Iowa farmer: just barely getting by. Nonetheless, he made ends meet with his moonlighting and also did well enough to improve his land and make a 400% profit on it in four short years. Even better, he had the gift for being in the right place at the right time. He had arrived in Sterling in 1856 when it was coming off its booming year, and ten years later he returned just in time for its post-war quantum leap.

Sterling did not really start growing until 1867, when Sterling businessman, Augustus Smith, who had made a fortune filling government contracts for mittens and gloves during the Civil War, bought land on the south side of the Rock River. He built a millrace there and founded a new city, Rock Falls. The brilliant, mercurial Mr. Smith was a musician and poet, industrialist and booster, and thoroughly quixotic visionary. He had a flair for promoting, and he could move real estate. Offering cheap land and factory space for start-up industries, Smith quickly drew new businesses to his burg and also to Sterling. His first great coup came when he enticed Hugh Wallace's cousin, Thomas A Galt and his partner George Tracy, to move their farm implement factory and door shop over to the south side of the river. There, the partners founded Keystone Manufacturing, which for the next 30 years was one of the nation's leading farm machinery manufacturers. By 1870, the Twin Cities had established themselves as a manufacturing center. On both sides of the river, water was powering factories that ground flour and turned out tools, machinery, buggies and wagons.

Although the Panic of 1873 ruined Smith, he had done his work. The industrial center envisioned by Wallace was well on its way. Perhaps Smith's greatest gift to the community was not the businesses he lured there, but the people who flocked to Sterling and Rock Falls in search of jobs and new opportunities, not only in the factories on the river front but also in the shops and stores that supported these industries. Three of the Twin Cities greatest industrialists, Washington Dillon and John and Edwin Lawrence, all came to the Twin Cities after the Civil War to run hardware stores. In the late 1870s, they got into manufacturing, Dillon jumping into the brand new barbed wire industry and the Lawrence brothers making builders hardware and inventing the first steel barn door roller. With Galt, Dillon, and the Lawrences leading the way, the Twin Cities began to develop a concentration in hardware that by the turn of the century would become even more pronounced.

Also arriving in these years were two other immigrants: John Benson and his wife, who came from Sweden by way of Chicago, where their first child was born in 1869; and Herman Bittorf who came from Germany and would marry another German immigrant and start a family. The sons of these two families, Will Benson and Herman and Louis Bittorf, would be the first local boys to work their way up through a factory (Lawrence Brothers) and start a manufacturing firm of their own, National Manufacturing. They typified the spirit of improvement, which Lincoln celebrated, "The hired laborer of yesterday labors on his own account today and will hire others to labor for him tomorrow. Advancement—improvement in condition—is the order of things in a society of equals."

Frederick Wahl also fulfilled this vision. Sweat and stick-to-itiveness put him in the position to be daring when the time was right. In post-war Sterling, he saw his opportunity and quite literally bet the farm on it. In his first two years back in the area, he rented a farm and, though he "made a comfortable living," he was not about to rest there. In 1868, another Smith, Aeterm Smith, sold him a 160-acre farm in Deer Grove, south of Rock Falls. The sale price was $17 an acre, at 10% interest and no down payment. At first it looked like a bad bet. That first year, "a prairie fire came and burned everything except the house, my new harvester, some straw, 5 hogs, and a low stable." Wahl thought he was ruined, but Smith gave him another chance, probably figuring it was his only hope of getting a return on his investment. Smith's patience was rewarded. The crops and the prices were good next year, and in 1870 Wahl was able to exchange his farm for an 80-acre farm that had much better land. When The Chicago, Burlington, and Quincy Railroad arrived in Deer Grove the following year, it was clear that Frederick Wahl had chosen very wisely. The road of progress was running through the Rock River Valley, and he was on it. When the swamps south of Rock Falls were drained, he was able to secure some very fertile land.

It was more than good luck, though, that enabled Frederick to improve his holdings and prosper. That new harvester which survived the 1868 fire indicates that he was invested in his own productivity, and he equipped himself to make good use of the good land that came his way. The farm machines produced by Keystone in Rock Falls, McCormick Works in Chicago, and a host of other Midwest companies were revolutionizing agriculture and making America the breadbasket of the world. Illinois farmers had moved far beyond subsistence. As Frederick's Memoirs demonstrate, their livelihood, including their harvester payments, depended on bringing their crops to market and getting the best price they could.

> In 1874, I put the 80 (rented acres) in wheat, and my 80 in corn. I let the cattle run in the prairie all summer. I made money on the wheat, which sold for $1.20 per bushel. In 1875, I took 270 acres to plow up; it being prairie. I had to plow it all up the first year. I did well the first year, as I sowed 40 acres of flax, and sold the seed for $ 1.70 a bushel. I got 600 bushels this year. The next year I raised 1800 bushels of wheat. I then bought another 40 acres at $32.00 per acre and 8 years to pay it back at 10%. In this time I was determined to make some money, so I bought another 8 acres, and hired some help; then I made some money.

He made some money. He bought more land and eventually owned 560 acres. By that time, he certainly had other people working for him and was as much a capitalist and staunch Republican as the shopkeeper or factory owner who lived in town. He became a pillar of the Deer Grove community. Over the next twenty years he served in various capacities, as road commissioner, school trustee, and school treasurer.

He was truly blessed with a happy, fruitful marriage. He and Anna had twelve children, four girls and eight boys, and they were able to grow old together, free of financial concerns. When Frederick retired in 1890 and moved to Sterling, he still owned 360 acres. He sold these to two of his sons, William and Charles, and moved into town, where he and Anna lived in the home his father had left him.

Later they built another house on an adjacent lot, and it was there they celebrated their golden wedding anniversary in 1908. Three and four generations of the Wahl family, about thirty people in all, gathered to pay tribute to their long, happy life. In the picture taken that day, fourteen year old Leo Wahl is standing in the back row, first on the left, looking like a younger version of his two uncles, Dr. Edward Wahl, fourth from the right in the third row, and Sheriff J. Frank Wahl, fourth row, second from the right. In just four years, the two uncles would go into business with their nephew making and selling his first invention. Anna lived another seven years, dying on February 6, 1915, and Frederick, the sturdy and stalwart pioneer from Oppenweiler, survived his wife by eight years, and died March 13, 1923 at a good old age of 89.

5. Will: Well on Way

Young William, Frederick's and Anna's oldest son, also had a mind of his own, and in these two years made two choices, which were decisive for his descendants, one of whom was Leo J. Wahl. On April 26, 1890, the 27 year- old, Lutheran farmer was married to Elizabeth Hein, a Catholic, at the St. Mary's Catholic Church in Tampico, a few miles southwest of Rock Falls. In an age that theologically and socially was closer to the Wars of Religion than to the September 11, 2001 War on Terrorism, the young couple must have had a love that indeed conquered all or, at the very least, all the objections and obstacles that accompanied their courtship and marriage.

At this time, the Twin Cities and surrounding countryside were as strongly Protestant as they were Republican. At the St. Johns Lutheran Church in Sterling, which Frederick Wahl attended, Reformation Sunday at the end of October was a major celebration, and the pastor's sermon that day on the significance of Luther and his 95 theses was guaranteed to be quoted at length in the Monday editions of the *Standard* and the *Gazette*. As for Catholic parishes, they were springing up throughout Northern Illinois, and they were growing. The tide of immigration was on their side, but the American Catholic Church was still two and three decades away from coming into full power as a force in American public life. These local parishes were still immigrant churches living and thriving in a state of siege. With Protestantism still dominating American culture, their survival depended on solidarity, discipline, and militant devotion to the Faith as embodied by Holy Mother Church and taught by the Pope and the Magisterium.

Before getting married, William attended six classes on Catholicism and agreed that he and Elizabeth would raise their children in the Catholic faith. This fundamental choice, combined with a third one that he made, opened William and his family and the Catholic Church to a host of consequences, as blessed as they were unforeseen. Shortly after the birth of their first child, William decided that he and his family would do better in town. In 1892, they left the farm and moved to a house on West Sixth Street in Sterling. They opened a butcher shop a few blocks away on First Avenue in downtown Sterling, which by then was attaining its current dimension of 20 square blocks north of the industrial district along the river.

William's relocation was a good career move. He was going where the people were and where the money was. Massive industrialization and the mechanization of agriculture, to which the local giant Keystone Manufacturing was a significant contributor, were revolutionizing food production and the demographics of town and country. Whiteside County reflected this shift of the population from the farm to the city. From 1870, when the Twin Cities began to industrialize in earnest, to 1890, the population of Sterling and Rock Falls grew by 62%. By contrast, the largely rural population of Whiteside County grew by 12%. In 1870, the Twin Cities accounted for 15% of the population of Whiteside County. In 1890, their share had climbed to 23.3%, and by 1930, it would be 36%. The location of Wahl's shop on First Avenue between 3rd and 4th Streets put him in the heart of downtown Sterling, which was just the right place for a shop owner to ride out the five year depression ushered in by the Panic of 1893.

Over the next four decades the Twin City economy would prove remarkably resilient during panics and depressions. Twin City industries in 1890 were amazingly diverse and included flourmills, wagon factories, farm implement shops, and even a gas engine works. However, since the founding of Lawrence Brothers and Northwestern Barb Wire in the late 1870, Sterling and Rock Falls were developing a marked concentration in hardware. Which, in the vicissitudes of the American economy between the Civil War and World War II, stood the community in good stead. While hit by panics and depressions like the rest of the nation, the Twin Cities did not hurt for as long or as hard as most areas. Their wire mill and hardware factories seemed to put it on the front edge of any economic recovery.

At their home at 5 West Sixth Street, Will and Elizabeth would raise their family—4 boys and 2 girls—buoyed by the rising tide of Catholicism in Sterling and the nation. In 1898, a half block away from their home, the newly built St. Mary's Church opened its doors. Ten years later, the Rockford Diocese was organized with Bishop Muldoon as its first bishop. In the next two decades, under the dynamic leadership of MSGR Andrew Burns and the generous support of parishioners, the two local Catholic parishes erected St. Mary's grade school and then added a high school. With the church up the block and the school across the street, the Wahls were connected to a circuit subtler and more wonderful than anything even Mr. Edison could devise. And so it was that on one fine Sunday afternoon in April in the Year of our Lord 1927, William Wahl announced that he was going for a stroll which took him to a mission service at St. Mary's Church. There, he continued his stroll by walking up the aisle to be baptized as a Catholic. When he returned home, he brought Elizabeth the good news that he too had embraced Holy Mother Church and had been embraced by her.

By this time, William Wahl was a respected businessman whose shop enjoyed a large clientele. With his sound business sense and winning disposition, Will made the most of his shop's central location. When he retired, he sold the business to his oldest son, Fred, who had helped his father at the market since graduating from eighth grade. It is said that Fred Wahl had a basement under the butcher shop, and on some busy days he would go down into the basement to catch a quick nap before the afternoon rush. One day he didn't return and they found that he had quietly passed away in his sleep.

As Jack Wahl remembers, "I remember Fred as a kidder. One day when I was just home from Navy boot camp, I was dying for a really good steak. So I went down to see Fred. I asked him to find me what he considered to be a really good steak. He argued with me and sat up on the counter about the ugliest looking piece of steak I'd seen. I told him that I was getting mad, and he proceeded to tell me that steaks are graded Commercial, Choice, and Prime, and if I wanted the best, that was Prime. He then gave me Prime and proceeded to tease me about it every time he would see me."

When Will Wahl died in 1934, Sterling's centennial year, the Gazette's obituary included this tribute,

> Mr. Wahl was of a quiet genial disposition, always even tempered, courteous, and attended strictly to business. He was much liked by all with whom he came in contact. His home life was ideal, coming of a large family of brothers and sisters. He had a good sized family of his own. The Wahl home was one in which parents and children alike were happy, parents were honored, the children were a pride, and habits of industry and a religious and patriotic spirit were inculcated. As a citizen and a businessman, Mr. Wahl was always ready in his quiet way to respond to the call of progressive citizenship. His memory will be cherished in the hearts of many friends.

The warmth and stability of the Wahl home gave Leo Wahl the right start in life and helped him uphold the family heritage. In his three-fold devotion to God, country, and family, he was very much the son of his father. Like so many Wahls before him, he had a head for business, a willingness to work, and the family's gift for choosing wisely. He also had something more: a love of science that made him quite at home in the new world that American industry and invention were creating. Indeed, Leo would take his place in a long line of Sterling inventors. And, like so many Wahls before him, he would pass on the family business to his sons, in whom he had already instilled with the virtues and skills to keep it going.

CHAPTER 2

CHILDHOOD AND YOUTH

The Mt. Morris Index *says that work has
been commenced on the tearing down of "Old
Sandstone." In a few weeks nothing will remain
to show where once stood the first college building
in northern Illinois. So one by one dissolve the
links twixt the present and the past.*

STERLING DAILY STANDARD, JULY 6, 1893

*The fight goes not always to the strongest
and swiftest, but that is the way to bet.*

A saying which Leo Wahl kept under the glass of his desk

1. The Business of Science and Invention

Business skill was clearly part of the Wahl family heritage, something almost genetic, and it is little wonder that Leo Wahl grew up to be a businessman. What is marvelous is that the businessman was also a scientist and an inventor. Business, science, and invention when combined in one person can make for an unstable, even volatile compound. "It was proverbial, notes Matthew Josephson in his biography of Edison

> that inventors for the most part starved, or even went mad, like poor John Fitch, or at least were ruined in the end, like that talented Yankee Charles Goodyear, creator of vulcanized rubber...Now, the 'business talent' for promoting an invention and bringing it to market, as Jeremy Bentham, the philosopher of utilitarianism, had written long ago, seemed to occur in men 'in inverse proportion to the talent for creating inventions.[1]

The great Edison was so successful because he did have a head for business. Very early in his career he learned to invent for the marketplace, to recognize a demand and to meet it with inspiration, cogitation, and experiment's remorseless trial and error. Nor did the great man go it alone, proving adept at winning investors and directing talented assistants in completing a multitude of projects. There was also a bit of Barnum in the wizard of Menlo Park, whose ability to cultivate the press and secure free publicity would make him the envy of Hollywood and Madison Avenue. Even so, Josephson's biography makes it clear that as ambidextrous as Edison sometimes seemed, the business side of invention was where Edison sooner or later struck out, not being able to handle the curves of Wall Street or the shifts of his competitors.

Leo Wahl was one of those rare inventor-businessmen who neither starved nor went mad. Wahl's genius, while substantial, never approached the Olympian heights that only Edison commanded; on the other hand, it was also free of the eccentricity and irascibility that characterized Edison. Lacking the master's prodigious gift, he nonetheless shared his approach to invention: inspiration and insight, he knew, were only the beginning; they were necessary but not sufficient. The proof and the perfection were in experimentation and testing and failing and trying again. "I know I've got it right," Leo Wahl would say, "because I have tried everything else."

It is at this point that Wahl parted company with the Master, whose intellect and ambition could not remain long in the Midwest but had to test itself in eastern capitals and join the forces of Capital that dwelt there. The exemplary proportion, balance, and wholeness of Leo Wahl's life proceeded from the ties of faith, family and community. Edison, the towering genius whose work made Wahl's inventions and business possible, grew up as a problem child whose genius did not begin to emerge until his late teens, when he was a rolling stone telegraph operator going from job to job, studying, experimenting, tinkering, and rebelling. When his genius reached critical mass, Edison made his way east, to Boston and New York and New Jersey, and there his gifts matured and flourished.

By contrast, Leo Wahl was almost conventional. He was a Midwesterner, liked his home town and did not need to go East to get financing. A man of science, he was not a village atheist or pugnacious agnostic. Raised a Catholic, he remained a devout Catholic though educated in the public school system and at the state university. He generously supported his parish and the local Catholic schools and sent all his children there and then to Catholic colleges. A tireless worker, who believed that perspiration was the key component of inspiration, Wahl could never do as Edison and so many have always done—pursue achievement to the neglect of his wife and family. Wahl's Catholic upbringing and marriage anchored his life and gave it direction. While the children of Edison found themselves on the periphery of the Great Man's life and work, Leo Wahl made it his business to train his children in the way that they should go. Without strain or compulsion, his three oldest sons grew up and grew into the family business almost simultaneously.

The author of *Main Street* notwithstanding, there was nothing mean or mediocre in the Midwest virtues that Leo Wahl embodied. Born in 1893, at the very beginning of the Progressive Era, Wahl carried into the 20th century a spirit of progress that had thrived in Sterling since its establishment sixty years before. Scientist, inventor, businessman, husband, father, philanthropist, citizen, patriot, and pilgrim: he distinguished himself in each capacity. And yet, for every mark he made, there was also something in reserve, a mysterious well from which his actions and achievements sprung. Handsome, athletic, intelligent, Leo Wahl was an impressive figure, a public man characterized by reserve and modesty. Like all who are truly articulate, he did not waste words, especially on himself. More often than not, he let his actions do the speaking.

With his intellectual gifts and his passion for science, Leo Wahl could not have been born in a better place or at a more opportune moment. Those who share his faith would call it providential that Leo Wahl should be born in Sterling and Rock Falls so near the turning of the Twentieth Century. This factory town had a long tradition of invention that Leo himself was to enrich. Leo was born at the very moment that electrical science, manufacturing technology, and finance had matured and created America's electrical power industry. By the time Leo reached adulthood, the development of that industry, which was based on alternating current, had created a market for products that he would invent—electric massaging vibrators and hand-held electromagnetic clippers, both of which did their work by means of alternating currents' rapid back and forth motion.

If the time was right, so too was the man. The life of Leo Wahl is the story of a man who made the most of the moment given him.

2. "It's here they got the range and the machinery for change."

Leonard Cohen, "Democracy"

As the last decade of the 19th century began, the little Twin Cities of Sterling and Rock Falls had good reason to face the future with confidence. They had a strong economic base built on three sectors, agriculture, industry, and commerce that re-enforced and nourished each other. Many of the local factories made products for agriculture—hardware, tools, machinery—and some of these industries had their origins in retail. Thomas A. Galt, John and Edwin Lawrence, and Washington M. Dillon, all began as hardware retailers with a knack for invention and an eye for opportunity. They invented or manufactured products needed by local farmers, found the manufacturing of it profitable and full of potential, and soon were operating factories and selling products regionally and even nationally.

Those shop owners who preferred to stay put and had the requisite business skills and experience could do quite well in Sterling and Rock Falls. The national chain stores would not arrive for another few decades, and while mail order houses were a threat, most local merchants cultivated a customer base that extended far beyond the city limits. As the largest towns between Dixon to the east and the Quad Cities to the west, and between Freeport to the north and Peoria to the south, the Twin Cities were where local farmers went on Saturdays to shop and socialize. The cities also welcomed more permanent infusion of farm capital when wealthy farmers retired. It would be another two or three decades before the warmer climes of California and Florida began to beckon local retirees. For now, though, the Twin Cities would do just fine. There, everything was close at hand—people, shops, churches, library, and the theater. As Leo Wahl's grandfather and great grandfather both demonstrated, successful local farmers in the late nineteenth century moved into the Twin Cities when they retired, and with them came new homes, another welcome boost for the local economy.

Sterling, in particular, was a buoyant place, with several banks, three newspapers, a theater, churches for almost every denomination, and good schools. The community's leaders—manufacturers, merchants, ministers, educators, and editors—were united as Lincoln Republicans and Evangelical Protestants. The victories of the Civil War were as yesterday even for Leo's generation. In 1890, Civil War veterans dedicated the Civil War monument in Central Park, a fifty-foot high obelisk topped by a statue of a Civil War soldier loading his musket. As Leo Wahl and his classmates progressed through the Sterling school system, they could count on February convocations commemorating Lincoln and Washington. Distinguished elders from the community would share their experiences in the war and hand on the lessons that American youth must learn and never forget. Memorial Day and the Fourth of July were also big celebrations in which the community made every effort to nurture the mystic chords of memory. School might be out, but Americans then were not yet too busy or too mobile to remember. One of the most stirring events was Independence Day, 1900, when Civil War hero, General O. O. Howard gave a speech that noon at a local park, and in the evening at a gathering at the monument at Central Park,. He and the local G. A. R., many of whom had served under him, reminisced about the war and sang patriotic hymns. Lincoln, too, was an abiding presence in the community. Many were still alive who had heard him speak there in 1856, and there were even a few local elders, who had known him personally.

Patriotic ardor, religious fervor, and civic spirit, combined with remarkable local talent, made Sterling a bustling progressive community for the next four decades. Many of its business leaders were not content to make a success of one enterprise. They branched out into others—manufacturing, finance, real estate—and more often than not were also active in public affairs, serving as a mayor or city councilman, a school board member, or a trustee in the local churches. In the 1890s, as in the 1850s, the spirit of revival began stirring in the Midwest, and Sterling was a particularly fertile ground. Local churchgoers appreciated fine sermons, and local papers were generous in their summaries of Sunday sermons. If people still remembered the Civil War as yesterday, they also recalled the way the Spirit moved through Illinois in the years just preceding it. Not surprisingly, a revival that gave a particularly strong boost to Billy Sunday's career was the one he held in Sterling in February 1904.

While ministers and evangelists led the call for spiritual reform, it was the local papers, *The Gazette* and *The Daily Standard*, that were the community's chief evangels of progress. In addition to representing rival factions of county Republicans, the papers exercised a three-fold mandate of printing the news, booming Sterling and Rock Falls to the world, and spurring locals to make the community a place that any crusading editor would be proud to boom.

The progressive spirit of the local papers often gave prophetic insight into the direction of the community, where it was going and where it should be going. Town therefore could counsel country. In a January 17, 1890 article, the *Gazette* urged local farmers to change their way of doing things and adopt more scientific methods of farming. The soil in Northern Illinois, it said, was not as productive as it had been 25 years before, which, of course, was the time when Leo Wahl's grandfather had come back to stay in the area. A quarter century after the Civil War, local farmers were experiencing lower yields of wheat (their staple crop) because they were not taking care to replenish the soil. They needed to increase their drainage and become more knowledgeable. Local schools could help by teaching agricultural science, but the farmers would have to make an investment not only in time but also money:

> The improved methods of agriculture will cost a little more money than the present exhaustive system does, but the farmers will get benefit in the long run. With better methods,

much larger crops could be raised…Local farmers make money here (but if better methods were pursued here by all, much more money would be made and the land would always remain good.

The Rock River Valley, said the reporter, could then claim quite justly to be "the Garden Spot of the West."

The *Gazette* also demonstrated 20-20 vision on manufacturing. Two weeks later, it reprinted an article on hydro-electric power, which had appeared in a Minneapolis paper. In commenting on the piece, the Gazette urged Sterling to build a second dam and a hydro-electric power station on the upper rapids at Broadway Avenue: "There are many thousands of horse power of undeveloped water power at the east of this city, from which could be distributed power for a distance of several miles at a very low cost, and much cheaper than steam." There was no bombast in this booming, and Sterling was to regret not acting sooner on this advice.

It was sad but true: local editors often found themselves to be prophets without honor. Then too, their sage words could not overcome local divisions, the rivalry between the east end of town—the community's traditional "garden spot"—and the west end, the home of Sterling's factories and its new business district. There was also the tension between the two twin cities. In 1877, leaders could build a bridge between the two towns, and another generation could build a bigger and better one in 1924, but there was no getting over the distrust that Rock Falls felt for any movement to consolidate the two towns. The same January day that the *Gazette* was championing scientific farming, it was also urging the merger of Sterling and Rock Falls, arguing that one city could operate more efficiently than two and attract more industry, promote prosperity, and lead to more investment on the south side of the River.

The *Gazette* was never more ahead of the curve than it was in this cause. At the very dawn of the Progressive era, it was advocating the very thing that Progressives and Robber Barons would champion for the next three decades: progress, efficiency, and prosperity through consolidation into large operating units. Unfortunately for Sterling progressives, the people of Rock Falls refused and continued to refuse to budge from their bend of the river. The very word, annexation, created visions of their proud community being reduced to nothing more than South Sterling. Indeed, the founder of Rock Falls, Augustus Smith, late in life expressed the regret that he had not given his town precisely that name. Citizens there, he reasoned, would then have gotten used to the idea and been inclined to fulfill their destiny as inhabitants of a greater community that straddled both banks of the Rock River.

While the newspaper was identifying flaws and pushing change, there were already new forces at work in the community, equipping it for the next century. Lawrence Brothers, the community's first hardware manufacturer, was quite literally on the move. Its steady growth required it to move to larger quarters every few years. By the time it moved over to Rock Falls in the 1890s, it was one of the nation's leading manufacturers of builders hardware. The Twin Cities' second hardware manufacturer, Northwestern Barb Wire, was also doing very well under the direction of its founder Washington M. Dillon. After surviving the Barbed Wire patent battles of the '70s and '80s, Dillon had won the respect of the DeKalb barbed wire barons and their mercurial protégé, John "Bet a Million" Gates. In 1889, Gates organized the Columbia Patent Company, a trust that administered the barbed wire patents; Northwestern joined it, and not only got free of the tonnage tax, but was one of the few members that survived the hard times of the 1890s. In 1892, Dillon formed a partnership with eastern steel maker, J. Wool Griswold, who wanted to establish operations nearer the recently discovered ore deposits in the Mesabi Range. The two withstood the Panic of 1893 and completed a large new mill in Sterling, the Dillon-Griswold Wire Mill.

Elsewhere on the Sterling millrace, another company, John Charter and his Charter Gas Engine Company was pioneering in the development of the internal combustion engine. A German immigrant, Charter had gotten into cigar making at an early age and had invented a cigar mould used throughout the industry. After starting Sterling's first cigar factory in 1863 and operating it for 14 years, he sold his interests and became involved in Williams and Orton, another local factory that made mill machinery. Elected president in 1877, Charter began taking the company in a new direction suggested to him by a gasoline engine exhibit at the Centennial Exposition in Philadelphia in 1876. He hired a mechanical engineer and inventor from the east, Franz Berger, and set him to work developing the first gasoline engine that would use liquid fuel. It took several years and several thousand dollars, but Berger eventually fulfilled his commission. An editor of the *Gazette*, Ed Hoover, later recalled that day in 1886:

> I saw Franz Berger take a wad of wire wool, stuff it into a pipe, push it through a chamber of an experimental gasoline engine and get an explosion that drove the piston forward. That was the first carburetor ever devised by man. A better method was later devised by Mr. Berger. I have investigated the records and find several patents for gas engines before that date, but Franz Berger and John Charter of Sterling devised the first gasoline invention has materially affected the whole course of modern civilization.

Regardless of the disputes over whose engine was first, the facts are indisputable. When Charter sold his first gas engine to Lawrence Brothers in 1887, it was the first gas engine to be sold commercially. Charter bought out his partners, renamed the company to Charter Gas Engine Works, and set the company on a four- decade career as a manufacturer of small engines. Other inventors built on his break-through and developed the internal combustion engine for automobiles. Henry Ford was so impressed with the achievement of Berger and Charter, he later tried to buy the stone factory where it was developed and transfer it from the Sterling millrace to his museum in Dearborn, Michigan. National Manufacturing, a hardware company founded in

1902 by three former employees of Lawrence Brothers, owned the building at that time and politely declined Mr. Ford's offer, explaining that the old building still figured in its manufacturing operations.

Besides adding a brand new industry to the local economy, Charter know-how also made another key contribution to the industrial expansion of the Twin Cities. The local YMCA, which E. Le Roy Galt (son of Thomas A. Galt) had organized in 1889, was like other Y chapters, a non- denominational center for education and edification. One of its most important services was a night school that included Bible Study, business classes, and industrial arts training. George Hanson, a mechanical engineer at Charter who had helped Berger develop the gas engine, was one of the founding members of the Y and also an instructor in mechanical drawing at the night school. This class proved to be of enormous value to the community. Reporting his death at home in Washington D.C., the May 18, 1929 issue of the Gazette noted that

> a number of our most substantial citizens studied in his classes at the YMCA, and it was the result of his class in mechanical drawing that some of the largest industries of this company owe their inspiration. By all who knew him in any capacity, Mr. Hanson is remembered as one of the finest Christian gentlemen.

Among Hanson's prize students was Louis A. Bittorf, the factory superintendent at Lawrence Brothers. Bittorf himself became a teacher at the night school, and in 1901 and 1902 helped organize National Manufacturing. Bittorf's own inventions were to contribute several key products to National's line and help it to become a leader in the manufacture of builders' hardware.

Myron Detrick, one of Bittorf's associates on the Y night school faculty, provides another instance of the spirit of invention that was so vibrant in the Twin Cities. An instructor in steam engineering, Detrick had already built his automobile, a steam powered vehicle, and while National was starting up, he was starting an automobile factory right next door. After a hopeful start Detrick and his backers found that they could not compete with cars run by gasoline-burning, internal combustion engines and they closed Sterling's first and only automobile factory. This setback, though, did not deter Detrick, who within ten years had invented a wall and arch system for boilers. He founded his own company, the Detrick Wall and Arch Corporation, which sold boilers throughout the world.

When he visited the Twin Cities in the 1930s, Detrick provided the *Gazette* with his unique perspective on the local tradition of invention, "I have been in all but two states of the union, and I have not seen a community the size of Sterling to match its abundance of inventors and inventions." Clearly, Leo Wahl was born in the right place to be an inventor and launch a business with that invention. If the place was right, so was the time, especially for a devotee of the arts of electricity.

3. An Age of Miracle and Wonder

The 20th century was still seven years off, but its rays were already on the horizon, when Leo Wahl was born in Sterling, Illinois on October 24, 1893, the second son of William and Elizabeth Hein Wahl. No fanfare attended Leo's birth, but the local papers did have snippets that now look prophetic. The Sterling Gazette contained a notice from Germany about Europe's greatest diplomat. Four years after being cashiered by the new emperor, "Bismarck is allowing his beard to grow, not being able to handle the razor." The electrical grooming products that Leo Wahl and his sons were to invent and develop came too late to help the Iron Chancellor in his dotage. Their first appearance in the 1920s also came too late for the empire that Bismarck had founded. The two decades following Bismarck's death produced no diplomatic or military instrument strong enough to deter Bismarck's nemesis, young Kaiser Wilhelm II, from becoming Europe's nemesis and a catalyst for the Great War.

Other stories, though, gave clearer hints of the new world being born. One hundred twenty miles to the east, Chicago's Columbian

Exposition, commemorating the discovery of the New World, was entering its final week. Dedicated on October 21, 1892 but not open to the public until May 1893, this world's fair marked Chicago's emergence as a metropolis and showcased America's genius for invention and innovation. Located along the lakefront and spreading across 630 acres of Chicago's south side, the fairgrounds became known as the White City because of its exposition buildings and the lighting that kept them white even after sundown. America's leading architects had designed these large, white temporary structures, whose "endless array of stucco pillars, stucco ornaments, and stucco statuary," set off a Neo-Classical Revival in America. Situated on an avenue known as the Court of Honor, these building housed exhibits from all over the world that showed the latest advances of modern civilization. It was quite apparent and difficult not to notice that much of what was new was made in America.

The Columbian Exposition revealed that Yankee ingenuity, which was proverbial in the 19th century, had now attained a whole new scale of productivity. Americans were harnessing new energies, inventing labor saving machines, and creating entire new industries. Correspondent Walter Wellman, who later won renown as an aviator and explorer, acknowledged that America was still catching up with the Old World in the crafts and fine arts, but also assured his American audience that in all other areas of production—agriculture, forestry, machinery, and consumer goods—the United States was clearly dominant.

> "When you come to walk through the manufactures building day after day, noting and comparing, you will see, as I have seen that we…excel any other people in the houses, clothing, food, conveyances, books, education, furniture, apparatus for heating, drainage and cooling, in household conveniences and domestic luxuries of all sorts, in methods of travel and transmission of intelligence which the great body of our population is able to enjoy. This is civilization, no class superiority; it is in this kind of civilization that America finds its glory and pride. "
>
> (*Sterling Daily Standard*, August 3, 1893)

Indeed, the fair achieved its magic because the boundless wonder of things American extended beyond the utilitarian and flourished in entertainment and refreshments. The Court of Honor may have been an artistic and technological triumph, but for most tourists, the best part of the fair was the Midway, with its mile long run of booths, novelties, and amusement rides. Here America and the world first encountered the Ferris wheel and hamburgers and carbonated soft drinks. America's mass culture, which would spread all over the world after World War II, was already here in its infancy, tempting the nations with its sweet delights.

Equally wonderful was the electricity that powered many of the new inventions and kept the Court of Honor and the Midway bright even at night. On display were electric incubators, electric sidewalks, electric irons, electric chairs for executions, electric sewing machines, electric washing machines, an early fax machine that sent pictures by telegraph wires, and Thomas Edison's latest invention, the kinescope, which played the first motion pictures. Within five years, residents of the Twin Cities would see the instrument demonstrated at the Academy of Music in downtown Sterling. Also on display was Edison's earlier invention, the incandescent light bulb, which most visitors had not seen until they came here to the exposition.

That invention was the practical result of an inspiration—one might call it a vision—which had burst upon Edison fifteen years earlier. It was in August 1878, after he had seen a demonstration of an arc light, that "it suddenly came to me, like the secret of the speaking phonograph" (which he had just invented): it was "the indefinite subdivision of light." In a newspaper interview in October 1878, Edison announced his vision long before it became reality. "Edison," says his biographer, Matthew Josephson,

> "communicated…his vision of a central station for electric lighting that he would create for all New York, and from which a network of electric wires would extend, delivering current for small household lights. In some way (as yet

unknown) the usage of electric light would be measured, that is, metered, and sold. He said he hoped to have his electric light invention ready in six weeks (Josephson's emphasis). He was building additional shops adjacent to the Menlo Park laboratory in which to carry out his large undertaking. Then he would erect posts along the roads there, connect lights with all the residences and hold 'a grand exhibition.'"

(Edison, A Biography, p. 179)

The invention of the incandescent light took not six months, but a year. As for the "grand exhibition," the grandest came at the Columbian Exposition. Samuel Insull, Edison's protégé who had recently arrived in Chicago, later recalled that the fair was "the first really successful effort in electrical lighting of very large spaces…It was also the occasion of the first real effort in the direction of elevated electric transportation, and the production of electric energy from large marine-type economical steam engines directly connected to large electric generators."[2]

Significantly, the light bulbs used by the Columbian exposition and the electrical current that powered them were not Edison's. Only two years before, on July 14, 1891, the long court battle over Edison's carbon filament lamp was finally decided in Edison's favor. Federal Judge William A. Wallace ruled that Edison's carbon filament was a breakthrough in light bulb technology, one that was radically superior to those of his competitors, George Westinghouse and Thomas Houston. The victory, which came with only two years left on Edison's patent, was pyrrhic in the extreme. It had cost the Edison company $2 million in court costs, money that Edison would rather have spent on building up his business. His opponents, Westinghouse and Houston, were not stopped but merely inconvenienced. Indeed, they had lost the battle but would win the war.

The great man who had conceived of the "indefinite subdivision of light," had not anticipated the very definite subdivision of competition, nor the resistance of Wall Street financiers, nor the sudden inexplicable short-circuiting of his own vision. Once Westinghouse and Houston weathered two years of royalty payments, they again drew on their own considerable strengths: Westinghouse's control of alternating current technology which permitted the transmission of electricity over hundreds of miles with only a slight diminishment of power, and Houston's system of power plants, which was more extensive and more efficient than Edison's.

The Wizard of Menlo Park had not helped himself with the public or with Wall Street when he stubbornly championed direct current against Westinghouse. Ignoring the limited range of direct current—his power stations could provide electricity for a radius of only one mile—he refused to adapt his equipment to the new technology and, instead, warned of the dangers of alternating current which reached 10,000 volts. Edison's public campaign against A.C. ended in disaster when he tried to use capital punishment against Westinghouse. The state of New York was looking to replace hanging with a more effi-cient, more "humane" method of capital punishment, and Edison proposed that the state use A. C. He reasoned that the public would turn against this technology once they saw how lethal it was. With a bit of Edisonian mischief he even proposed calling the electric chair the Westinghouse chair. The execution, though, was a disaster. The first 17 second dose of electricity was insufficient to kill the convicted man, and the second dose, 72 seconds worth, did the awful work but left his body a charred, smoking monstrosity.

Fortunately for Leo Wahl, Edison's scheme backfired. Edison had succeeded in turning the public against him, at least temporarily, but had not prevented alternating current from being adopted by the electric power industry. Leo Wahl's inventions were based on A.C.'s regular and rapid reversal of current. It is this change of direction that drove the blades of his clippers back and forth and created their cutting action.

With his reputation for sagacity in shambles, Edison suffered fur-ther humiliation when J.P. Morgan and other bankers merged Edison's and Houston's companies to create General Electric. Seeing the greater efficiency of Houston's plants, Morgan put Houston in control of operations. Edison opposed the consolidation from the start but lacked controlling interest to stop it. Though as a scientist Edison pioneered the research lab as an engine of invention, he was a businessman of the old school, one who believed that competition spurred efficiency and progress. In this crisis, he became like any other Midwest populist who cried bust the trusts, and beware Wall Street. Like many a poor, foreclosed farmer, he could do nothing but watch as Morgan held sway, delivering this swaddling industry from the inefficiency of competition, just as he would later deliver steel and harvesters.

Disillusioned, Edison turned his back on light bulbs and electric power and devoted himself to other projects. He improved one of his favorite inventions, the phonograph, and developed a process for extracting iron ore from the worn out mines of the Appalachian mountains. Edison devoted enormous time and energy into this latter project, which was designed to help eastern steel mills reduce transportation costs by supplying them with iron ore that was closer to home. For all the time and energy poured into the enterprise, it was ultimately quixotic: there was no way that Edison could ever develop an extraction process efficient enough to compete with ore from "the bountiful Mesabi Range deposits," which Josephson notes, were "enough for most of America's needs over the next sixty years" and "gave a tremendous geographical advantage to the Midwestern steel mills over the older ones in the East." Of course, New York steelman H. Wool Griswold, who was in partnership with Washington Dillon, could have told him that, but Edison, the émigré from Ohio, was all too accustomed with alliances in the East.[3]

Not so, Samuel Insull, his young protégé and associate. Rather than accept an insignificant post at General Electric or have anything more to do with New York bankers, Insull moved to Chicago in 1892 to become head of a small power company. The White City was inspiration enough for this bold wheeler-dealer. His keen grasp of electrical science and keener grasp of finance and politics enabled him to gain control of Chicago traction companies and within fifteen years, begin expanding outward. By the time Leo went off to college and began conceiving of the electro-magnetic hair clipper, Insull's Illinois Northern Utilities was positioning itself to gain control of the last independent water power on the Rock River, that of the upper and lower dams of Sterling-Rock Falls. For the next two decades, Insull built holding company on holding company until he electrified 30 states and created a market for inventions like Leo Wahl's electric hair clipper.

4. Childhood: Catholic Boy, Public Schools, Early Signs

Leo was a little more than two months old when William and Elizabeth Wahl had him baptized at Sacred Heart Catholic Church in Sterling on December 31, 1893. The family homestead on West Sixth Street, was already conveniently located and would only become more so. The downtown, as we have seen, was only a couple blocks to the east, and Sacred Heart was only three blocks away, north by northeast, on—First Avenue and East Seventh Street. In the next two decades the city and the local Catholic Church were both growing in the Wahl's direction. They would soon have new neighbors— a new Catholic Church and a new parish—and young Leo, born too soon to attend the schools that this parish would build, would nonetheless receive a diploma from one of the finest high schools in the state. Young Leo became a shining example of local public education and of Catholic achievement.

Catholic presence in Sterling dated back to the late 1840s, when missionary priests first came to Sterling a few times each year to hear confessions, celebrate mass, and minister to souls. Catholics through-out the county flocked to the masses, and as the flock increased in the next decade, so too did the frequency of the masses. In 1859, Sterling's first Catholic parish, St. Patrick's, was organized. In the next thirty years enjoyed the Parish spectacular growth, suffered financial reverses and, like the American Catholic Church as a whole, wrestled with the problem of ethnic division. In 1870, the German Catholics who comprised the second wave of Catholic immigrants to Sterling formed their own parish, Sacred Heart. With the increasing population and industry of the local German community, Sacred Heart soon became a flourishing parish, replete with a new brick church building, a rectory, and, in 1875. a grade school that operated until 1910. In a good solid Yankee community that prized education, Sacred Heart Grade School gave Sterling a clear sign that Catholics and Protestants could agree on at least one thing, the importance of education.

By the time Leo Wahl was born, the community was contemplating some new advances. Civic leaders were beginning to plan for a township high school, a progressive and relatively new institution which first appeared in Illinois in the late 1860's, when settlers from New England established a township high school in Princeton, a community about forty miles southeast of Sterling. As for local Catholics, they were about to take the first of several large forward leaps. In November 1893, but a few weeks after Leo's birth, Father J.J. Bennett became pastor of St. Patrick's Catholic Church in Sterling and almost immediately began working with the parish trustees to establish a building committee that would erect a new church and rectory. The two projects, the civic and the parochial, would dovetail providentially and not only create a public high school and a new church building, but also provide the foundation for a Catholic school system. Such undertaking would also start the ascendancy of the Catholic Church in this most progressive and Protestant of communities.

St. Pat's, which had been in Sterling, for almost 30 years, was a growing parish sorely in need of enlightened leadership. That it would get from Father Bennett. Since 1876, St. Pat's had occupied the Old Presbyterian Church Building, which was built in 1852 and was the first church constructed in Sterling. Not only was the building old and second-hand—an adaptation of a Calvinist edifice (!)—it was poorly located, being on the east side of town while most Sterling Catholics lived on the west side. Father Bennett and his parishioners began planning not only a new church building and rectory, but a whole new parish, relocated on the west side of Sterling and renamed to make it more than just an ethnic church.

The Panic of 1893 and its four-year depression put everything on hold but only temporarily. Just as Washington Dillon and C. Wool Griswold had to halt construction of their Sterling wire mill, so did the parish and the cities shelve but not abandon their grand designs. By 1896, when McKinley and the Republicans were beginning their campaign to recapture the White House, the parishioners of St. Pat's and most of the citizenry of Sterling and Rock Falls were confidently preparing for the better times to come.

Protestants and Catholics, the public schools and the Catholic Church, found themselves working hand in hand. After a series of referendums in 1896, the Sterling and Coloma Townships chose a site for the new high school, which, marvelous to behold, was the corner of Fifth Avenue and East Fourth Street—St. Patrick's Church and the grounds it occupied. The sale was completed in the fall of 1896, and the following year construction was under way. In Autumn 1898, St. Mary's church and Sterling-Coloma Township High School were both up and running.

The transformation of St. Pat's into St. Mary's typified the direction and the dynamism of the Catholic Church in the Twin Cities and throughout the nation. What was in a name? A most catholic embrace of the future. Under either name, the parish remained largely Irish, but guided by its Irish-American pastor, it had chosen a saint that all Catholics could embrace. Whatever, the next wave of immigration brought—German, Irish, Polish, Italian, or Hispanic—any Catholic who came to Sterling could find a home under the name of Mary. Just as the frontier served as a safety valve for the pressures of the melting pot, so too the American Church, with its predominantly Irish hierarchy, did not resolve its ethnic tensions but gave them an outlet in the Catholicity of the Church and the universal authority of the See of Rome. There, ethnic fervor could find room to cool and co-exist and carve out a place in the new land that was Catholic and American and, yet, connected to their Old World origins.[4]

In the next three decades local Catholics were to be blessed with extraordinary leaders. Father Bennett, who designed the new church and rectory, was the first of three Catholic Clerics expand the Church's prestige and influence in the Twin Cities. Bishop Peter J. Muldoon became the first bishop of the Rockford Diocese and, at that time, made Father Bennett his Vicar General, and named Father Andrew J. Burns to succeed Bennett as pastor of St. Mary's. During World War I, Bishop Muldoon headed the American Catholic Church's relief efforts and, after the war, headed the National Catholic Welfare Conference which issued a statement on post-war reconstruction that America would have been wiser to embrace in the '20s rather than the '30s. Father Burns directed the construction of St. Mary's Grade School and High School, and in 1929 was eventually made monsignor. He served at St. Mary's until his death in 1957, a few months before Leo Wahl's. All three pastors were men whom the civic leaders of Sterling could not help but admire and respect: well-educated, articulate, and forceful; they were skilled administrators who exercised moral and political authority most adroitly.

5. BMOC

These two new structures, St. Mary's Church and Sterling Township High School defined the two public realms that young Leo Wahl inhabited: the Sacred realm of Scripture and Tradition, Word and Sacraments, Church and family; and the secular world of the public school, whose goal was to educate students to be good citizens and productive members of the world's most modern, most democratic society. As Leo grew up, he excelled in school, was a scholar, athlete, and class president. At the same time, he remained devoted to the Church, growing strong in faith as he grew in years.

Leo was too young to remember the depression that devoured the heart of the 1890's. Prices were low, but few people could take advantage of them; what jobs there were did not pay much. *Gazette* reporter and local historian, Scott Williams, later remembered that "a number of people" worked "for wages of 5 to 15 cents an hour, and those who made over $10 a week were envied."[5] By the time Leo was old enough to attend school, McKinley had been elected President and prosperity had returned. Sterling was again becoming the city of the full dinner pail, a situation that certainly helped business at William Wahl's butcher shop.

Leo's first two years of grade school were at Sacred Heart, but in the fall of 1902, Leo's parents enrolled him at Wallace School, the public grade school about four blocks west. Unlike his younger brothers and sisters who were able to attend St. Mary's Grade School, Leo received his grade school and high school education in the Sterling public school system.

Though his mother certainly regretted that Leo was not receiving religious instruction, the Sterling schools were already well-known for excellence. In the following year, the school board of Sterling High hired a Michigan educator, Elliott T. Austin, to be Principal of the high school. During Professor Austin's 29-year tenure, Sterling High School gained a statewide reputation for excellence. The University of Illinois School of Education, which at that time examined high schools, consistently gave Sterling the highest rating. It is little wonder. The faculty then numbered graduates from the Universities of Michigan, Wisconsin, and Illinois, from Columbia University, Wellesley, Northwestern University, the Art Institute, and the University of Chicago. Austin, a University of Michigan grad with an advanced degree from Wisconsin, also taught history at Sterling and later conducted summer tours of Europe. Under Austin, the high school developed an interscholastic athletic program, expanded its courses, and developed a comprehensive program of home economics for girls and vocational courses. The high school also offered night courses for people in the community who wished to continue their education. With Austin, the township high school replaced the YMCA as the center of higher learning in Sterling.

For young Leo Wahl, though, learning was not something that took place only in the classroom. He showed an early interest in electricity and quickly demonstrated an aptitude for it. He conducted electrical experiments at home and filled one friend with wonder when he connected a string of pans on the wall of the barn and sent a bolt of electricity dancing from pan to pan. By the time he was a teenager, he was making his electrical research work for him in school. In seventh grade, he sent wireless messages to his classmates across the room. When his teacher found out about this inspired shenanigan, she was too impressed with Leo's precocity to punish him. Rather, she turned it into a teaching opportunity and had Leo demonstrate to the class how he had set up this high-tech mode of passing notes.

Precocity, was but one side of young Leo Wahl, and by no means the major side. As the second oldest child in a large family, he had his share of chores. One of these was to take the family cow from their home on West Sixth Street out to pasture in the morning and to bring it home in the afternoon. Fred, Leo's older brother, had the responsibility of milking the cow. The pasture was located a mile north on Locust Street and later was the site of the elegant Mediterranean style home that Leo built in 1926.

In high school, Leo was an outstanding student-athlete who was popular and well-liked. In his sophomore year, he was President of his class. The treasurer was Charles Larson, who later founded the Charles O Larson Company.

Tri-County Athletic Meet in Sterling, May 9, 1909

By the time he entered high school, he was already a powerful, gifted athlete. In the spring of his freshman year, he was Sterling's outstanding medalist at the Tri-County Track meet. He finished first in the shot-put with a toss of 37'9," first in the running broad jump with a leap of 18'9," first in the hundred yard dash with a time of 10.45 seconds, first in the discus with a throw of 90'9," and first in the 200 yard dash with a time of 26 seconds. Leo's dominance in track and field—he won five of Sterling's seven first place finishes—enabled the Golden Warriors to win the meet with 53 points. Tied for a distant second, with 23 points, were Lanark and Oregon. These athletic performances seem almost unbelievable, and they should be. It seems that sports writers use only last names. Our research for this book showed us that there were two Wahls in the school and often on the same team. Gifford Wahl, we eventually realized, was truly a gifted athlete.

6. "The Straight Forward, Not Afraid to Go Ahead Boy"

It was a packed house in the auditorium of The Academy of Music on June 14, 1912. Sterling Township High School was holding its 14th annual commencement ceremonies and Leo Wahl and his 29 classmates were taking leave of the hallowed halls of Sterling High. It was undoubtedly a typical graduation ceremony filled with its mix of memory and hope and high-toned advice. The accounts of such occasions, though, suggest that the elders of education back then were a bit more eloquent and witty than they are now. At the exercises the year before, W. W. Davis, local polymath and president of the school board, had praised the graduates,

We congratulate you on your success. You are heroes. You have shown the perseverance of the saints. To begin school at six, spend eight years in the grades, then four more years in the high school, day after day, rain or shine, requires more courage than some boys and girls possess. So many fall out by the way.

And he had challenged them:

Now you are free. The world is before you. Plenty to do. The South Pole remains to be discovered. Gas should be cheaper and every cabin lighted by electricity. We need safer and slower automobiles that will not turn turtle and kill people. Airships should be invented that will not drop passengers until they reach the end of their journey. Someone is to write a great novel or poem that will put his name into the Hall of Fame. Yes, there is no limit to your field of labor. Hitch your wagon to the proverbial star.

Summer rest will soon be over, and when autumn comes we bid you Godspeed in your chosen work.[6]

On this night a year later, he would tell Leo and his classmates, "All honor and success to the class of 1912. May you attempt much and leave the world better and brighter than you found it."[7]

Before Mr. Davis issued this charge and handed out diplomas, the graduates heard a commencement address that in retrospect seems to be addressed to Leo himself. Professor Harmon Hall of Mansfield, Ohio spoke on initiative. By today's standards, Professor Hall's approach was politically incorrect in the extreme, and even then might have raised a few eyebrows in the audience. Though most of the graduates were women, Hall confessed,

With apologies to the girls of the class, I love the boy—the boy of the Indian type. The straight forward, not afraid to go ahead boy. This is his greatest day. He has no doubt whether things are worthwhile. The world to him is bright and shining, big with mysteries worth penetrating, and hung with prizes worth all a man's strength to win them. He increases our faith in ourselves. He increases our joy in life.

On this point, Professor Hall was careful to explain what he meant.

In his youth and strength and comeliness, we need him for something more higher and much more important than the tasks he thinks he is called to solve. We are ready to worry along with the labor problem and the tariff question, with matters of demand and supply and the yellow peril. We really retain the graduate on a far more momentous issue than any of them--to pass on the question whether this old world and the life we live in it are still worth our best and utmost.

We watch the light in his eyes, listen to his ringing words, and are reassured. All's right with the world. The graduate fresh, unspoiled with the light of youth in his eyes and the dreams of love whispering in his ears has looked on the world and again pronounced it good.[8]

In his conclusion, Professor Hall identified character as the most important attribute a human being could have, character and sympathy. His motto was, "A rose in life is more than a hundred wreaths after death."

Young Leo Wahl was already started on the straight forward, not afraid to go ahead with activity that was to characterize his life. In the fall, he was planning to attend the University of Illinois at Champaign-Urbana. A top student in high school, but without the scholarship opportunities available today, Leo was able to afford college by staying with his mother's great aunt, Liva Heins. At the university Leo was to study electrical engineering. He would also begin developing plans for a portable hair clipper powered by an electro magnetic motor.

It was not his first stab at invention. While still in high school, Leo had begun investigating electromagnetic motors. In his junior year, at the urging of his uncle, Dr. E. W. Wahl, he had invented an electro-magnetic massaging vibrator, starting his predisposition to tailor his inventions to things people would use and, ultimately, buy. According to Sterling reporter Scott Williams, Wahl took out his patent on the electric vibrator in 1913, just a year after he graduated from high school. Leo went into partnership with his uncles, Captain Frank J. Wahl and Dr. E. W. Wahl, who provided the capital and initially oversaw the manufacturing and marketing of the product. As the business was just getting started in 1916, history intervened when Uncle Frank was called into active duty to serve with American forces in Mexico hunting Pancho Villa. The following year, the United States entered the Great War, and soon the two Wahl uncles and their nephew and partner were all in Europe.

Chapter 3
The Sterling Clipper

Anyone who has a good product to sell should find ways to make that product better and cheaper than anyone else can make it. That's all there is to manufacturing success. Make something people want, concentrate on one or two items and eliminate serious competition.

LEO WAHL[9]

Invention was a creative gift that would not let my father rest. He was smarter than I. He had a brilliant mind. He had a large family, built a big house. I think he was committed to getting us into the business.

JACK WAHL

1. Eureka: A Moment Years in the Making

Those guns that had begun in August 1914 had at last been stilled. The troubled peace established by the November armistice was peace enough for most doughboys, including Leo Wahl. Leo was serving in the legendary Rainbow Division in motor transport. He drove and maintained the trucks that maintained the troops on the Western Front. He had not served in the trenches, but he had still seen plenty of action and enough danger for one lifetime. With the Rainbow at the front almost continually from March 1918 to the end of the war, Leo had been exposed to shelling and all the uncertainties of transport in history's first motorized war. Truck drivers were casualties of war, too, and one of them had been a friend of Leo's: Merrill Benson, the son of Sterling industrialist William P. Benson, had been wounded in October 1918 and shipped home. With the great flu epidemic hitting its peak, troop ships could then become floating coffins, and that was what this hospital ship was for Merrill Benson. A day out to sea, young Benson contracted influenza and died just outside of New York harbor.[10]

Leo, though, had been spared and was now working in a motor repair shop just outside of LaHavre, France. Except perhaps for aeronautics, still a very fledgling science, the motor pool was about as good a job as the army could offer someone with an electrical engineering degree from the University of Illinois. The work had a certain interest without being all consuming. Delivered from the Great War and its deadly strain, Leo now had time to breathe and to contemplate the rest of his life. He could concentrate on that project that had occupied him since college: the invention of an electromagnetic hair clipper. He had long pondered the problems, had conducted his share of experiments, and had clung to this task during the war. Meditating on the electromagnetic clipper had been a refuge and a promise of hope. It was also something more than therapy, though. Leo Wahl was reflecting, not daydreaming, and the calm that descended after November 11, was the medium that an inventor's mind needed. One day early in the New Year of our Lord, 1919, he exclaimed, "I have it!" It had come to him just like that. In an instant he understood what it would take to make a hand-held electric hair clipper.[11]

Just like that. It was a moment of eureka, of discovery. It was a sudden flash of inspiration that had been years in the making. Indeed, it went back to high school and pre-dated Leo's first invention. Like so many flights of genius, it was launched with a simple premise. As Leo explained later, his trips to the movie theaters had got him to thinking about adapting "vibrating armatures with tuned harmonica motion to a small organ suitable for use in the thousands of small moving picture theaters which were springing up all over the country." Though he never carried through on this invention, the conception is doubly and triply significant. Leo forsook the organ but kept the electromagnetic principle. Alternating current sends electric current flowing in one direction, stops it instantly, and pulls the current back in the other direction, repeating this cycle several times in a second. In the process, it generates power and does enormous amounts of work. Leo's first two inventions, the electric massager and the electromagnetic hair clipper, both used alternating current to create vibrating armatures.[12]

The conception of an electric organ also shows the young scientist exercising Wahl business sagacity. Not only had he found practical applications for the principles of electromagnetism, he was showing himself to be a shrewd judge of the marketplace. Movies had not been in Sterling much more than a decade, but Leo could already see the potential of the film industry and was anticipating its needs. Science and business both required keen observation and speculation about the causes and consequences of events. Throughout his life, Leo showed great skill at sizing up the marketplace and inventing for it. Blessed with a good eye and good instincts, he was one on whom nothing was lost. His foresight, more often than not, was also twenty-twenty.

When Leo got to the University of Illinois campus, he went to work, both in the classroom and out. There were no scholarships then, and though his father had a good business, it was not good enough to pay Leo's entire way through school. Leo was able to afford room and board by staying at his aunt's and working part-time. One of his jobs was peddling his invention to barber shops in the Champaign-Urbana area. Leo's sales work not only generated business for his uncles who were managing the shop back in Sterling, it also opened his eyes to even greater business possibilities. He observed the new motor-driven hair clippers that barbers used. They were expensive and cumbersome. A flexible shaft connected the clipper to its power source, a motor which weighed several pounds and was supported by a trolley. Leo realized that he could improve on them. He could make a light-weight, hand-held clipper, sell it at a lower price, and make an excellent living doing it.[13]

All Leo had to do was adapt the principle of his electric massager to the operation of a hair clipper. Between that idea and the invention, though, would fall several years study, work, and a number of false starts, not to mention a police action and a world war. In 1914, Leo helped finance his junior and senior years at college by selling his interest in the vibrator massager to his uncles, who formed the Wahl Vibrator Company. The brothers located their business office and shop in Sterling, and employed Doctor Wahl's son, Henry, an employee of Commonwealth Edison, as their Chicago rep.[14] Leo completed his studies at the University of Illinois, got his degree in engineering, and went to work for Wagner Electrical Company in St. Louis. By this time, he was beginning his experiments with the electromagnetic clipper. Meanwhile, his Uncle Frank was looking forward to devoting himself full time to the company once his term as sheriff had ended.

Leo and Uncle Frank had to change their plans quite drastically after June 16, 1916. On that day, Pancho Villa attacked Columbus, New Mexico, and President Wilson responded by calling up several

National Guard units, including the Illinois unit in which Uncle Frank was a captain. Under the command of General "Black Jack" Pershing, these units guarded the border and engaged in the fruitless search for the fabled Mexican revolutionary. With his uncle gone, Leo returned home to take over management of the company. His job had changed, but his clipper research and development continued.

By March 1917, tensions on the border had eased, the Wahl Vibrator Company was beginning to grow, and Leo and his uncles entertained the hopes of returning to what Warren G. Harding was to call "normalcy." At this point, foreign atrocities again intervened, and the sinking of merchant vessels by German U-Boats drew the United States into the Great War in Europe. The National Guard units which had served along the border, soon found themselves reactivated and organized into the 42nd Division, which their commander, General Douglas MacArthur had given the nickname, "The Rainbow Division," because "it would stretch over the United States like a rainbow."[15] By August 1917, these 27 National Guard units began gathering for training at Camp Mills, Long Island, New York; by October and November they were sailing to Europe.[16] Among them were Captain J. Frank Wahl and his nephew Leo, who had been one of the first Twin City boys to enlist, though not the first to make it "over there." That distinction went to Leo's friend, the ill-fated Merrill Benson, who had enlisted as an ambulance driver in the Canadian army.[17]

The Wahls—Leo, his cousin, and his two uncles—saw a lot of war but all survived. Of them all, perhaps Dr. Wahl had the hardest time, suffering exhaustion and illness and returning to the States in May 1919 in broken health. At that time, he told the local paper that "if he had the choice of going all over again or being taken up to Riverside (Cemetery) and buried, that he would choose the latter."[18] The good old-fashioned Yankee choler in that remark suggests that Dr. Wahl had regained his health. As for returning to the states Leo was the last Wahl to do so. Rather than making him rush back to the states, his eureka moment made him decide to stay a little longer and do graduate study at the University of De Poitiers in Paris. He had taken an exam and won a scholarship to that prestigious university.[19] The coursework would deepen his understanding of electricity and help him finalize his invention and market it. Besides, the flu epidemic which had claimed the life of his friend Benson and of so many others, made him reluctant to return home just yet. In March of 1919, while the rest of the Rainbow prepared to return to the states, Leo received his early discharge from the U.S. Expeditionary Forces signed by General John Pershing in France. Any free time Leo had was spent working on his prototype hair clipper.

2. When Leo Came Marching Home

The French Family was nice enough to provide room, board, and a work-shop in exchange for Leo doing a little plumbing and wiring in their home. After awhile, Leo found an urgency to get back to America and on to work. On a hot August day, when Leo stepped from the train onto the red brick platform at the Sterling Station, he certainly had mixed emotions. He had heard about the big celebrations, music and everything, when the Sterling group of men returned triumphantly to their homes. Here was Leo standing all alone. Moving on, he picked up his bags and began walking up the hill to his home on 6th street. The more powerful emotion was to focus everything onto getting his electric hair clipper into production.

3. Patent

On October 14,1919, Leo Wahl filed a U.S. Patent on his newly designed electric hair clipper. On July 8,1920 another patent was filed. In the next few years he was to file another half dozen patents on improvements in electric hair clippers. Leo told me that in those early days he would set up a routine. The first week he would build about a dozen hair clippers. The second week he would drop off the hair clippers, teach the barbers a little bit about how to use them, and tell them he would be back in a week to collect $20.00 for the clipper if the clipper hadn't broken down and the Barber liked it. The next week, he would do the same thing with larger quantities. The clipper worked and the Barbers liked it. Leo had many things to do and often he would work through the night on various aspects of the fragile growing business. It was still 1919 and Leo Wahl was in successful production of the world's first high speed hand held electric hair clipper, in fact the company had produced and sold almost 1000 by December 31, 1920. His younger brother Clyde Wahl, at the University of Illinois, sold a majority of the clippers. Wahl Clipper was incorporated January 29, A.D. 1924. Leo J. Wahl of 1308 Locust Street, Sterling, Illinois subscribed to 120 Shares and paid $12,000, Verna Wahl subscribed to 15 shares for $1500 and his younger brother Clyde Wahl subscribed to 15 shares for $1500 of the Wahl Clipper Common Stock. The three people listed above were elected as Directors until the first annual stockholders meeting. Clipper manufacturing was originally done by hand operation. Coils were made by hand turning a crank, winding insulated copper magnet wire. The coil was removed from the mandrel. It was immediately wound with a special tape so it could be dipped in varnish and then baked. A measured stack of laminations was then pushed into the coil. A small group of women did this hand assembly of hair clipper parts on the second floor of one of the down town merchants stores.

The blades were a critical item on the hair clipper. The fine sharpening finish on clipper blades is called precision lapping and is the key to good hair cutting. Leo spent a lot of time researching and especially studying the technology of lens grinding. He designed and built his own precision lapping equipment. Until Leo was able to process his own blades in house he had to look elsewhere. He went to Racine, Wisconsin to the Andis O.M. tool company where he had some blades made to his specification. The company was owned by

Patented Jan. 1, 1924.   1,479,486

UNITED STATES PATENT OFFICE.

LEO J. WAHL, OF STERLING, ILLINOIS.

ELECTRIC CLIPPER.

Application filed October 14, 1919. Serial No. 330,547.

To all whom it may concern:

Be it known that I, LEO J. WAHL, a citizen of the United States, residing at Sterling, in the county of Whiteside ˄ ˄
Illinois, have invented certai˄ ˄
ful Improvements in Elec˄
which the following is a

My invention relate·
especially designed fo·
though it is suitable
other ways where '
employed, such as ˄
or shearing of anir

One object of ɪ
duction of a devicᴄ
ing elements as w
produce the moti
per which is han

Another object ᴄ
vision of means wɪ
is imparted to the
mechanism may bᴇ
netically without tl.
form of circuit break.

Other objects of the ɪɪ.
and be described in the specincaᴜᴏ.

The novelty of my invention will be nᴇ.
inafter more fully set forth and specifically
set out in the claims.

In the accompanying drawing:

Fig. 1 is a plan view of a device er
ing my invention, the casing being sh
section.

Fig. 2 is a longitudinal sectional side eɪ.
vation of Fig. 1, the section being taken
through the solenoids.

The same characters of reference are used
to indicate identical parts in both figures.

I am aware that electrical clippers have
been produced wherein the reciprocating
motion of one of the clipper blades has been
derived from an electric motor through the
medium of a flexible shaft and suitable mo-
˄ɪᴏ˄ translating apparatus; also clippers in
˄ᴏving clipper blade has beeᴇ

dle are easily rendered inoperative and require considerable attention to maintain them
in proper operating condition, while those
˄ᴛ˄res which operate electro-magneti-   60
ᴅireᴄᴛ current require a vibrator
˄ions to the flow of
ɪal voltage avail-
has been found
'uce a vibrator   65
red ineffective
˄ this voltage.
˄tages inherent
˄ypes and to
˄perate con-   70
˄ut either a
˄ing mecha-
˄ompanying
med.
nd to show   75
my inven-
ng of suit-
˄ped by the
the handle
ent is guided   80
Electro-mag-
˄ounted on a suit-
˄˄˄ᴇ 4, and suitably secured to one ᴏf
the walls of the casing, the terminals of ˄he
coils being connected as by leads 5 and 6,   85
throʋ˄¹
˄y suitable sᴡitch,
˄ng currenᴇ sup-
˄connection with
ᴄtric lights,
current supply   90
˄inary plug and
to so install the
device that it may ʋe reaᴅily disconnnected,
or in any other manner desired.

A bar 8 which either carries or comprises   95
an armature for the electro-magnet 3 and 4
and which is mounted, as at *a* in the handle portion 1, extends to and is operatively
connected with the moving clipper blade 9,
which rests upon and is held in contact with   100
˄ clipper blade 10, the latter
˄˄ handle portion 1.

INVENTOR.

Leo J. Wahl,

BY *Walter N. Haskell,*

his ATTORNEYS.

**REPRODUCTION OF THE FIRST WAHL PATENT
COVERING VIBRATOR MOTOR HAIR CLIPPERS**

Filed October 14, 1919

Patent of January 1, 1924, Leo J. Wahl, inventor.

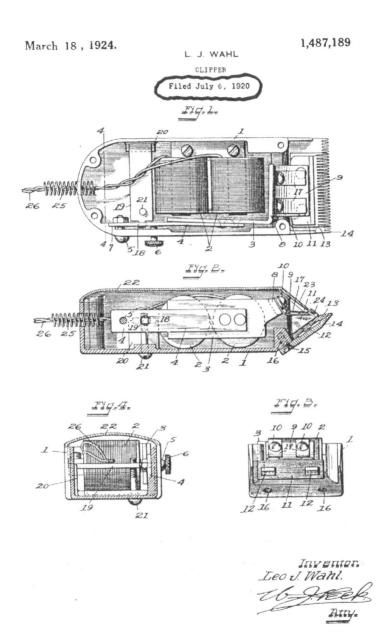

March 18 , 1924.

L. J. WAHL

CLIPPER

Filed July 6, 1920

1,487,189

Patent of March 18, 1924, Leo J. Wahl, inventor,
filed July 6, 1920.

Mathew Andis Sr., John Oster and M. Meltzer. The company had experience with blades for hand clippers and became interested when Mr. Wahls orders grew. It seems that the three owners had a major breakup culminating in the midnight opening of the safe with a sledge hammer, according to Matt Andis. Each of them decided to get into the hair clipper business. Oster hired an electrical engineer to design a universal motor with a gear head to drive its cutting blades. Mr. Meltzer started Master Appliance and Allover Hair Clipper Manufacturing Company. Mathew Andis Sr. went into production in early 1921 with a product having a yielding driving connection very similar to Wahls. Mr. Wahl needed to and did take action against Andis. Exercising his ability to make the right choice he selected an up and coming Patent Attorney, Max Zabel from Chicago. After negotiations with Mr. Andis, it was agreed there was infringement and Leo settled for a royalty of $2.00 a clipper. This was to be paid by Andis to Leo Wahl. Further, it was agreed that Andis would get an exclusive license to continue manufacturing and pay Wahl $1.00 each for every clipper manufactured by Andis. You can imagine what that influx of cash meant to a company struggling to grow. Jack recalls Leo saying, "I think we make more money when Andis sells a clipper than when we do." This license was to remain in effect for the remaining portion of the 17 year life of the patent. By 1927 Wahl and Andis produced 275,000 clippers. By December 1934, 398,000 were sold with about half produced by Andis and half produced by Wahl. As a result of the licensing agreement, Andis paid Wahl approximately $343,000. But that wasn't the whole of it relative to hair clippers patents. Hair Clippers were a hot commodity and Leo Wahl had to protect and defend his patents and stop infringers, as in 1930 actions against Nordstrom and 1933 and 1936 against Brown & Sharp. The company had truly turned a corner in the hair clipper business.

Leo's Mother, Elizabeth, was quoted as saying, "Leo knows how to make money—and he sure knows how to spend it." His younger

IN THE

United States Circuit Court of Appeals
For the Seventh Circuit

Nos. **5675** and **5676**

BROWN & SHARPE COMPANY,

Appellant,

vs.

LEO J. WAHL,

Appellee.

Counsel for Appellant:
MR. C. PAUL PARKER,
MR. FRED O. FISH,
MR. ALFRED H. HILDRETH,

Counsel for Appellee:
MR. MAX W. ZABEL,

Appeals from the District Court of the United States for the Northern District of Illinois, Eastern Division.

Front page, Bill of Complaint, Leo J. Wahl v. Brown & Sharpe Company, filed Oct. 4, 1933.

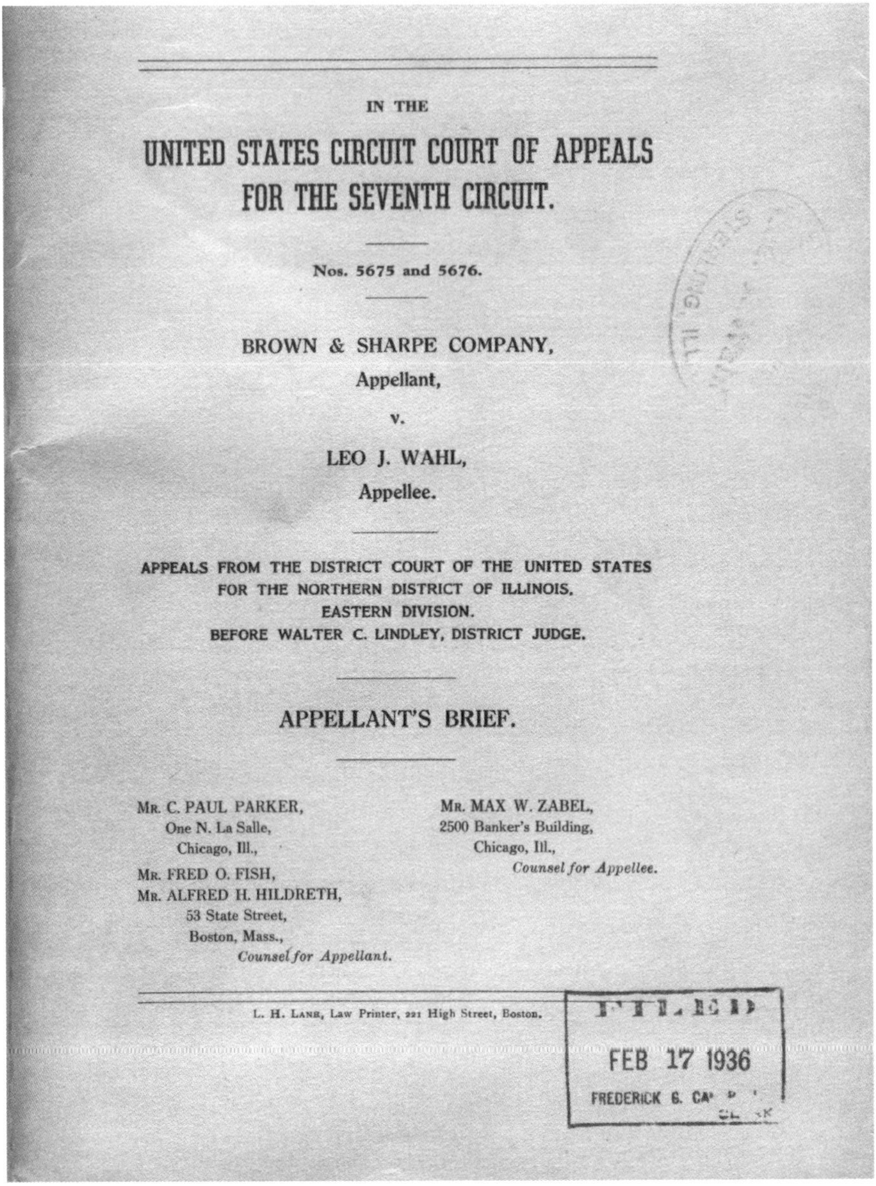

IN THE

UNITED STATES CIRCUIT COURT OF APPEALS FOR THE SEVENTH CIRCUIT.

Nos. 5675 and 5676.

BROWN & SHARPE COMPANY,

Appellant,

v.

LEO J. WAHL,

Appellee.

APPEALS FROM THE DISTRICT COURT OF THE UNITED STATES
FOR THE NORTHERN DISTRICT OF ILLINOIS.
EASTERN DIVISION.
BEFORE WALTER C. LINDLEY, DISTRICT JUDGE.

APPELLANT'S BRIEF.

MR. C. PAUL PARKER,
One N. La Salle,
Chicago, Ill.,
MR. FRED O. FISH,
MR. ALFRED H. HILDRETH,
53 State Street,
Boston, Mass.,
Counsel for Appellant.

MR. MAX W. ZABEL,
2500 Banker's Building,
Chicago, Ill.,
Counsel for Appellee.

L. H. LANE, Law Printer, 221 High Street, Boston.

FILED

FEB 17 1936

FREDERICK G. CA...

Patent Infringement Lawsuit, Feb. 17, 1936.

brother Wayne says, "Leo had made it Big. He had a Big House, a Big Family, and a Big Car. Corbetts Cadillac Dealership was next to the factory and Leo couldn't resist trying the new technology in automobiles. One Day while in Chicago, Leo parked his car in a lot, and, when the attendant brought back his 12 cylinder La Salle, all he kept saying was, Man that's protection." When (Verna) mother needed her own car, Leo bought her a bright yellow coupe with an all aluminum body. Too small to hold all of the kids, Leo traded it in for another yellow four door Lincoln Continental Convertible. For a very reserved, quiet woman she was not too happy with that car either, but the kids liked it.

Going to Court on Patents is difficult and Leo spent a lot of time fighting legal battles to protect his patent rights and the exclusive license he gave to Andis. In the Brown & Sharp case, two of their attorneys shook hands with the Judge, who seemed to be an old friend. At one of the early infringement Court meetings, Mr. Zabel told Leo, who was still a young man at the time, that he could show his confidence in the case by not appearing in Court. They did win the case. In 1925 Mr. Wahl estimated that since 1920 his company had saved the barbers of the U.S. and Canada the sum of 4 million dollars— the difference between the cost of buying the clipper made in Sterling and buying the old and much more expensive style clipper apparatus formerly used. At that time there were 40 people working in the factory at their location on East Third Street. The first floor was previously occupied by Sterling Ice Cream Company. After winning his lawsuit, Leo Wahl leased both the first and second floors and expecting to double in size by midyear, bought a lot of new machinery.

4. Building the Business

The business grew rapidly as Wahl improved manufacturing processes and productivity. The lower case of the clipper was available in plastic now as well as in painted or brushed aluminum finish.

Another interesting finish was crinkle finish where the paint shrunk up as it dried and was an excellent grip finish. Jack can recall that during Christmas Holidays, while still in high school, Jack remembers running the aluminum die-casting machine. It was a tough job and he will show you the burn scars that he got when the melted metal squired out on him. Wahl added other products that could be purchased by barbers to be used in their shops. The product line on June 15, 1934 consisted of an electric clipper (named a small 89), a handy electric vibrator, a silent electric hair dryer, and hand clippers. A Gazette Ad at that time showed the products that were produced in the Sterling plant and available for direct sale at very competitive wholesale prices. I believe they were testing the market to see if there was consumer demand. Two of the first salesmen were Vic Bein (December 16,1951-long term), and Bob Propheter (for the short term). Sales in 1965 were $3,115,000.00.

5. Home and Florida

Marriage

The young man from Oppenweiler, Germany certainly helped Leo to make the right choice in the Patent settlement with Andis. Leo tried to tenaciously focus on the business, but that didn't always happen because one of the sweet Glafka girls caught his eye. Leo J. Wahl and Verna A. Glafka were married May 9, 1922. In 1926, when their third son, Jack, was born they moved out of their modest home at 1308 Locust Street and into a large new Mediterranean style home at 1701 Locust Street. The factory was successfully growing and Leo managed it with both hands. He would arrive home at noon for lunch. His ritual was to come in the door, take off his hat and coat, get the mail from the box, and take it to the closet in the front hall. Item by item, he would throw it into the trash basket without opening it. Invariably, one or two items would catch his eye, and he would go into the living room and read them while everyone sat at the table and waited. No one ate or complained because they knew business came first, before anything else. It was hard for the boys, who were playing sports, to have only 30 minutes for lunch before going back to school. It was years later that I remember my Father telling someone that his kids learned more about business at the table that they would learn in a year of schooling.

Florida

With the telephone and air mail, Leo was able to monitor operations and direct the growth of the product line from Florida. Leo Wahl had a chronic sinus problem, and found that he was able to get relief by spending time in the hot humid salty weather of Florida. In order to be able to go to Florida without a hotel reservation he bought a small house near the hotel. He and Mother would stay there until space became available in a hotel. Quite often he drove the family to Florida in a brand new Cadillac touring machine.

And that was not always without problems. On one occasion the water boiled out of the radiator as we passed through rather a remote area. He refilled the radiator from a nearby stream and off we went. Thirty miles later it boiled over again. This time Leo got water and a large rock. He found a thermostat that controlled air that stuck on heat. It didn't take him long to fix that new deluxe feature. He was a practical man, and he did what he needed to do.

A wife's wisdom

Leo visualized Florida as a great growth area. He could see the population of older retirees growing rapidly. The occasional hurricane would be a problem until construction was designed to withstand Natures wrath. Flagler felt the same about Florida and he committed large funds to railroad and deluxe hotels. Leo spent a couple of afternoons with a Real Estate Agent as he considered the purchase of a large piece of undeveloped property that extended from the Atlantic Ocean to the Inland Water Way, in Boca Raton, Florida at a very competitive price. This is where Mother (Verna) spoke up, told Leo that he had his hands full working with his sons in the Wahl Clipper Corporation in Sterling. Mother said, keep this as a vacation area and not another work area. Mother, Verna, won out!

CHAPTER 4

POST-WAR TRANSITIONS

You can't operate inefficiently,
pay top wages, and still stay
in business.

JACK WAHL, FEBRUARY 13, 1970

1. "Because I could not stop for death"

Leo Wahl was never short of energy; time, though, was another matter. After World War II, he talked of retirement and prepared for it, but his heart was not exactly in it. True, he groomed three of his sons to manage Wahl Clipper, and, in 1954, turned the reins over to them while he stepped upstairs to be Chairman of the Board. Stepping up, though, was not stepping aside. Leo Wahl had too many things to do, too many new ideas to explore, too much love of business and invention. Idleness was not for him, nor was he about to spend his time living in the past. He made it a point to spend mornings at the plant on East Third Street. There was still work to do, a future to build. He involved himself in all phases of the design and construction of Wahl Clipper's new plant on North Locust Street.

It was impossible for Leo not to get involved in the daily operations of the plant. He cared too much about the company and the people who worked there. One day, as he walked through the plant discussing production issues with his son Warren, they passed an employee who was laboring to push a cart up a grade that connected one wing of the factory with another. Leo broke off in mid sentence and hastened over to help the man with the cart. Together, the two quickly made the grade, Leo returned to his son, and picked up their conversation with not a comment about the chore just performed. A well-spoken, articulate man, Leo wasted few words on himself. On this subject he let his actions do the talking.

May 9, 1957, seemed to be no different than other days, except that it was the 35th wedding anniversary for Leo and Verna. When he came home from Wahl Clipper at noon, Leo had lunch and relaxed in the afternoon shooting pigeons, which clogged up the eaves spouts with their nests and carried germs and viruses, especially encephalitis. With the approach of evening, Leo went inside to get ready to take Verna out for dinner. He never completed this task. He suffered a stroke and was rushed two blocks east to Sterling Public Hospital. He fought for life but to no avail. He died eleven days later, with his family at his bedside. He would have been 64 in October.

Family and friends were shocked. It was hard to believe that such a vigorous man was gone. The sense of loss was overwhelming. Not long before, he had gone to the Mayo Clinic and had a satisfactory check-up, at least that is what he told Jack. The doctors did caution him about salt, but over the years, Leo had been doing a little maintenance on his own. He cut back on his pungent cigars and switched to cigarettes and then to Turkish cigarettes, with their reduced tar content. Perhaps, he could have done more.

Inevitable as such thoughts were, they were put aside as family, friends, and the community at large gathered to mourn. On the 22nd, Leo's casket was open for viewing and the next day, a Solemn Requiem Mass was celebrated at St. Mary's Church. Bishop Loras T. Lane came down from Rockford to preside, and Father Raymond Wahl, Leo's youngest son was the celebrant. In the homily, St. Mary's pastor Father Frank Bonnike extolled Leo's "religious zeal, scientific talent, deep humility, and wide-spread generosity."

A few weeks later, a newsletter of the Mayslake Retreat House expanded on this theme. Its lengthy obituary cited Wahl's dexterous combination of inventive genius and business skill, his active involvement in the Sterling-Rock Falls community, and his deep faith and life of devoted service to the Catholic Church. In addition to being a trustee at St. Mary's, a member of the Sierra Club, and a Fourth Degree Knight of Columbus, Wahl was also "a most generous benefactor and ardent booster" of the Mayslake Retreat House. His gifts, said the article, "reached up into five figures." Equally important, Leo made eight retreats there and brought others with him, often his sons, Warren, Robert, and Jack, as well as friends, relatives, and even employees (Who always came with him on company time). On his last retreat, just the previous December, there were 23 people in Leo's party.

Leo's death, sudden though it was, did not leave his company in disarray. The founder had been astute and prudential to the end. He had built his company in the heady days of the Coolidge prosperity, kept it steady during the Depression, and managed its conversion to wartime production of machine gun lifters and micro switches, all for military use and for which he voluntarily lowered the price. With the end of World War II, Wahl continued to thrive in the new Cold War economy that emerged in the late '40s and early '50s. The need for a strong defense and two-decades of pent-up demand now unleashed to coincide with crew cuts and the baby boom and the proliferation of suburbia—all these combined to create a prosperity unprecedented even for the United States.

Wahl Clipper was quick to embrace new possibilities. The company expanded its line to include hairdryers, shears, sharpeners, razors, foot massagers, attachments, barber combs, wrenches, and vacuums that could be used with clippers in barbershops and textile factories. Leo continued to look at all types of products that could be built utilizing his electromagnetic motor. For instance, four patents cover unique designs of malted milk mixers using electro- magnetic motors. Leo was keenly aware of the growing need for good mixers in the rapidly growing chain of Prince Castles and McDonalds. His mixer was too powerful, however, and never achieved production status. Wahl also streamlined the company's production. It introduced plastic housings, and began manufacturing almost all of its production parts except cords and screws. This vertical integration helped Wahl control quality and costs and become more competitive. In 1922 Leo Wahl offered his college roommate, Al Swenson, the opportunity to have exclusive rights to Wahl products in Canada. That handshake deal was to last over 80 years. In 1948, the company built a new warehouse at its factory on East Third Street in Sterling.

Having been an exporter almost from its very beginning, Wahl Clipper, in the 60's, was in a good position to take advantage of the free trade of the *Pax Americana* when it came. Wahl was an established name in the barber and beauty trade, and the demand went on for Wahl products as it cut across national boundaries. The company adjusted the voltages and cycles of its clippers to meet foreign requirements and expanded its sales handsomely. Establishing a partnership with English investors and opening a factory in England, it not only regained the business it had there before the war, but began expanding into other countries as well. In 1954, Wahl strengthened its position in Canada by opening a factory in Windsor, Ontario, just across the river from Detroit, where it manufactured parts for its Canadian products. Don Hennessey, who had been a popular coach and athletic director at Newman Catholic Community High School in Sterling, worked closely with Warren and became the first manager of the new plant. The operation was very successful because there was a 22% duty on finished products from the United States to Canada and a 20% duty on parts. Further, a Canadian dollar was worth a $1.25 U.S.

2. The Second Generation

As already noted, 1954 also marked the passing of the torch. While the founder became Chairman of the Board, he handed leadership of his company over to his three eldest sons. Warren, the oldest, became President of the company; Robert became Vice-President and Treasurer; and Jack, his third-born, took over as Manager of Engineering.

These were not overnight moves. Leo Wahl had been grooming his boys from childhood. When they were still very young, he began communicating his love of work and invention. His children saw that he never stopped inquiring or exploring. He kept up with his studies at home and often returned to the factory in the evenings. Sometimes, he took the kids with him and let them watch him try out the plant's new machinery. They learned the value of work. He had them earn spending money by letting them take apart old, traded-in clippers and sell the copper and aluminum parts to junk dealers. As teenagers, they worked during the summer at Wahl Clipper. They embraced the idea of joining Dad in the family business as they grew older.

Formal education, including college, was, of course, part of the process. All of the Wahl children began on the same path—St. Mary's Grade School and Community High School (now Newman) in Sterling—but in time, each found his or her own way. Warren (1923-1981) went to Notre Dame and also to St. Ambrose, setting a precedent of Catholic higher education that many other Wahls have followed. Warren had completed two semesters at St. Ambrose, when World War II started. He enlisted in the U. S. Naval Air Corps, but before beginning active duty he was able to complete another semester at St. Ambrose in Davenport. Having learned to fly in high school, he also took more flying lessons at the Quad Cities Airport and was accepted into the U.S. Naval Officers training school. In the Navy, he took college courses while continuing his flight training at bases in Iowa, Texas, and Florida, and then went on to pilot a TBF torpedo plane.

Warren was a passionate, adventuring spirit. He was a gifted musician who could play the violin by ear. His style was thoroughly romantic. He would hear a tune on the radio, pick up his violin and begin to play it while dancing wildly about the room. The flights that music provided, though, could not compare with those of the airplane. The skies were his second home. There he found freedom.

He learned to fly under the tutelage of Gene Jacoby at Whiteside County Airport, which was then only about a half mile north of the family home on Locust Street. During World War II, he went to flight school at Pensacola, the cradle of the U. S. Naval Air Corp. Some of the things that Warren could do with an airplane, though, neither Gene Jacoby nor Uncle Sam ever taught him. The unverified story is that, one winter day in high school, when Rock River was frozen solid, Warren flew his craft under the Nelson Railroad Bridge east of town. There was also that day, when brother Jack and his mom were in the backyard taking care of the wash. Jack was holding the basket while his mom was hanging the clothes. All of a sudden, they heard a voice from on high calling to them, "Hi Mom! Hi, Jack!" Mom and Jack looked up. It was Warren. He had cut the plane's engine and was letting it glide low over the old homestead, while he got a better look leaning out the side door. 'Mom about had a hemorrhage," said Jack, remembering the incident years later. Perhaps it was also no coincidence that Jack never took to flying like his two older brothers did, nor did he ever relish being in a plane that Warren piloted.

Warren's daring as a pilot was not recklessness but the Wahl penchant for calculated risks translated to the heavens. On the ground, Warren, the musician, could give himself to frenzied fiddling, but the cockpit was where he exercised skill and cool nerve. On one Sunday morning flying out of Pensacola, his engine quit at low level just after taking off and flying over the edge of the Florida Everglades. Luckily, his plane plowed into a stand of small trees and finally stopped in a mushy swamp. Warren was shaken-up but walked away from the plane. That day he was flying alone and the navigator who usually flew with him said, "I don't ever want to fly with a pilot who can't walk away from a crash landing."

As much as he loved the thrill of flight, Warren was preparing for a future on the ground. On November 7, 1944, he married Mary McKenny of Dixon, and they had two children, James and Theresa. Warren joined Wahl Clipper after the war and quickly became Director of Production and Manufacturing. In 1954, when his dad was ready to step upstairs, so was he.

Almost two years younger than his older brother, Robert Wahl (1924-1998) graduated from high school in 1942 and also went to Notre Dame. After one year of classes there, he was drafted into the Army, where he served as an engineer and gunnery inspector and eventually became a pilot. On August 12, 1945, he married Mary Drew of Sterling, and they had three children, Leo, Elizabeth, and David. After his discharge from the Army, Bob went back to school and graduated from St. Ambrose with a B. A. and a B.S. in accounting.

He returned to Sterling and joined Wahl Clipper as an accountant working with Leslie Black, the chief financial officer.

Bob and Warren shared a love of flying, and they brought it with them to Wahl Clipper. Their dad had always been interested in air travel. He had been an early member of the board of directors of the Whiteside County Airport, and his family's flight to Yellowstone for a vacation in 1936 had been the subject of a Northwest Airlines magazine ad. Leo saw the possibilities of a company airplane, especially since he already had the pilots, and before too long, Warren's duties included being company pilot. He made flights to meet vendors, pick up machinery parts, or to visit Sunshine Industries, the small service and sales station that the company had started in Fort Meyers, Florida, to serve the South. Bob, who did not usually mix business and flying, said on one occasion that the wing of the plane took a damaging hit from a large duck on take off from a visit to the Ft. Myers service station. He eventually bought his own open cock-pit biplane that was rigged for acrobatics.

Son number three also found his way to Wahl Clipper but did so by way of land and sea and his father's discipline, electrical engineering. Once established in the family business, Jack Wahl found that flying with Warren and putting in 60 or more hours a week were sufficient reasons for not acting on any impulse to take to the air himself. Of all the kids, Jack Wahl was most clearly the chip off the old block. He liked to build things, like model airplanes, gas and electric motor scooters. At age 13 he enjoyed riding all over the countryside on his home made scooters. Given his scientific aptitude and his deep filial piety, he did not choose his career so much as it chose him. "When most kids were playing with tinker toys," Jack Wahl recalled several decades later, "I was taking electric motors apart. I never really gave my future much thought. I always planned to be an electrical engineer."

Jack and Bob were still in high school, when a little wrestling match gave Dad some new thoughts about their future—that it was no longer remote, but, indeed, quite near at hand. One Sunday after-noon, as he and his boys always loved to do, Leo and Bob had a wrestling match in the living room. And, as always happened, Dad emerged victorious. Indeed, Leo loved to take on his kids two and three at a time. Even though he always came the winner, the kids loved it and came back for more. This day, though, one match was enough for Bob, and for Leo too, though he realized it a little too late. When Jack joined them in their tussle on the floor, the match was to have a very different outcome. Jack, athletic like Bob and Leo, gave Leo all he could handle and more. Dad, who was fast approaching 50, suddenly found himself thrust into an awkward position with all his weight (and Jack's too) on one leg. Jack heard a loud snap. It sounded like a tree cracking in half. Dad went down with a howl, and that was when Mom rushed into the room.

"What happened?" she asked in amazement.

"I think I sprained my ankle," Leo said, his denial greater than his pain.

"No, you broke it, I heard it break," said Jack.

And so he had. At first, Leo did not know whether to be angry or proud. With pleasure, Leo would tell others how his strong young son had bested him in the living room.

Of course, Leo wasn't one for convalescence and certainly not one for depending on others for transportation. Soon, he was driving himself to work, having to use the emergency brake to stop the car. And pretty soon, his strong young son was taking the vehicle into the shop to have the burned out emergency brake repaired.

After a semester and a half at St. Mary's College in Winona, Minnesota, where he started on the football team until cracking his thigh bone, Jack was drafted into the Navy and assigned to Great Lakes Naval Training Center, north of Chicago. There he went through boot camp and was then accepted into a 13-week course at their machine shop Industrial Engineering School. Next was a 30 day refrigeration school at Carrier Corporation in Syracuse, New York. Next he was given a travel voucher to send him on a five day cross country train ride to Seattle, Washington. In a few more days he was ordered to take a train down to Treasure Island in San Francisco Bay and be ready to ship out at a moments notice. It was the beginning of a Navy experience that showed Jack how fortunate he was to be and gave him a taste of the Far East that would, indirectly, shape later decisions at Wahl Clipper. On the ship everyone had a responsibility, with a couple thousand marines on board, my main one was to see that the frozen food and meat lockers were in good shape.

Jack's Navy career opened with what seemed to be "the world's largest blackjack game running 24 hours a day." Feeling like the Navy didn't know what to do with him and his buddies, all at once, Jack found himself on a troop transport heading west under the Golden Gate. He, along with everybody else, was terribly seasick. Neither fortune nor favor smiled on Jack when he was assigned to garbage detail, with the task of also, keeping the scuttlebutts operating (refrigerated drinking fountains). Bad as it sounded, it was, like many dirty jobs, extremely important. Navy ships saved all their garbage, which they dump all at one time, in the dark. Afterward, the ship makes a sharp turn so that birds or submarines could not follow.

Despite the blackjack beginning, this was serious business. The war wasn't over. Jack's ship was part of a convoy bringing Marines and supplies to the battle area of the Pacific. It was the next stop, Leyte Harbor in the Philippines, where the ship heard about the A-Bombs dropped on Hiroshima and Nagasaki. The crewmen didn't go ashore. Instead, a group of about 40 were transferred on to LCI's (landing craft invasion) and set off heading north to Okinawa. The group arrived there about midnight I don't know what day it was and went ashore in the middle of a thunderstorm. "We carried everything we owned in our duffel bag as we climbed around in mud looking for a dry place to spend the night," Jack recalled. Life on Okinawa was a challenge. The group's records hadn't arrived, so the men hitchhiked, sightseeing around the Island. Then the first typhoon came. "It ripped our 30 man tent to shreds, and in the dark, we looked for protection," Jack said. "We found it in a cave recently evacuated by the Japanese." The group spent a few days unloading bags of cement for punishment, I think, and working construction jobs, then we were moved to a "receiving ship", which was no more than a large floating hotel. The ship had no motors or propellers to drive it and sat with four or five ships holding an anchored position in Buckner Bay, Okinawa.

After a few days, the ship received a warning that another typhoon was coming. Any ships that could, were to go to sea to get away from the storm. The Navy ships moved away from Okinawa as rapidly as possible, but because Jack's ship had no engine or propeller, it couldn't move. The second typhoon struck, and it was the mother of all typhoons. "We had five solid anchors keeping us from being blown onto the beach," Jack remembers. "We were riding the storm out as the waves would lift us and then drop us. Other ships unsuccessfully tried to attach themselves to our ship, then we saw it. A large green freighter steaming under full power came into Buckner Bay on one side and tried desperately to circle around to the other side and go out. But it couldn't go against the wind, which clocked at around 140 miles per hour. It smashed directly into the side of our receiving ship. We were blown together into the shallow coral. And all night the merchant ship pounded against us. Now we were afraid that when the typhoon would swing the other way, we would be blown out to sea."

Jack's ship was lucky. By 10 the next morning, the sea was almost calm; but the ship's trials were not over. As a receiving ship, it had large cooking facilities, and that morning a lot of people came to our ship to be fed. The air all over the ship was full of fuel oil vapors, which for some reason exploded in the kitchen," Jack recalls. "Some sailors, with fire burning on their backs, jumped over the side without a life jacket into shallow coral waters. I was just leaving the kitchen area when the explosion occurred. I grabbed a life jacket and ran toward the bow of the ship, fully expecting another explosion to

Every wave lifted the ships and then dropped them back down on the Coral. When the eye of the typhoon passed and the winds blew in the other direction, Jack and his mates feared that they would be blown back out into the sea and sink, Oct. 9, 1945.

Many ships fought and lost their battle to stay off the Coral beach. The anchors on Jack's ship begin to drag during the night, and his ship ended up on the Coral beach, Oct. 9, 1945.

Gallery 14

Many sailors jumped to Jack's ship when their slammed up against his. A large green freighter steaming full speed ahead rammed into the side of Jack's ship and pounded into it through the night, Oct. 10, 1945.

Looking from the mess hall to the starboard side, a huge hole had been ripped through the side of the ship. Many sailors lost their lives, Oct 10, 1945.

Gallery 15

blow the ship in half. Believe me, I was scared to death and, days later, I realized a portion of my hair had turned instantly gray."

The next day, the sailors were called together to hear a presentation at the Anchor Theater in Okinawa. The Navy had a special mine sweeping project in mind. Those who wanted to join this project would immediately be moved onto a ship and away from the mess at Okinawa. We would also get 6 extra weeks of shore leave when we got back to the States. It seemed that the problem was to get rid of a number of pressure mines that had been dropped by U.S. bombers all over the Japanese Inland Sea. "It was stupid," Jack said in assessing the experience. "But the whole group volunteered each other, and we were locked in."

On October 4, 1945, just one month after the surrender ceremony, a storm began to form in the Pacific. The winds started slowly in the Marianas, where General Curtis LeMay's B-29s had once taken off to strike Japan. As if in a revengeful fury, the storm gathered mass and strength as it blew northward. Navy weathermen tracked the storm for days and predicted it would sputter into China. But on October 9, the kaze seemed to change its mind and headed straight for where the Americans were massed on Okinawa.

By 2p.m. the kaze was blowing ninety-five miles an hour. The rain blew "horizontal, more salt than fresh." Huge U.S. Navy ships anchored off Okinawa were blown sideways, their heavy anchors dragging the bottom. Forty-foot walls of water came roaring through like locomotives. A muddy darkness fell on "a scene of indescribable confusion as dragging ships collided or…disappeared into the murk."

By 4p.m., the kaze was blowing 115 miles an hour with gusts up to 140 miles an hour. As if to intentionally inflict maximum damage, the wind shifted and tore grounded boats off reefs and blew them back across the bay, "dragging their anchors the entire way." Ashore there was only misery. "Twenty hours of torrential rain soaked everything, made quagmires of roads and drowned virtually all stores, destroying most of the tents and flooding the rest." Some quonset huts were lifted whole and moved hundreds of feet, others were torn to bits, the galvanized iron sheets ripped off, the wallboards shredded and the curved supports torn apart. The kaze destroyed 80 percent of Okinawa's houses.

When it was over, 12 ships lay on the bottom of the ocean and 222 were grounded. One hundred thirty-three of these were damaged beyond repair. Famed U.S. Navy historian Samuel Morison later concluded: "This was the most furious and lethal storm ever encountered by the United States Navy."

In 1281,the kamikaze killed 150,000 Mongals who dared to attempt to invade the land of the gods. That typhoon left the Japanese mainland unscathed. It seemed to target the seaborne invaders.

The October 1945 typhoon also skipped the main islands of Japan. If the Flyboys had not brought Japan to its knees and it had continued with the war as the Spirit Warriors had insisted, the typhoon off Okinawa that day would have torn through a U.S. invasion fleet of thousands of ships and millions of American boys.

When Jack came home from service, he had two months of leave made up of overseas duty survivor service and another month for serving on the guinea-pig mine sweeping fleet. Around the house, Jack took it easy. Much too easy for his father's liking. It bothered his father when he walked by the room and saw his son sleeping after being out half the night. When Jack came down for breakfast, he could see that his father was upset. "Aren't you ever going to work," his father asked.

"I'm being paid by the government," Jack said. "I'm on leave. I'm still in the Navy."

Leo was such a workaholic, it was hard for him to see a son of his goofing off and wasting time, especially when he had plans to train his sons in the business.

Leo took those plans extremely personally. In a later serious discussion, Jack talked about how much he had enjoyed the course at

Carrier Refrigeration School in Syracuse, New York. He told his dad that he thought he might like to pursue that type of work. At this, his father got up, turned, and walked out of the room. A little later, his mother asked him, "What did you tell Dad?"

Jack informed her and she said, "He was extremely upset." She later told him that he was almost crying when he was telling her about what Jack had said. He had his mind made up that three of his sons would join him at Wahl Clipper and carry on the business that he had started.

When Jack was discharged from the Navy on July 26, 1946, he returned to St. Mary's College for a year and then transferred to Marquette University in Milwaukee. By then he was back on course to Wahl Clipper, pursuing a degree in electrical engineering and taking a special lab course his senior year which allowed him to do an important in-depth analysis of the electro-magnetic motor, and the tune of the hair clipper. He spent more time on that course than any other. After a session in the lab, Jack would call his father, and they would talk for two or three hours. Jack was not only learning the mechanics of the electromagnetic hair clipper, he was also learning about the mind of its inventor.

Leo wanted well-rounded sons, so he saw to it that Jack got some sales experience as well. Dad sent him samples and instructions to call on customers in Minneapolis. When he got to the third customer, Jack was met with laughter. The man knew what Jack did not know: that the factory was way behind on orders and that any order he would give Jack would be worthless, for the factory would not be shipping it for three or four months.

On August 21, 1948, shortly before beginning his last semester at Marquette, Jack and Margaret Keefe of Deer Grove, Illinois were married at St. Mary's Church in Tampico, the same parish where his paternal grandparents were married 58 years earlier. The couple had six children: Rosemary, Gregory, Joan, Ellen, Laura, and Mark. Margaret succumbed to cancer after 48-1/2 years of their marriage. After Jack graduated with a B.S. in electrical engineering in December, 1949, he and Margaret returned to Sterling, where Jack went to work at Wahl Clipper and learned all facets of the business. He began on the factory floor, running punch presses and grinding machines. Then he did a stint in the plastics molding department, first as assistant foreman, then as foreman. In 1952, he was transferred to the assembly department.

From the time that the three boys came to work at Wahl Clipper they punched a time clock the same as everybody else working there. After nine months of work, Leo announced that he was putting his three sons on salary. Their salary would be exactly the same as it had been including any overtime that some of them had worked. It was the beginning of Wahl Clipper Corporation's effort to compensate employees based on performance.

These stepping stones were all part of the post-graduate education of the young engineer. So too was overtime, when Jack got to use the skills he had learned in college. Jack had been with the company less than two years when Leo had the drawing board moved upstairs from the tool room, where the foreman there, Jim McNinch, had been using it. McNinch, though, had left Wahl to start Sterling Electronic Door Control Corporation, which manufactured an electronic door opener that he had developed. Manning the drawing board after 3:30 each day, Jack Wahl started Wahl Clipper's first engineering department. In the next three years, as his engineering duties expanded, he hired people to assist him, and, in 1954, he was named Manager of Engineering in addition to his duties as assembly department foreman. Two years later, in 1956, he was made Vice-President and joined the Board of Directors.

When Leo was in Florida, he still kept a close eye on the operations of the factory. He was particularly interested in the design of the new products. The sketches sent from Leo Wahl to Jack showed his latest thinking regarding his new home clippers and how he would like to see Cadillac-like Tail Fins incorporated into the design of the clipper. Another sketch dated March 1955 showed his

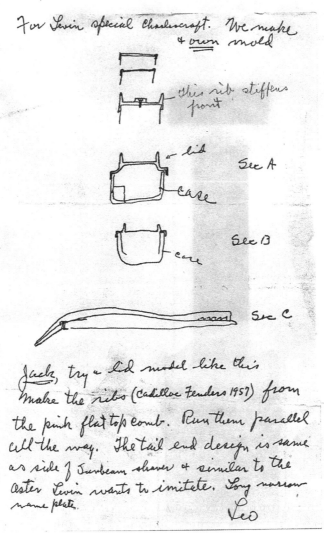

For Levin special Chaslescraft. We make
+ own mold

this rib stiffens
front

a lid

Sec A

case

Sec B

care

Sec C

Jack, try a lid model like this
Make the ribs (Cadillac Fenders 1957) from
the pink flat top comb. Run them parallel
all the way. The tail end design is same
as side of Sunbeam shaver + similar to the
Oster Levin wants to imitate. Long narrow
name plate.

Leo

*Memo from Leo J. Wahl Jack Wahl on design for a new
hair clipper lid, 1957.*

Gallery 44

thoughts on the new electric shaver cutting heads that would cut both long and short whiskers. Jack was to immediately begin work on these projects along with his other duties. Quote, "This one can do everything."

Indeed, Jack was already demonstrating a gift for invention and a large appetite for work. In 1956, he and his brother, Warren, President of Wahl Clipper, became restless about who owned the company and who did all the work and started Mallard Plastics, Inc., a company that did custom molding and later made conveyor systems for warehouses and factories. Soon thereafter, Jack invented a new conveyor system that featured wheels with an angle flange that kept boxes rolling straight. This invention gave the fledgling company a foothold in the marketplace. Actually the company has been operated by its own general manager with little attention from Warren or Jack. Today, in the age of lean manufacturing, focus factories, and just-in time-production, the market for its pallet and carton flow systems continues to be strong. Mallard counts among its customers Anheuser-Busch, Chrysler, Hewlett-Packard, Whirlpool, Nestle Foods, and Coca-Cola, to name just a few in the private sector. In the government sector, the U. S. Navy and the U. S. Post Office have both acquired Mallard systems.

At its start-up, Mallard moved into the first floor of the 3rd Street factory recently vacated by Wahl Clipper. By 1956, Wahl Clipper was expanding again, and this time on a whole new scale. With no way to add on to the old plant, Wahl Clipper began constructing a new factory north of Sterling just off Illinois Route 88 (now Route 40, or North Locust Street). The new structure housed the plastic molding departments, and, by September of 1957, Wahl Clipper had moved its entire operation there. The brick, concrete, and steel structure was built for heavy machinery and featured a large loading dock. There were tiled washrooms and a large parking lot. This last amenity was impossible at the old factory which had been located in a well-established residential area. Even better, this site contained land, lots of land, for the additions that the growing post-war economy would most certainly require.

Leo Wahl and his sons made the right move. In time, the company would grow almost exponentially, no sooner completing one addition before having to begin another. In the meantime, though, Wahl Clipper faced some major trials. Indeed, the time of testing had already begun. Death deprived Leo's sons of his guidance. Though he had taught them well, no amount of prudence could anticipate the actions of a work force recently unionized, or of the Age of Aquarius, whose dawning in another decade or so was to change (at least for awhile) everybody's idea about hair.

3. "The New Men of Power"[20]

World War II not only delivered America from the Great Depression, it also made organized labor a new power in American life. When the war started, labor and management had declared a patriotic truce. The government promoted union contracts that included "maintenance of membership clauses" requiring union workers to stay in their union until the war ended. Unions were quick to consolidate these gains and expand their influence. They recruited more vigorously than ever before and met with surprisingly little resistance. Buoyed by patriotism and handsome war profits, business avoided doing anything that might provoke strikes. Between 1940 and 1945, union membership increased from 9 million to 15 million.

After the war, labor renewed its battle for better pay and more benefits. It had the leverage of larger numbers; it also had a war record of restraint and patriotic sacrifice. The unions made their demands; management resisted. The unions struck; deadlock ensued. Work stoppages in 1946 were the largest in history. Pressed by both sides, as well as by a host of other crises at home and abroad, the Truman administration found capitulation the quickest way to compromise. It allowed business to hike prices by 19% in return for granting raises amounting to 18%. Truman had established an unfortunate precedent of using inflation to end labor disputes, but the chickens would not come home to roost for another two decades. In the short term, mollification of both sides enabled America to get back to work and produce its way to prosperity. By 1948, the economy had begun to catch up with post war shortages and began a period of prosperity, so enormous and so sustained that even labor joined the middle class, with the rank and file buying homes and new cars and making plans to send the kids to college. The 1950s proved to be the high tide of the American labor movement. Union membership peaked in the mid-50s at about 27% of the work force.

It was at this time that the union movement caught up with Wahl Clipper. In the early '50s, the International Association of Machinists of the American Federation of Labor (AFL) began trying to organize Wahl factory workers. They got a willing response from employees who saw what union membership had done for workers at Northwestern Steel and Wire and International Harvester, the two largest companies in Sterling and Rock Falls. Leo Wahl's first impulse, naturally enough, was to resist. He consulted a Chicago law firm that specialized in dealing with unions. His Chicago attorneys advised him to counter with a letter writing campaign in which he addressed employees personally and appealed to their loyalty. Wahl entertained the counsel but ultimately rejected their advice. A reserved man, he was not comfortable with this kind of chumming. He would not be someone he wasn't. "You can have your union," he told the workforce, "but we will run the factory." Leo only lived long only enough to see the union implemented. He was not around when his proviso was tested.

The unionization of Wahl Clipper went smoothly enough. Early in 1955 Wahl employees voted to join the Machinists union. By September, union and management had hammered out an agreement on compensation, vacation, rules and grievances for the next year. Six weeks later, in early November, union representatives and

Wahl management, under the direction of President Warren Wahl, finalized details of a comprehensive health and welfare program for all Wahl employees. At that time, J. George Eichorn of the machinist union declared, "We are certain that this is the most complete insurance program in this area and will do much for the good relations of everyone concerned."

Twelve months later, Wahl Clipper narrowly avoided a strike, but only after the union gained new concessions. The negotiations involved three days of intensive talks and produced a pact that made Wahl a union shop, placed a union label on all Wahl products, and provided an average hourly increase of 9.5 cents. The contract also included more vacation days, additional incentives, and new procedures for transfers, job bidding, layoffs, leaves of absences, and grievances. After Warren Wahl presented the details of the pact to his workers, he and the management team left the meeting and let the employees,(a group of not quite a hundred) discuss the merits of the plan. The employees found little to dislike, and on September 24, 1956, Wahl employees voted unanimously to accept the contract.

Afterwards, union representative Milo Himes was jubilant. It was a victory for both sides. "We are on the threshold of an era of industrial cooperation and good will at the Wahl Corporation," he said and then vowed that Wahl management would not regret the good faith that it had shown. "As the company has agreed to be fair with us, so must we be fair to them by giving them the cooperation and loyalty they have proven they deserve. We will do everything possible in making and keeping Wahl Clipper an unrivaled leader in its field. I am also sure that there will seldom be any shortage of applicants for work with this growing, progressive company."

The era of good feelings did not last long. In 1960, the contract expired without a new agreement being reached. The union allowed negotiations to continue another week, but when these proved fruitless, Wahl's factory workers, (85 in all,)walked out at 7 in the morning on September 30. The union set up picket lines, and the Wahl management closed the plant for three days to let tempers cool.

It took another eleven weeks and perhaps the Spirit of Little Lord Jesus, for minds to meet. On December 23, 1960, the workers voted to accept a new three-year contract providing a schedule of wage increases ranging from 19.5 to 26.5 cents an hour over three years. The workers also gained another half day of paid holidays, which increased their total to 7.5 paid holidays. The next morning, Jack Wahl, who with each new contract was playing a larger role in the negotiations, announced the settlement and said that the company would re-open the plant after Christmas and have all employees called back to work by the end of that week. Wahl concluded on a note of guarded optimism, "With the signing of the new contract, the management of the company is looking hopefully to peace and prosperity for all the year to come."

The peace and prosperity actually lasted much longer than that. The machinist union and Wahl management had established a cautious truce that got them through another nine years and two more contracts without any work stoppages. On November 18, 1963, a few days before the Kennedy assassination and more than a month before the current contract ran out, the management and the union came to terms on a three-year contract that went into effect immediately. In addition to raises of 10 to 20 cents an hour phased in over three years, Wahl employees also gained a pension plan to be funded by the company. Three years later, the parties came to terms with ten days to spare. The pact of November 8, 1966 gained the workers an immediate 4% wage hike with increases of 1.43% each year remaining on the contract. They also received a new 4-week vacation plan, pay for jury duty and bereavement, and one more paid holiday, which brought the total 8.5 days.

These negotiations were typical of the new accommodation between labor and management. In the first two decades of the post-war era, labor unions pursued the middle class agenda of the rank and file. Rather than assaulting the structure of American capitalism, they had sought a fair share in its growth. Meanwhile, corporate power continued to consolidate and found that it could also do business with Big Labor. Worker productivity, the ongoing blessings of the Baby Boom, and the lack of foreign competition, all allowed business to increase compensation and benefits and pass the cost on to the customer. The Kennedy administration calculated that annual pay increases of slightly over 3 per cent would not be inflationary, given the productivity of American industry and the steady growth of new markets.

The sixties were good years for Wahl. After the 1960 strike had caused sales to dip from a record high $3 M the year before to 2.5M, sales began gravitating upward in the first half of the decade sales then took off in 1965, which bettered the 1959 total and mounted steadily each year until peaking at about $4.5 M in 1969, the year that the next strike, the Mother of All Strikes began.

Wahl Clipper was not just rising with the decade's rising tide. It was expanding its operations and introducing new products. In an effort to diversify and expand its operations, Wahl Clipper was anxious to promote its custom molding of thermoset and thermoplastic. They advertised and received a very large thermoset molding job from General Electric in Morrison. As a result they learned how to run a company 24 hours a day and 7 days a week. In early 1960, Wahl purchased L.C. Wrench company, whose wrenches were used by automotive and airplane mechanics.

Wahl had for years pioneered the market for handheld hairdryers. Their product had a centrifugal fan aluminum housing with a wooden handle, known as the Silent Dryer.

Warren and Leo Wahl retooled the hairdryer in thermoset material for the housing including the handle and the fan with cost reductions and improved manufacturing methods, Wahl produced over 2000 a day to meet the demand of another product called the Thirty Minute Dryer which had a hairdryer stand and a soft bonnet. The success of

these products was not ignored by our competitors who concentrated on higher wattage (600 to 1000) for faster drying.

Wahl's next effort in hair dryers (350 watt) was the Collegiate in 1963.
All of the parts were injection molded in Wahl's plastic department.
The dryer gave the user freedom to do other activities while drying
the hair, the cord and hood could be packed into a compartment, the
tambourine door closed, and it was ready for travel or storage.
However sales were disappointing. By the time the product was on the
market, dryer wattages averaged 1200 watts and were imported by very
well known companies like Sunbeam, Norelco, and General Electric.

In 1965, Wahl introduced a men's electric shaver whose patented,
disposable flexible blades anticipated later developments in the
industry. 15,000 were sold. That year, Wahl produced the Clipper
Vac, whose revolutionary attachment vacuum amazed tradeshow
crowds that year. The Clipper Vac could do a full haircut without
depositing a strand of hair on the recipient's clothes. The next year
the company produced in-house its first rotary motor clipper and
strengthened it the next year by changing the wound field to a permanent magnet motor. That same year, Wahl also introduced the first
cordless hair trimmer powered by a rechargeable battery and was
sold in the Professional Beauty and Barber trade. They also produced
a new high-powered animal clipper, an enlargement of its first rotary
replete with permanent magnetic motor field. This product assumed
new importance in the early '70s when the craze for long hair forced
Wahl to expand its sales of animal clippers.

4. Goodbye to All That

As the '60s drew to a close, so did the dynamism of the post-war
expansion. "The times," indeed, "were a changin'." Having
rebuilt Western Europe and brought democracy to Japan, America
now had to live in the world that it had made. After a fling in
Camelot, the nation would in time rue the changing of the guard her-

alded by the Kennedy Presidency. The "greatest generation and their children" would miss the leadership of their elders—FDR, Truman, and Ike; Marshall, Nimitz, and Acheson. In time, businessmen, factory workers and families everywhere would look at free trade "from both sides now," from lose as well as win. As the tumultuous sixties blazed to a close, so much of American life was in turmoil: assassinations, the Vietnam war, protests, polarization of generations and races. The Johnson administration's decision to wage war on the Vietcong in Southeast Asia and on poverty at home gave a sharp inflationary boost to the economy at the same time that productivity of the American worker was beginning to decline. The coupling of these two problems threw the American economy in to a strange funk, which soon gained the label of stag-flation and was characterized by a decline in the stock market, corporate profits, and real income, and the rise in interest rates, prices, and unemployment. Richard Nixon, who succeeded LBJ as President found this economic malaise as intractable as the war in Vietnam.

It was at the dawn of this new era, with the rise of both unemployment and inflation, that Wahl Clipper celebrated its 50th birthday with an open house. On Friday afternoon, August 4, 1969, tour guides led small groups of employees and relatives through the plant, stopping in every department where representatives from that area explained its operations and answered questions. The tours began in the tool room and concluded in the office where guests had cake and punch or coffee and mingled and enjoyed each other's company. It was just the kind of occasion that was a specialty of the family-owned companies that still dominated Twin City industry. Within a couple months, the congeniality of this occasion would seem like only a dream.

On September 22, 1969, the contract negotiations began with a shock. Under the direction of the International Representative of the United Machine Workers, the local union presented Wahl management with a 40 page proposal. The length was unprecedented; so too were the demands. One sticking point was a proposal so radical it promised to overturn Leo Wahl's proviso: the union wanted all disagreements between workers and management referred to a board of arbitration. With such a revamp, the employees would still have their union, but the union and a government board of arbitration would effectively run the factory. This demand for unconditional surrender did not square with the union's roots in the AFL nor did it have any contact with modern reality. The Roosevelt coalition was no more; the Rust Belt was already in the making, with Sterling and Rock Falls on its western edge; and here, the local machinist union was seeking control of the means of production.

5. "What a Long Strange Trip"

The machinist union and the little twin cities on the Rock River went a long way back--back before 1912, when American Steel and Wire, a major affiliate of U S Steel helped Paul Dillon and Northwestern Barb Wire buy the bankrupt Griswold Wire Mill; back before the Panic of 1907, which raged in New York while Sterling and Rock Falls were celebrating the opening of the Hennepin Canal; back before 1903, when Keystone Manufacturing went into receivership and International Harvester purchased it secretly to avoid TR's trust busting; back before the turn of the 20th century, before October 1900, when war hero and VP candidate Teddy Roosevelt spoke in Central Park; and before the previous month too, when Sterling held its first Labor Day parade; back into the shadows of the grim Gay Nineties, when the Panic of 1893 threatened to prevent the construction of the Dillon-Griswold Wire Mill, which Washington Dillon and eastern industrialist, C. Wool Griswold were building in Sterling, right across the river from Dillon's Northwestern Barb Wire.

Back then, the Twin Cities still breathed the Yankee spirit of Lincoln and the Civil War. Sterling prided itself on being the city of the full dinner pail, whose factory workers were not the proletariat, not bomb throwing radicals, but day laborers, who worked their ten hours, collected their day's wages and, if their wives and families were blessed, made it home without stopping at the saloons that lined Third Street, just two blocks from the mill race and the factory district.

The local labor movement gained respectability one Sunday afternoon in May 1901, when AFL President Samuel Gompers gave a two-hour speech before a packed house at the Academy of Music in downtown Sterling. Earlier in the week the International Machinists Union had gone out on strike in the United States and other countries. Its goal was a nine-hour day, a 12.5% wage increase, and safer working conditions. These conditions now seem unobjectionable, but at the time they marked the divide between labor and capital and provoked Gompers to great eloquence. He appealed to the audience's sense of justice, its patriotism, its faith. He aligned labor with the Gospels and the Union's cause during the Civil War. Idealism and high-tone principle were not his only weapons. He could also appeal to prudence and the profit motive. Justice in the workplace, he argued, was simply good business.

> The American wageworker should be given a better wage so that he will have a greater power to consume. He should be given shorter hours so that he can have more time for thought and recreation and that his mental powers can more fully develop. We deny that long hours and low wages are essential. If they are, then China leads the world.

This reference to China a hundred years ago, so true then, now possesses an almost unbearable pungency. The combination of lower wages and steadily improving productivity has made China the fastest growing economy in the world, one that continues to take manufacturing jobs away from America.

Thirteen years later, Henry Ford raised the minimum wages of his workers to an unprecedented $5 a day. The enormous productivity of his assembly line gave him the option of paying higher wages or lowering the selling price. He opted for the former, shrewdly reasoning that American workers could not buy his cars making low wages and that who better to start boosting American income than the industrialist who would benefit the most from it.

After the Panic of 1907 subsided much earlier in the Twin Cities than in most communities, Harvester began expanding and modernizing its operations. In so doing, it transformed the Twin Cities into a worker's market. To keep workers from bolting to Harvester, other factories had to raise their pay. In 1909, wages at 75% of the local plants went up more than 12%. A year later, the community's newest hardware manufacturer, nine-year old National Manufacturing matched Harvester's progressivism by introducing an annual bonus that paid its most experienced workers a bonus of 10% of their year's wages. The next great boost in pay for workers came seven years later, when the United States entered World War I and converted its industries to war production. Some of those gains were lost a couple years later, when the depression of 1920 and 1921 forced local factories to cut wages.

In 1969, it was clear that the nation, organized labor, and the machinist union had all come a long, long way since Samuel Gompers took a train ride from Chicago to Sterling and raised the consciousness of the Twin Cities. Sorting through the union's 40 pages of demands, the Wahl brothers figured that some things had perhaps gone too far. Many months later, union leaders were forced to arrive at the same conclusion, but for very different reasons.

Three decades of hindsight do suggest that the Machinist Union overplayed its hand. Samuel Gompers himself might have dismissed its proposal as he did his Socialist adversaries, whom he called "economically unsound, socially wrong, and an industrial impossibility." In 1969, the nation, which was still fighting the Vietnam War, was also beginning a prolonged period of economic stagnation. Worker productivity was dropping, while Big Business and Big Labor were doing the familiar 3-step inflation shuffle: strikes, pay raises, price hikes. The less than benign neglect of Washington allowed this cycle to continue unchecked round after round from industry to industry. No one was clairvoyant enough to see OPEC's 1973 oil embargo, or, further down the road, the Japanese miracle. But at least a few people on Capitol Hill and in shops and offices across the country could agree with Jack Wahl, who in a letter to employees observed, "You can't operate inefficiently, pay top wages, and still stay in business."

6. Winning Hearts and Minds

In autumn 1969, negotiations on the new contract went nowhere and stayed there well into the next year. When the contract expired on October 31, 1969, union and management agreed to continue meeting in the dim hope of avoiding a work stoppage. This time, though, the union's patience did not even last a week. On November 4, 1969, it called a strike and the company's 96 factory employees walked out, leaving the 44 office workers and supervisory personnel to mind the shop.

Wahl management had dug in for a long siege. At the recommendation of its counselor, Rockford attorney Ed Fahey, it had anticipated a strike and built up inventory. Wives of supervisory personnel volunteered to help out and salesmen came in from the field. At first they had neither the numbers nor the skills to do basic production, but with a little training they were quickly able to take care of the repairs in the service department and eventually run some assembly lines. After the company presented the union with a proposal on November 5, the parties did not meet again until December 4. Though a representative from the Federal Mediation Commission chaired that meeting, no progress was made. The next meeting was a month later, on January 6. It was the same old story: picket lines outside the plant and no progress at the bargaining table, nor did the parties adjourn with any date set for another meeting. The winter temperatures outside were warm compared with the chill that had settled over these negotiations. The next meeting two weeks later provided more of the same, except that two federal mediators presided and got 5 hours of frustration for their pains. Emerging from the deliberations, they announced that they would not sit in on another meeting until the two parties reduced the number of issues dividing them. The first real movement came a month later, when management and the union met with another mediator and were able to report some progress. To keep the momentum going they met the next day.

A week later, on February 13, Jack Wahl sent the employees the first of several letters on the progress of the talks and management's position on the issues. Having sat in as an observer on all of the union negotiations since the '50s, Jack Wahl, with the Personnel Manager, Dave Kilburn, and Warren looking his shoulder had become the company's head negotiator. The triennial contract wars had exhausted Warren's patience and he had turned the bargaining over to Jack, whose temper was less volatile. In these letters Jack proved to be an adept communicator. He discussed the issues in detail and showed that management was flexible on matters of compensation, but he defended its right to manage and make decisions to protect jobs and keep the company profitable. "The company believes," he wrote,

> The economic and non-economic improvements are substantial. Employees have been and will continue to be treated fairly, but the Company must not sidestep its responsibility to manage and operate this plant in the most efficient manner. Many people who have lived in this area can list any number of factories, which are no longer here because they failed to do this.

He then closed the paragraph with the previously quoted statement: "You can't operate inefficiently, pay top wages, and still stay in business."

There could be no concession on the point of who ran the plant. After listing the various concessions on pay, discipline, union activity in the plant, grievance procedures, layoffs, overtime, and safety and health, Wahl then discussed the issues that were non-negotiable: management's right to subcontract work that the local factory could not do profitably, the freedom of foremen to do production jobs in emergencies, and the right of management to resolve disagreements with workers internally rather than submitting each one to a board of arbitration. This last union demand, Wahl argued, would allow arbitrators to refashion the union contract with each new appeal. Any concession on this point would give control of Wahl Clipper over to a third party whose decisions could change the course of the company and harm its competitiveness and profitability.

The strike intensified in April. No longer content to let things drag on the way they had for six months, Wahl management took two steps that would resolve the strike one way or another. On April 1— April Fool's Day—it presented the union with one more proposal, and it took out a full page ad in the Gazette announcing that Wahl was now hiring permanent factory workers. Some employees resigned from the union and returned to work. The Company received threatening phone calls and picketers began stopping people trying to enter the plant. To prevent violence, local, county, and state law enforcement officers began standing guard at the plant. The second day, 13 people who had gone into work were stopped by angry strikers who punched a hole in one of the workers gas tanks and roughed up the driver. That night, the leader of the group, Dean Bess, had a flare thrown through his window. When Dean considered quitting and Jack volunteered to personally drive him into work, he decided to stay the course.

The union tried to maintain discipline by fining defectors. Its argument was that there was no leaving the union except by expulsion. Management complained of this action to the National Labor Relations Board, and eventually won a favorable ruling which forced the union to withdraw its fines. In late April, the union filed a counter complaint, charging management with bargaining in bad faith, but the NLRB dismissed this suit. On May 15, a sniper fired five shots into one of Wahl Clipper's transformers. The company had to send everyone home until Commonwealth Edison repaired the damage. This work was finally complete early Sunday morning.

The turning point of the strike came on June 16, 1970. A group of disgruntled workers petitioned the NLRB to have the machinist union decertified at Wahl Clipper. Fearing that it would lose the rank and file, union leadership quickly came to terms, accepting the last offer on the table. On July 20, the strike was over. The new pact called for wage hikes of 7%, 6%, and 5% for the three years of the contract. Second and third shifts also received pay boosts of 12 and 17 cents an hour, respectively. New Year's Eve became a full day holiday instead of a half. Vacation days and insurance and pension benefits also increased.

The International Association of Machinists and Aerospace Workers paid dearly for these concessions. The new contract made Wahl Clipper an open shop. Even worse, a vote was coming that would eject the union from Wahl Clipper. Legal maneuvers and the inertia of federal bureaucracy might delay judgment day, but they could not prevent it. On March 17, 1972, with the vote on de-certification only a week away, Jack Wahl sent the employees another letter that reviewed the history of the strike and its aftermath. He closed with this exhortation, "We have all suffered bad experiences during the past years because of this union. No one has escaped. Now you have the opportunity to free yourself—and me—of this burden. As it was suggested to me recently, "No dues is good dues.""

The vote on March 24 was decisive. With 83 of the 88 employees voting, 28 voted to retain the union, 54 voted to expel it, and one ballot was contested. After almost 17 years at Wahl Clipper, the machinist union was out. This hard-won victory was a chastening experience for the Wahl brothers. They and their company had been delivered. Now it was up to them to run their business so that no worker would ever want the union back. Such a consensus, though, would take time to build, and would occur only after much healing had taken place.

The vote had expelled the union, but the memories of the strike and of the old Wahl Clipper would remain and have to be reconciled with the new company that was emerging. When Wahl management decided to hire replacement workers in April, 1970, it had decided that replacement workers and former strikers who rejoined the company would for initial job bidding purposes all be treated as new employees. The strike had temporarily erased years of seniority. If a striking veteran worker; job was filled, he would be like any new hire, started at the bottom. He or she was not doomed to stay there, by any means. Indeed, most of the strikers who came back were able to climb back up the ranks rather quickly and attain positions that were equal to or even better than their old jobs. As a result of a court hearing on activities, one non-employee picketer spent a few weekends in jail.

It was the interim period, though, that was difficult. Having to work at lesser jobs and rub shoulders with replacement workers tested the mettle of many and provided the company with a challenge almost as stern as the strike itself. Under such conditions, a new threat to Wahl's existence came as a blessing in disguise. Nothing focuses the mind of various factions and forges new unity as outside threats to their survival. While Wahl was battling through its last and longest strike, American culture was undergoing some seismic shifts which threatened to alter Wahl's market place. The times had been changing so much that Wahl found the only way to survive in the early '70s was to go to the dogs.

7. "Gimme a Head with Hair, Long Beautiful Hair"

The counter-culture changed hair grooming habits in America. Jack Wahl had taken notice in 1969 when he visited his son's prospective engineering fraternity at Purdue. On the wall, pictures of the previous year showed young men with their hair trimmed and their faces shaven, but the photos of the current year disclosed a new collective shagginess—long, streaming hair, curling locks, ear covering sideburns, mustaches and beards. It was a manginess not seen since frontier America a century before. Something had happened and Wahl did not know just what or how, but the businessman-engineer knew he could quantify it. He compared the two fraternity pictures. Approximately 70% of the men in the currant photo had ear covering long hair, whereas in the previous years photo only 20 percent had long hair. Personal aesthetics aside, the huge increase in shagginess had to alarm a manufacturer of hair clippers. Upon his return to Sterling, he brought his concerns to the board of directors. Such developments, he said, did not bode well for the business.

Jack Wahl wished he had been mistaken, but he was not. His observation was all too correct. The early 1970s were very difficult for Wahl Clipper. Weathering the strike had been difficult and there was no quick recovery. The long wait for the union vote made matters worse. While these issues were tearing at the company, sales in Wahl's traditional line of clippers, both consumer and professional hair care products, dropped sharply. In 1970 they had dropped to $3.5 million, and plunged again in 1971 to $3.25 and rose no higher the following year. American men were not getting haircuts like they used to. There was a whole lot less demand for Wahl hair clippers.

The post-union Wahl Clipper, though, proved resilient and turned adversity into a blessing. The business downturn forced the company to diversify and, in so doing, build the foundation for a resurgence later in the decade. To make up for losses in its traditional lines, Wahl Clipper began developing the animal clipper market. By letting its business "go to the dogs"—i.e., increasing sales to veterinarians and dog groomers—Wahl was able to weather the high tide of the counter culture. This diversification bought Wahl just enough time for its engineering department to achieve another breakthrough. In 1971, the company found another application for its rechargeable battery technology and developed the first worldwide successful cordless-rechargeable soldering iron. By 1973, the Wahl soldering iron dominated 90% of the American market.

That year, 1973, was Wahl's comeback year. It did not simply halt the three year slide in sales, it set a new record with almost $5 million in sales. Sales continued to climb. By 1980, Sales had reached $10 M. Though this was an era of high inflation, a 100% increase in sales in only 6 years indicated some very real, very substantial growth. Wahl was growing through new products. Once again, Wahl built on previous technological breakthroughs. In 1975, Wahl introduced a complete line of foot and back massagers, which employed Wahl's superb electromagnetic motor and feature controlled vibration and heat. Two years later, Wahl put another innovative product on the market, the hygienic, battery-operated nose and brow trimmer, a grooming tool that would have had no takers just seven years before.

This nose and brow trimmer showed that somewhere in the 1970s, the faithful, followers of fashion had done an about-face. The fact was, the utopian and revolutionary aspirations of the '60s had exhausted themselves. Under President Nixon, the nation had meddled and muddled its way out of Vietnam and, as distressing as the fall of Saigon was, most Americans were glad that the war was over, even in defeat. Without the war hanging over the heads of young America, the left had no one to mobilize. Demonstrations died down; student radicals, graduates or not, sooner or later had to get jobs, and the vagaries of earning a living reconnected many baby-boomers with traditional trains of thought. The generations could begin making peace. That other shock to the American psyche, Watergate, had removed Richard Nixon from the halls of power. It came just in time, allowing the Republic to celebrate its bi-centennial with genuine, though tempered, enthusiasm. Long hair persisted, but it was no longer a proclamation of rebellion and revolution. It had become a fashion, and like any other fashion, it too would and did pass. Given the acceleration of 20th century life and the popular craving for novelty, it passed rather quickly.

Interestingly enough, its passage from popular culture in 1973 was the year of Wahl's resurgence. One of the hit movies that year was George Lucas's *American Graffiti*, a coming of age story set in the late '50s. In 1974, Ron Howard, one of the stars of American Graffiti, began the hit television series, *Happy Days*, depicting the '50s as a simpler, happier period. As interest in the '50s awakened, so too did preferences for shorter hair. There was more demand for barber products, and the rejuvenation of Wahl's traditional lines, coupled with its array of new products, started a growth surge that has continued for two and a half decades.

In retrospect, it is now clear that the age of Aquarius, dawned and now gone, had been a blessing in disguise. While threatening Wahl Clipper, it did not destroy it and, with Wahl's talent and resilience, served to make it strong. The counter-culture had expanded the consciousness of American males just enough to make them aware of fashion and hair as a vehicle of self-expression. By equating style with substance, the '60s had convinced the younger generation that life was style (hence, lifestyle itself a word coinage of this period). Good grooming thus was more than a duty to be performed before one went off to work or to school or to chauffeur the kids. It had an aesthetic dimension crucial to the image that one wished to project in the world. Oddly enough, a stanza from "Hair" offered good news for Wahl's very productive, very profitable future:

I want it long, straight, curly, fuzzy
Snaggy, shaggy, ratty, matty
Oily, greasy, fleecy, shining
Gleaming, steaming, flaxen, waxen
Knotted, polka-dotted;
Twisted, beaded, braided

Powdered, flowered, and confettied
Bangled, tangled, spangled and spaghettied!

This catalog of configurations is comic yet prophetic. Gone were the old restraints on what men and women could do with hair. Fads and fashions in hairstyle only added to the market for clippers and hair grooming products. Oddly enough, the Woodstock generation had changed the way everyone looked at hair. As new possibilities became apparent, Wahl Clipper was there with a wide range of products, new and old, to help people be well groomed or make a statement or simply try a new look. In the last quarter of the 20th century, Wahl Clipper would develop more new products, open new markets all over the globe, and become, as its recent ads proclaimed, the place "where the world goes to look good."

9. Making the Grade Together

For Wahl Clipper, then, the last transition of these two tumultuous decades proved to be one of renewal and resurgence—the very kind of transition that all successful companies must make sooner or later if they are to survive. The pivotal year of 1973 was the beginning of three decades of enormous growth in which Wahl became a most remarkable player on the world stage. In the last quarter of the 20th century, it showed that a family-owned company from a small town in America's rust belt could thrive by maintaining its reputation for excellence and combining it with innovative new products, deft advertising, and bold development of foreign markets.

As they rebuilt Wahl Clipper after the strike and adjusted to the changed marketplace, the three Wahl Brothers realized that they needed to expand their board of directors. Ever since their father's death, they had been the board. Since all were active in the day-to-day operation of the company, they could meet at a moment's notice, deliberate, and decide quickly. While this arrangement had the advantage of convenience and speed, it did not always encourage documentation, nor was it always long on deliberation. With the business becoming more complex, the three brothers decided that they needed help. The help they wanted at this time was support from other members of the family.

It was also becoming apparent that they needed to create a board that includes some experts outside the family. As in all family businesses, friction had developed. One important issue concerned performance bonus compensation plans. Another concerned the company airplane and the rules governing its use. In a solution that pleased everyone, the brothers settled this later issue by selling the plane to Warren. Other problems, though, did not admit to such amicable resolution. The company needed a board of directors that was independent and could also give expert direction. In particular, they needed people with national and global business experience.

In 1973, the brothers added Wayne Wahl, their father's youngest brother, and William J. Gearns, their sister's husband to the board. Though they were still family, the two men brought a wealth of skill and experience to the company. As a manager at IBM, Wayne Wahl was well versed in computer technology and the practices of one of the world's most successful companies. He kept Wahl Clipper abreast of the latest developments in data processing.

Gearns was a New York businessman who had founded his own plastics film company and was skilled in international sales and marketing. He was interested in developing new business and also hired a strong, energetic business consultant who produced several suggestions that helped the company.

Change being change, there is something lost even in times of progress. So it was with the company's second president and chairman of the board, Warren Wahl. At Wahl Clipper's Directors Meeting in 1977, Warren announced that he was retiring. Leo's oldest son had worked at Wahl for 31 years and, for the last 22, had served as President. Under his leadership, the company had moved to its north

Locust Street location and had substantially increased its sales. At 54, he was at a young age to be retiring, but two decades as president had exacted a heavy toll on his health. The last eight years had been especially tough. In March 1969, he and his wife Mary divorced after almost 25 years of marriage. Eight months later the Big Strike buffeted Wahl and ushered in four years of travail for Warren and the company. On June 6, 1975, Warren married a high school classmate, Joan Tracy, and two years later, he decided to leave Wahl and devote himself to flying, carpentry, and enjoying his cabin in Watersmeet, Michigan.

Sadly, his well-deserved years of retirement were all too short. On June 13, 1981, he died of a heart attack at his cabin in Michigan. Even in death he imitated his father's generosity: he left 10% of his gross estate to charities to be determined by his brother, Monsignor Raymond Wahl. Wahl clipper, 1981 Annual Report paid tribute to Warren: "His strong leadership and manufacturing skills matched his complete dedication to this corporation and brought us thru a long series of profitable growth years." Even in the turbulence of the late '60s and early '70s, Warren had helped the company continue its unbroken string of dividends for its stockholders.

When Warren announced his intention to resign, the board had to decide on a successor. Both Robert and Jack expressed interest and each man made a presentation outlining his plans as President. The board voted for Jack, who became President and Chief Executive Officer, and Robert succeeded Warren as Chairman of the Board.

Like his father, Jack combined engineering and business and salted the mix with a good dose of invention. During his career, Jack would assign 46 inventions to Wahl Clipper, and in 30 of these, he was the sole inventor. He also had six other patents with Mallard for a radio transmitter that plugged into the cigarette lighter of the automobile and opened the garage door. In addition there were also three patents for self-guiding conveyors. Jack Wahl, a self-confessed workaholic, was also very much a family man. As Leo had done with his sons, so Jack and his brothers raised their sons to continue the family business.

Jack brought to his post a love of work and a competitive spirit that made him uniquely suited for the rough and tumble world of global business. In 1994, when he was inducted to the House Ware Hall of Fame, Wahl observed,

> It is a great honor to be singled out to join the entrepreneurs, the real movers and shakers…I bet most of them have been hard driving workaholics: the true entrepreneur really enjoys work. None of these Hall of Famers were working just to put bread on the table. So why are we doing it? We are working because somehow the lazy bones have been purged out of our bodies, and the fact is, we love to be in the game, especially when it's tough and we are winning.

By the time Jack Wahl became President, Wahl Clipper knew what tough was, and he knew a thing or two about winning. Under his leadership, the company would take winning to the far corners of the earth. It was able to do so, partly because Wahl management made good use of the lesson it had learned from its labor troubles. In resolving to run the company so that workers would never want the return of a union, Wahl and his management team worked hard at earning the trust and good will of the workforce. With the union gone, the company maintained and expanded its benefit package and, in addition, began introducing incentives that gave employees a stake in the company's success. Wahl Clipper now has profit sharing, a 401K plan, and multiple performance incentives for each worker.

Like the Age of Aquarius, the awful strike of 1969 and 1970, proved to be a blessing in disguise. It gave Wahl Clipper, management and workers alike, the chance to learn a lesson that most of America did not learn until much later, when it was already too late to save jobs and companies from foreign competition. On the day after April Fools Day in 1973, the same year of Wahl's turnaround, the Sterling Gazette ran a story entitled, "Wage Earners Believe They Could

Accomplish More During Work Day." It reported the finding of a recent Gallup Poll: 60% of American workers believed that they could increase production by 20% or more, 56% agreed that American workers could produce more, and 50% thought that they personally could do more if they tried. On the issue of job satisfaction, 77% of American workers were satisfied with their jobs, down 10% from April 1969 when job satisfaction had peaked at 87%.

Clearly, Wahl had come to a fork in the road and taken "the road less traveled by." In the next two decades, workers and managers developed a new relationship in which teamwork replaced confrontation and self-interest merged with that of corporate profits. With the rust belt proliferating, and first, Japan, and then Southeast Asia and China on the rise, everyone in the company could see that productivity and efficiency were good for everyone: they meant job security, increased pay, and greater satisfaction at work.

Significantly for the Twin Cities, Wahl Clipper was right in step with National Manufacturing. This hardware manufacturer was founded in 1902 by the first local industrialists to emerge from local factories: William P. Benson, Louis Bittorf, and his brother, Herman Bittorf, who was later Leo Wahl's associate on the board of Central Trust and Savings. Leo J. Wahl served as President of Central Trust and Savings Bank from 1931 to 1938. Serving as President of the Bank during the Depression, his Bank was the first to reopen after the Bank Holiday. Leo made the statement " that you really learn banking during a depression." National had begun its resurgence a decade earlier and, by the mid-seventies, was hitting full stride under President Bill Benson—like Jack Wahl, an engineer—and Plant Superintendent, Joe D. Bittorf. In the last quarter of the 20th century, both companies strove successfully to improve productivity and profits by introducing new products, automating, and giving workers greater incentives to improve plant operations.

Among Twin City industries, Wahl and National had taken a middle course that might be called progressive non-unionism. Through attention to fair compensation and benefits, incentives, and good communication, the management of both companies had created workplaces in which unions were neither wanted nor needed. The growth of Wahl and National in the fourth quarter of the 20th century testified to the wisdom of such a course. By 2001, they were the two largest industrial employers in the Twin Cities and stood in stark contrast to the community's two oldest manufacturers, Northwestern Steel and Wire and Lawrence Brothers, both of whom wound up in bankruptcy court that year. Northwestern, with its high union contracts and aging equipment, had lost out to domestic mini-mills and to European and Asian competitors. Lawrence Brothers lacked the means and motivation to stay competitive with the on slot of Asian imports.

It had been a long, strange trip indeed, but at the start of the 21st century, there were few people in the Twin Cities who could take issue with what Jack Wahl had said 30 years before about wages, efficiency, and staying in business. In 1981, President Ronald Reagan took the first step to curb union power when he fired the striking air-traffic controllers. This is when the tide turned. The United States improved its productivity and reduced the antagonism between labor and management. In the next chapter, we will look at how Wahl Clipper became "the place where the world goes to look good."

CHAPTER 5

A HIGH FLYING CONSERVATIVE COMPANY

*We're a conservative company. We're not wild
flyers. We work at staying ahead of the competition
and for that reason have been an early user of
computers for office, tooling and product design.
Our products are designed to solve people
problems, and as long as hair keeps growing
24 hours a day, our product has a place
in the market.*

JACK WAHL, 1983[21]

1. A Thousand Words & the Rest of the Story

One time when Jack Wahl was a boy, the Wahl family had sat down to eat dinner, and young Jack noticed a wet spot on the table, then another. To his surprise, more drips followed in rapid succession, faster and heavier. It was then Jack remembered: His mom had called out that dinner was ready and he had rushed downstairs; from the bathroom. He had been running water in the tub but hadn't turned it off. It was an understandable error—any lad with three brothers did not want to be late for dinner—but the water was still running and the consequences were soggy. Drip-drop, drip-drop, drip-drop, the water began to run off the ceiling light fixture, which happened to be a clipper ship. The whole family began to laugh. "Jack," they said, "has launched a clipper ship."

Several decades later, they and the rest of the Wahl stockholders might have said the same thing when they looked at the 1990 Wahl Annual Report. On the top half of page 3, there is a picture of John F. Wahl, President of Wahl Clipper; next to it is his letter to the shareholders. Wahl is smiling and so were the shareholders once they read the letter and looked at the lower half of the page. There, a bar graph of Wahl Clipper's annual net sales for the previous 25 years shows a decidedly upward thrust, one that began in the late 1970s at about the same time Wahl became President. Indeed, this little chart shows the Wahl Clipper ship going airborne.

Take-off had been gradual but successful. Wahl's net sales increased from $5.24M in 1976, America's bicentennial, to $7.6M in 1980, an average growth of at about $.6 million per year. The next three years showed a steeper ascent, with increases of about $1.5 M per year. Then in 1984, the Orwellian year of woe that hurt Democrats but not democracy, Wahl sales climbed sharply, and for the next six years increased about $5.25M annually. In 1990, the year of Desert Storm, Wahl ascended like a space shuttle. Net sales jumped almost $14.7M and reached a total of $58.2M, more than double what they were in 1986 and ten times the 1977 figure. With the triple boosters of booming international sales and growing market shares in the professional and consumer divisions, the Wahl Clipper ship had attained earth orbit.

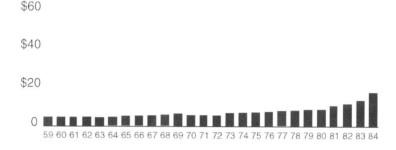

DOMESTIC SALES 1959-1984
(in $ Millions)

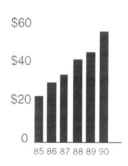

DOMESTIC SALES 1985-1990
(in $ Millions)

Wahl's earning had jumped 36% in 1989 to $18.84 in 1990. The company paid a dividend of $4.20 per share, and its after tax profit margin was 13.3%, which put it well above the leaders on the Forbes List of Consumer product companies. Not surprisingly, Wahl's productivity was outstanding. The company had earned $14,800 per employee. What a long way the company had come in thirteen years. In 1977, when Jack Wahl had become President, Wahl Clipper earned $1.33 a share.

Impressive as these numbers are, they have allowed us to recap a quarter century of Wahl history in far less than a thousand words—they can be misleading. It is all too easy for the eye to cross the page, step up through the years, to 1990's dizzying peak and jump to the conclusion that there was something inevitable about the company's growth, or that it is all summed up in these dollars and cents. Here is where history with its millennia and millennia of words becomes useful. Here is where we can draw close and see the people who made this growth possible, and their times, the stumbling blocks and stepping stones which were part of their daily walk at work. Here—in the words of Paul Harvey, who for several years advertised Wahl products on his radio show—is the rest of the story.

2. April 30, 1977: The Flight Plan

Jack Wahl was in the prime of his life when he became President of Wahl Clipper. He was healthy, physically strong, smart, well-educated, and blessed with the Wahl business savvy. Both instinct and experience taught him what made a company work. The successful executive had to look for every edge. One edge was the company that his father had built and which he and his brothers had maintained. As it entered the last quarter of the 20th century, Wahl Clipper faced enormous challenges, but it had a good foundation of manufacturing expertise, prudent management, and good market reputation. The company had always paid a dividend and was free of debt.

However, Jack knew that Wahl's solid track record was not enough anymore to guarantee its future. In a fast growing industry, Wahl Clipper had to grow even faster or it risked being squeezed out of new markets and crushed by bigger players. Raised, trained and educated to be an engineer like his father, Jack had also inherited Leo Wahl's visionary streak, his questing spirit, and a thirst for new challenges. He had brought all these before the Wahl Board of Directors when it was considering a successor to Warren Wahl. In January 1976,

Jack had proposed a five-year plan to increase Wahl sales to $15 million. That notion was so intriguing, so inviting, so irresistible, that Jack and the board eventually set the figure at $18M. Weighing Jack's innovative growth strategy and the more cautious, accountant's course laid out by his brother Bob, the board had opted for growth and picked Jack. Evidently, the engineer-visionary was also a bit of a salesman.

The selling job, though, was only just beginning. Having convinced the board to make him President and Bob Chairman of the Board, he now had to convince the rest of the company to follow his lead. Having started at the top of the company, he proceeded to work his way down to the rank and file. On April 30, 1977, shortly after becoming President, Jack held a breakfast on Saturday morning at the Holiday Inn in Rock Falls for all salaried personnel and all employees who had a stake in the company through Wahl's Dividend Equity Program. Jack's aim was to inform them of the company's new strategic plan and to enlist their support. He knew that he could not mobilize Wahl's workforce without their help.

The salesman-engineer began with what a later American President would call the "vision thing." Jack had to show his people that his vision of the future was good for the company and good for them. After announcing the five-year plan to increase annual sales to $18 M, he told his audience that:

> We've got about the best marketing, administration, and manufacturing team anyone could put together—and they're right here in this room . I've told them that each of you will want to see this company grow and will work to make it happen. Why? Because you know that if this company grows, you grow with it. Your departments and responsibilities grow, and if you're up to the challenge, your opportunities for advancement, salary and benefit increases grow.

Jack then pledged himself to the success of this mission and asked his managers to do the same, "I'm over fifty years old now, and I've spent my whole life in this business. I hope I've gotten smarter besides getting older. I'm giving an all out effort to making this Plan. I'm committed to giving it my best shot. I'm going to ask you to do the same."

Jack then explained how they would reach the $18 MM mark in five years. "We're going to work a little harder and a lot smarter" and "take a few more calculated risks in all areas." Jack knew that all companies started out with the same two resources: time and people. These would have to be Wahl's edge. Each day, each week, every person, every company had the same amount of time to use. The supply was limited, but it was also sufficient. Jack realized that the company whose managers made the best use of time and were willing to work longer, harder, and smarter, would be the company that was more competitive and able to capitalize on opportunities for growth. As soon as he became President, he had issued a directive: all salaried personnel would work a minimum of 45 hours a week. They would have flexibility in the hours they chose to work, but they had to work a minimum of 45. "This is the bottom line," Jack explained at the time, "put in 45 hours and we will be more competitive. The jobs you are doing, are important to Wahl, and if you are willing to do what is necessary to do the work and do it well, the company will be profitable and grow and everyone here will benefit."

At this breakfast, though, Jack took a cue from the motto of IBM, (Uncle Wayne's company): *Think*. He challenged all salaried personnel and stakeholder to bring ideas and imagination to their work. "We expect you to do more thinking about your work. You're all very intelligent people and we expect you to put your mind to work to initiate ideas at all levels and send them up for approval." For the company to become more innovative and dynamic, they would have to be problem-solvers and innovators too. Such an enterprise required patience, honesty, and teamwork. "Any complaint," Jack urged them, "can be submitted by anyone to any level of authority, as long as everyone in the chain of authority is also informed. My door is always open. "I'm interested in solving problems—not in creating them."

Wahl Clipper growth then began with the growth of its people—these people, Jack's associates, and the people who worked for them—but the process would not stop there. Personal participation, said Jack, would lead to corporate transformation, because the company was also "going to

> do much more budgeting and planning with individual department goals tied to the corporate objectives…smooth out the chain of command and make authority and responsibility more visible…continue to add new and innovative products to our line…expand our sales force to get more people out there pushing our products…target a product and a market and go all out to reduce manufacturing cost and lower the selling price drastically…do this on back massagers now…lower prices to bring in much larger sales volumes"

Jack hoped, that expanded sales would eventually require a second shift at the plant. Larger production runs would lower the overhead cost per unit and gain back some of the earnings sacrificed to price cuts.

Here, lest anyone get swept away in euphoric visions, Jack interjected a cautionary note. It was the voice of his father and his father's father, all of whom took risks, but, to use one of Jack's favorite expressions, never bet the farm. "We must be careful. My father used to say, 'There is no sense in wearing out the machinery for nothing', and it's true!" The Visionary had yielded the floor to the clear thinking, plain-speaking Businessman. "This is a risky business, but winning in a calculated risk can pay off in good dividends, and that's one of the things all of us want to see." It was this simple: "If we're right we'll see them; if we're wrong, we won't."

The Businessman held the floor, but now the voice belonged entirely to Leo Wahl's third son, who was determined that his father's company would not forget the lessons it had learned so painfully only a few years before. "We're going to have to look at another problem also;" he said, "and this is important. The 'word' has to get to everyone. We are dead if an expansion of the work force brings on a flood of extra wage and benefit demands because business looks good. I expect you to take this information back to your people. We all live in the Sterling area and this is where we should stay."

Jack closed his talk by reviewing what he expected from his managers and salaried staff and what they should expect from each other. The first thing he asked for was teamwork.

We expect full cooperation between every manager, every foreman, every assistant, and every department. The common corporate objective should guide all of our efforts. We must criticize ourselves and each other to assure that we are always doing our best. Self-defeating and self-interested pettiness is out.

He also wanted extra effort and leadership by example.

We expect every man in this room to care about his job. Every job is important to the whole, and we all expect to put in the time and effort to do the job right. That doesn't mean 45 hours with a couple of hours of 'bull sessions' on outside interests. Go the extra mile for the company and the company will go the extra mile for you. If you don't, your employees won't either.

Third, he required fairness and decency.

We expect our non-union plant to stay non-union! We expect and demand that every supervisor treat all employees fairly, uniformly and with respect. You are to continually demonstrate the fact that employees at this plant are much better off without a union!

The adversarial relationship between union and management had been a disaster for Wahl, a failed experiment that it dared not repeat. Besides, the company that Jack was proposing to build required the participation of everyone pulling together in a common cause.

It was to be a new day at Wahl, and it was to begin as every new day must, with people dedicating themselves to each other and working for a common cause. Jack opened the floor to questions, answered them, and prepared to adjourn the meeting, but first he let the Visionary have the floor again. Now as never before, his audience heard the Yankee Progressive and the Midwest Inventor. He spoke in a voice that was both national and local. Here was what the Twin Cities had always been, America in microcosm.

> I've traveled enough in foreign countries to see and compare the industrial opportunities of the United States with other countries. Let me tell you—we've got it all over them. The lack of capital to build facilities and buy machinery and tools, the barriers both real and artificial due to language, terrain, electrical power differences, the transportation and distribution problems, the raw material shortages, the pollution, the lack of an affluent buying market, and on and on.
>
> I tell you, everything is potentially better here in the United States. As a country, we should be able to compete with any foreign manufacturer. In most cases their only advantage is an extreme employee loyalty and willingness to work hard for very little. In other words, when foreign employees' productivity beats ours, they are not only winning but they are winning in a lot tougher league. Conversely, as a manufacture England is going down the tube because so many of the people have collectively lost the will to work.

Sterling had a long and eminent line of industrialists whose bold leadership made their companies and communities stronger. With this speech, Jack Wahl had stepped into that tradition and invited his lieutenants to join him. His plan was so breathtaking because it contained nothing futuristic or fantastic. The people who listened to him could recognize the Wahl Clipper he proposed. Even though much of it was still pure potential, it was something that everyone in the present company could build, should build and would build together. These Wahl employees were like generations of Twin City workers before them: clear thinking and plain speaking and they were committed to their task.

3. Captain, Crew, Craft

Jack's speech worked, but he had to keep making it work everyday: his exhortation now had to take the form of example. Having asked the managers to work long hours, he worked even longer, 60, sometimes 70 hours a week. He involved himself in all areas of the company's operations and made himself available. There was no mistaking his message: the higher a person's position in the company, the more that was expected of him or her. Jack made certain that the person he expected the most from was himself.

In leading by example, Jack Wahl was himself following the example set by his father. Jack often thought of his father as he went about his duties. Leo Wahl had died still in the prime of life. Every memory that Jack had of him was of a handsome, vigorous man who stood straight and tall, with his silver hair cut short. Leo Wahl was reserved but always the gentleman, always the model gentleman. He wore his hat with a brim and always tipped it to the ladies. He ran his company with vigor and prudence. He laughed at the sign that Warren put on the door of the tool room, "Do not start vast projects with half vast ideas." If he was really upset that no progress was being made on a project he might say, but only in the context of this prior and abiding counsel, "Come on Jack, Do it or get off the pot."

Jack's first project was to make the company more profitable. Profits were essential to the growth and long-term health of Wahl Clipper, or any company. Without strong profits a company could not continue to pay competitive wages, attract quality people, and invest in new products and labor saving technology. When profits dried up, a company stagnated and became uncompetitive. Death and dissolution could not be far behind. These notions did not figure in much of the public discourse then, but in time, they would. Oil embargoes and double-digit inflation in the late '70s, and the Japanese economic miracle and the ravages of the rust belt in the '80s, all gave America some sharp lessons in basic business. By that time, though, Jack's Clipper Ship was already launched and setting a course like that of other successful American companies.

Though Wahl Clipper, had always been profitable, the future that Jack envisioned required earnings and expansion of an entirely different order. As President, Jack soon realized that development required diversification. The hair cutting and styling market was really several markets, and for Wahl Clipper to grow, it had to create products for the various niches and customers in that market—the barber, the beautician, the vet, the animal-groomer, the mom cutting her children's hair, the fashion-conscious teen, and the go-getting business professional trying to make a good impression. Each of these customers needed Wahl products, but ones that met their particular needs.

In 1979, Jack began implementing his long-range plan for corporate growth. This project included product development devoted to identifying and meeting customer needs, more sophisticated marketing and merchandising, and substantial, sustained re-investment of earnings into labor saving equipment and processes. He began organizing a new management team around a radically restructured organization. Wahl Clipper, Jack realized, could grow strong through division—or rather divisions, separate sales and marketing organizations to develop Wahl's business in four distinct areas: professional barbers and hair stylists, consumers, foreign markets, and electronics, (where Wahl achieved startling success when it adapted its cordless rechargeable clipper technology to soldering irons and won 80% of that market from four very strong competitors).

The name of the game was growth. By diversifying its sales approach, the company aimed to expand its sales to established customers, open new accounts and develop whole new territories, all of which would warrant putting more salesmen in the field. Wahl Clipper could sustain this expanded sales effort only by improving productivity and developing new products. The company had to give its sales force more products to sell and maintain and increase its profit margin while doing it. The company's tradition of invention and quality engineering had positioned it to meet this challenge. Invention and engineering, as well as business smarts, ran in the family. The company had long been vertically integrated so that it controlled the manufacture of all its parts.

Equally important, Wahl's strong position in the professional market gave it a built in laboratory for developing new products for the consumer and international divisions. Trends, techniques, and fashions that surfaced with professional hair stylists eventually found their way to the consumer market. The Groomsman, a battery-powered beard and mustache trimmer, is a good example of a product that Wahl introduced in the Professional division and adapted for the consumer market. This product was Wahl's entrée into the high-volume, rechargeable rotary motor market. Wahl not only got its foot in the door, it kicked it wide open. When Sears marketed the Groomsman with its line of electric shavers, the Groomsman outsold them all. The beard and mustache SKU ("stock keeping unit) sold more than any other SKU.

Wahl Clipper's long experience as an exporter also gave it a head start on new growth. Leo Wahl had begun selling his clippers abroad almost as soon as he started the company. Later under Jack's direction, the company began developing new foreign markets. By 1983, he told a Rockford Register-Star reporter, "If America is going to keep its people employed, the market for its quality products cannot stop at the U. S. borders. One in four of our workers is employed because of exports." In the next seven years Wahl's dynamic growth in overseas markets attracted the attention of the federal government which was trying to encourage American companies to pursue foreign markets. In 1989 and 1990, the Small Business Administration named Wahl Clipper and its Sterling plant the Illinois Exporter of the Year. At this point, the interaction of Wahl's three major divisions became even more fruitful. In 1990, Wahl was able to introduce to the American consumer market, the Euroflex, a rechargeable shaver.

This multifaceted growth strategy makes perfect sense now—

hindsight basks in a 20-20 aura—but in the mid-seventies, it was still under development, and required Jack to do some difficult selling. It was part of his job to get the office and factory working at a new level of excellence. Indeed, Jack had been at this job for some years now—especially since the dark days of the strike when he emerged as the company spokesman and leader. What he had not anticipated was the resistance that he now encountered from his family within the company. The resistance was two-fold, arising from a conservative corporate-culture and family ties that would bind the hand of anyone who presumed to lead. Jack was calling the Wahl family to change the way it ran its company. He was calling them to look beyond the way Wahl Clipper had always done business and to see what the company needed to do in order to survive and thrive. He was calling them to let Wahl Clipper shed its parochialism and adopt procedures that worked for the world's leading companies. Any call for such radical change would be hard to accept, but when it came from a member of one's own family, it sounded downright unreasonable and presumptuous. A CEO, Jack learned, was not without honor, except in his own family. "Running a family business," he later recalled,

> is difficult, very, very difficult. Most people have no idea how much stress it puts on you to have your relatives on the board appraising your ability, your success, and your failure. In setting compensation and other benefits, at first I personally had a very hard time getting paid for performance. It is natural for family members to apply a leveling factor between relatives. Everybody isn't the same and that's not what makes for success. In a family company there can only be one head and that one has to have full authority and should be paid on performance.

Ultimately though, results provided Jack with his most irrefutable arguments, and the rising tide of sales, profits, and dividends carried away many objections.

Jack had significant allies in his efforts to re-energize Wahl

Clipper. He never would have gotten the job if the Board of Directors had not seen the merit of his strategy. Nor would the Wahl Clipper ship ever have taken to flight if the company had not come together to make the plan work in the shop, office, and field. Toward this end, Jack and the company received invaluable assist from board member Wayne Wahl, whose experience with IBM proved especially useful. Jack's uncle persuaded management to approve a compensation package for top executives that featured a very modest base pay, with very strong performance incentives that rewarded employees for making the company more profitable.

In 1981, Jack established a comprehensive package of employee benefits and incentives, including piecework, pension and profit sharing, perfect attendance award trips, Improshare, a fitness program, and a 401K deferred compensation plan and for key people dividend equivalent and Stock Appreciation Rights. Wahl Clipper's competitive package of benefits and incentives gave every employee a stake in the success of Wahl Clipper. People in all areas of the company contributed to the company's growth and could measure their compensation not only in larger checks but greater job satisfaction, personal growth, and career advancement.

The people of Wahl Clipper were helping Jack fulfill his post-strike vow that Wahl employees would never have another union nor ever want to have one. To grow, Wahl Clipper needed good people, which it had, and it only attracted more. In working very hard to develop new products and markets, the company was also developing a new kind of employee. As President, Jack could feel the new energy animating the work place and was spurred to even greater effort. "As the company grew," he recalled later, " I grew. It was a great joy to see Wahl employees acquire new skills and take on new responsibilities. Indeed, the opportunity for personal development that Wahl Clipper offered its workers was one of the things contributing to our long period of growth."

In the first few years after Jack became President, the company began growing gradually. The sales increases seem small in comparison with those of a decade later, but they show something quite remarkable: a small, traditional, family-owned company learning how to excel in a fiercely competitive industry. To break down the company's small town, small-scale mindset, he brought in new ideas through the managers, new board members, and consultants. Determined that this family-owned company would become a dynamic modern corporation, Jack sought the help of consultants to improve the company's marketing and public relations. For over a quarter of a century Ross Advertising provided the creativity for the consumer division. Jack continued efforts begun in the '70s to expand the board. In 1981 Wahl Clipper welcomed its first non-family member to the board: Barry Musgrove, the 46 year old President and CEO of Frantz Manufacturing, the Sterling-based garage door manufacturer. A successful executive from outside the company gave the board added expertise and a wider perspective.

Sometimes the consultants suggested a radical break with the past. Between 1971 and 1981, Wahl dividends had averaged 60% of its earning. In 1980, Peter Moffit advised the Board of Directors to take a different course. Paying out a high percentage of its earnings in dividends, he said, promoted neither growth nor the long term health of a company. It was not even in the best financial interests of the investors. By achieving a faster growth through reinvestment of a majority of its profits, the company would be transferring their earnings from annual income to capital gains, which were taxed at a lower rate. The *1981 Wahl Annual Report* noted that Moffit "questioned the ability of a company to remain the world's most efficient manufacturer of their products without reinvesting heavily to replace worn out machines." With the high inflation of the late seventies and early eighties, it was especially important for companies to maintain earnings and reinvestment at a high level.

Sometimes the visiting experts could be unsparingly honest. Wahl

Clipper became more savvy in its marketing after it hired Sue Taylor, who had successfully introduced a wet foot massage at Clairol, to be its marketing consultant. Reviewing Twix, Wahl's misadventure in home hair cutting, Taylor bluntly told Jack and senior management, "You can't expect to have a big success. You people don't completely understand what an end cap means!" Years later, Jack Wahl recalled the scene and admitted, "And we didn't!"

But Wahl Clipper, from the President on down, could learn. "They say when you fail," Jack said, "You learn more. We learned from ours, and we turned some failures into successes. The Wahl motto became *Ready, Fire, Aim*. What that means is take a shot. Learn from it, then aim for the bull's eye." The efficacy of this method was best demonstrated in Wahl's growing proficiency in product development.

New products were nothing new at Wahl Clipper. Leo Wahl had founded the company on a new product, and over the years the company had introduced enough of them for Jack to know what a necessary risk they were. New products had always been a key to success in the booming personal care appliance industry, which, since its inception in 1910, had offered steady stream of innovative products. In the last quarter of the 20th century, product development only became more important. Indeed, there was little growth without new products. In 1976, new products had accounted for $29MM in sales in the industry; by 1985 they reached more than $800MM. Enormous pitfalls, though, pocked this field of opportunity. Only one in ten new products in America make a profit. The prospect, though, did not daunt Jack, who was a product engineer at heart. He loved nothing better than to see a new product roll off the assembly line and land on the retail shelves.

His Ready, Fire, Aim approach combined daring and prudence in the best Wahl fashion. The company invested in new products yet kept calculating the prospect of success at every stage of development. Once the engineering department had developed a prototype and tested it thoroughly until it met Wahl's standards, the company introduced it in select local markets, selling it at different stores, at different prices and in different chains. To price the item to make it competitive yet profitable, Wahl figured in production costs, a small margin, and the cost of advertising, which was absolutely essential to get the product in the store and before the public's eye. If the local sales campaign sold enough to pay for the advertising, Wahl Clipper could do a large production run and go national with its campaign.

The sales force pursued a two-step approach: selling in and selling out. Radio and TV spots were essential for getting the line on the customer's shelf. The rep not only had to demonstrate the product, he or she also had to show the buyer the commercial that would bring the customer to his store in search of the product. If he liked the product and the commercial, he gave the product a try. This was the selling-in phase. If the advertising created interest and demand for the product, (getting the product off the shelves) the sales rep could return to the buyer and take a repeat order. This was the sell-out phase. Wahl hoped to sell out its initial inventory and do more products runs.

Advertising was one of the riskiest elements in product development. A new concept product could not get to market without TV spots, the point of purchase/packaging must be correct and move the customer to the point of purchase, but the high cost of commercials was itself a major barrier to profitability. Wahl Clipper, though, was not daunted. In 1985, the company spent more than $800,000 on rebates and advertising—a high risk proposition for Wahl. In fact, it showed a certain flair for getting its product before the public. In this period, and for several more years, it used such celebrity spokesmen as Art Linkletter, Paul Harvey, and Richard Karn, the co-star of Home Improvement. It also was adept at capitalizing on the opportunity for free publicity.

The approach of selling in and selling out worked. Consumer sales in 1985, which had a record number of new product introductions to that point, jumped 48% over the previous two years. The company had changed its performance from one of steady low profit margin sales into a dynamic growth division. For the first time, Wahl Clipper had a consumer product capable of selling a million units a year.

In 1986, Wahl found manna raining down, if not from heaven, at least from Hollywood. It was promoting its new beard and mustache trimmer that featured an attachment that trimmed the beard but did not cut it close to the skin. The resulting 3 to 5 day stubble was now no longer ugly but was the very image of manliness, thanks to the look that Don Johnson had popularized on the hit TV show Miami Vice. When the show's producers refused to let Wahl market the product under the name, the Miami Device, Wahl's Consumer Sales and Marketing did an end run, sending Johnson a couple dozen trimmers. He tried Wahl's stubble device, liked it, and said so. The national media picked up on the story and America learned of a new shaving product that was guaranteed not to shave as close as a blade. The trade journals found their own angle, citing Yassir Arafat and other public figures who preferred not to be clean shaven. Not to be outdone, local media focused on a local company whose new facial trimmer had caused a national stir. Johnson himself eventually did a commercial for Wahl by way of an interview that was picked up by national TV and became a wonderful 3rd party advertisement. It ended with the observation that there is something about a man who wears $1000 suits and a 5-day growth.

And there was something about a small-town Midwest manufacturer that was solid and conservative and yet hip and high-flying. Wahl made clippers with its accustomed excellence and yet it used new technology, new incentives, and new marketing techniques to make more of them for more people, and not only in America, but in the world as well.

4. Take-off, 1977-1980

It may have been coincidental that the two engineers, Jack Wahl and Jimmy Carter, began their Presidencies in the same year, but it was no accident that the former remained in office much longer than the latter. A nation emerging from the Vietnam-Watergate era, found that Mr. Carter was not what it needed in a world of Soviet belliger-ence and Islamic fundamentalism abroad as well as, rising inflation and economic stagnation at home. While "the times were a changin' "away from the Mr. Carter and the Democrats, things were falling into the lap of Northern Illinois' most famous native son, Tampico-born and Dixon-bred Ronald Reagan, whose wink and charm made Republicans suddenly ascendant and propelled him to the White House in January 1981.

As for Jack Wahl, he also welcomed the new direction the nation was taking. Shorter hairstyles were gradually coming back into fashion, and the nation was shedding the last vestiges of sixties tribalism and the unkempt pseudo-primitivism that went with it. Out was the Woodstock generation, many of whose members having reached their 30th birthday were already beginning to think about the rest of their lives. In was the Me-Generation, many of whom were the same boomers who used to wear flowers in their hair. They cared about how they looked and the impression they made. They needed the personal grooming products that Wahl Clipper was making. Wahl's business, which had gone to the dogs in the early '70s, could now swing back to its traditional role of helping humans manage their own manginess.

With the post-war baby boomers now entering into adulthood, assuming adult duties and resuming their upwardly-mobile aspira-tions, the personal care appliance industry was entering an era of new opportunities and new challenges. Between 1976 and 1985, the sales of personal care appliances almost tripled, jumping from $761M to $2.2B. Even factoring in inflation, this growth was substantial. Perhaps even more significant was the growing importance of new products. Their share of total sales had climbed astronomically from 4% in 1976 to almost 40% in 1985. If the market was now larger, its mentality was also different. The Me-Generation still carried with them significant vestiges of raised consciousness as well as memories of the 1973-1974 oil embargo and the trauma of waiting in line at the gas station. There were new traumas now that they too were paying their fuel bills. Like Americans of previous generations, they were still suckers for new gadgets and gizmos, but they wanted them to be energy-efficient.

At the same time, advances in technology promised to change the way these appliances were made, operated, and sold. The decade of the '70s saw the introduction of microprocessors, super computers, the Universal Product Code for retail scanning, and affordable personal computers. Humankind was also freeing itself of the cord. The first pocket calculators went on the market not long after Intel patented its first microprocessor in 1971. The next year, Hewlett Packard introduced the first hand-held scientific calculator, and by 1973, Sharp was producing calculators with liquid crystal displays. In 1979, Sony came out with the personal stereo, otherwise known as the Walkman, and a year later Eveready began selling its Energizer battery.

In this area, Wahl Clipper was already, pardon the expression, on the cutting edge. In 1967, it had introduced to the professional market the first cordless rechargeable battery operated hair trimmer. Four years later, in 1971 Bill Walton, one of Wahl's engineers found another application for its rechargeable battery technology. Walton invented and Wahl marketed the world's first successful cordless/rechargeable soldering iron, with detachable soldering tips. For the next three years Wahl dominated the industry and every year brought out additional tips. The business was very profitable. With this product Wahl established a new Electronics division and by 1973 captured 90% of the United States market. In 1977, Wahl came out with another innovative, battery operated product—the hygienic nose and brow trimmer. This product was brought to Wahl for marketing by an outside inventor Mr. Charlie Struck. As the '80s began, Wahl's Iso Tip line of soldering irons not only dominated this market, but provided Wahl's ever resourceful engineers with the technology for a brand new consumer product, Curls to Go, a cordless rechargeable curling iron/brush.

With these and other new products, Wahl had tapped into some very fundamental contemporary needs which would only become more urgent as the century came to an end. Modern Americans, always a very mobile lot, were only becoming even more so. This curling iron/brush should have been an ideal product for American women who were beginning to explore the possibility that they might have it all—home, family, career—and were busier than ever before. "It goes where you go," said one ad, "to add curls and body to your hair…anywhere." In similar fashion, Wahl billed its massager line as a personal care product ideal for active people who took their physical fitness seriously and might need to soothe their tired, sore muscles afterward. Wahl's Massager Station, the in-store sales aid that won the Point of Purchase Advertising Institute's 1980 Silver Prize for Outstanding Merchandising, was perfectly fitted for the self-serve shopping that had come to dominate modern retailing. One ad for the massager test station began, "Attention, Mr. Retailer, to cash in on the after golfing, jogging, cycling, gardening market, order today." The ad closed with the motto, "For the active life your customers lead."

Wahl Clipper was showing itself to be a company quick on the uptake, and in the coming years it would only become more so. Wahl Clipper was a company that brought a spirit of play and fun to marketing. The company's Seattle Slew Promotion in 1977 was an early example of Wahl's effort to use media events or celebrities to promote its product. That year, an employee of Wahl, director Bill Gearns, was a co-owner of Seattle Slew, the horse that won the Triple Crown. Gearns' connections enabled Wahl to use the champion steed to promote its line of animal clippers. The efforts were disappointing but could be chalked up to the fact that Wahl had very small penetration into the animal business. Oster was about 10 times as large. Wahl had obtained some success with poodles and other small animals, but not horses or large animals. The Wahl product at that time was low power, low cost and fine for small animals. The marketing flair was something the company could carry with it into the future and would use to build that future.

During these years of the Carter administration, Wahl was beginning to carve out a new niche for itself, one that set it apart from so many other American companies. While its growth may seem modest in comparison with what was ahead, Wahl Clipper was still outperforming most of the American economy which, in these years, remained sluggish if not mired in recession. From 1977 to 1980, Wahl Clipper's margin per sales dollar was 2.4% higher than the average American manufacturer and 4.6% higher than the average home appliance manufacturer. The company's four sales and marketing divisions gave it strength, resilience, and flexibility. It could offset occasional downturns in one market with gains in another. As it entered the '80s, Wahl also had several other things going for it: an energetic and cohesive management team, an excellent computer system, a talented work force that now numbered 171, and harmonious labor relations. Its goal continued to be to improve earnings and, in the next year the board would find that Mr. Moffit had some ideas along these lines.

It was in this period that the Twix self-styling hair trimmer provided the company with an education in new product rollouts. The trimmer was Wahl's venture into do it yourself (DIY) home hair cutting. Keeping its investment to a medium level Wahl decided to test the product in the market. A Ready, Fire, Aim project. With the investment in T.V. commercials, however, the project did not reach a break-even objective. The commercials were very effective and attracted the attention of Gillette. Though the Twix performed excellently, it could have been more attractive. After testing the product in its own labs, Gillette became even more enthusiastic. It asked Wahl to work up a quote for 500,000 units which Wahl did. In the meantime, however, Gillette decided to do one more market test. The results of this tests were not up to Gillette's expectations, so they decided to not proceed any further.

No amount of explanation could rekindle Gillette's enthusiasm. They were cautious, Jack felt, too cautious. Jack could not help feeling that Twix was simply ahead of its time. It was a learning adventure. We almost made it.

Another mishap with a big customer gave further evidence of the impact of the new global economy emerging with the rise of Japan and the Asian tigers. In 1980, Wahl's massager sales dropped 37% because one of its large private label customers began importing all of its personal care products from Asia. Wahl massagers also faced fierce competition from several other companies—Clairol, Polynex, Water Pick, Sunbeam, Oster, Northern, Norelco, Windmere, Conair and General Electric to name a few—all of whom were importing most of this line from Asia, where they could take advantage of lower labor costs. Most of them went out of the massager business after a year or two.

Having done business internationally almost from its inception, the Wahl company could look at foreign trade from both sides now. Its management could see that the new globalization could take, but it could also give. In 1980, Wahl's foreign sales jumped 42%. "This segment of our business," The 1981 Annual Report observed,

> Deserves special attention…Gross sales exceeded $2.5 million making exports important to our company. We will continue efforts to expand our product acceptance throughout the world and expect to further our recent gains…We also plan to evaluate the possibility of marketing products manufactured by others through our present Export Sales organization.

While recognizing the difficulties posed by the strong U. S. dollar, the report did not find it to be an insurmountable barrier. There were just too many opportunities out there in the wide world. Wahl management saw no reason why their company could not be a bigger player in the world economy, and that is exactly what Wahl Clipper did in the coming decade—that and becoming more proficient in developing new products, more productive through capital investments, and more adept at marketing and merchandising its products. Jack's Clipper Ship had taken off. Now it was ready to climb.

5. Ascent, 1981-1984
(This Brave New World)

In 1984, Wahl Clipper and Sterling, Illinois both reached milestones. The city where the Wahl family had settled and made such eminent contributions was 150 years old. It had a long, proud history that was rooted in the Lincoln-Yankee virtues of education and industry, civic pride and evangelical piety. Lincoln had spoken there in 1856. Billy Sunday had a rousing month long revival in 1904 that was a strong boost to his career. Teddy Roosevelt visited three times, each time being met with huge, enthusiastic crowds. The local schools, which still enjoyed a deserved reputation for excellence, and the township's excellent park system made Sterling a good place to raise a family. Sterling and Rock Falls, its feisty sister city across the river, had carved out a place in the American economy as a hardware manufacturing center. Most of the factories and mills that had made this name were eighty and a hundred years old and were still going strong—at least for now. At their outpost on the western end of the Midwest, also known as the Rust Belt, the Twin Cities were not immune from the maladies afflicting this once mighty manufacturing region: labor unrest, aging machinery, sagging productivity, intense competition from more modern plants in Europe and Asia. Within twenty years some of the major plants in Sterling would go bankrupt and either close or be reopened as much smaller operations.

So it was that Sesquicentennial Sterling was beginning to feel its 150 years. Wahl Clipper, on the other hand, was 65 years young. Bob Wahl, its Chairman of the Board, combined civic duty and good p.r. when he used Wahl Clipper's entry into the Spirit of Sterling Beard

Contest as a publicity op for the Groomsman, the brand new beard and mustache trimmer that Wahl was rolling out in the fourth quarter of 1984. This free publicity supplemented Wahl's heavy investment that year in a publicity campaign to increase the company's name recognition among consumers. The zest with which Wahl Clipper went after new business, even home town business, was a good indication that no rust was collecting out on North Locust Street.

Happily for the Twin Cities and the nation, Wahl Clipper was not the only thriving local manufacturer. Another Twin Cities company, National Manufacturing, was also thriving. This manufacturer of builder's hardware was 18 years older than Wahl Clipper and a little more staid in its public relations.

National like Wahl, had struggled through a period of transition in the fifties when their first generation of leaders passed from the scene. Under the leadership of Keith Benson, grandson of founder William P. Benson, National had been revived in the '60s on the strength of its ties with the dealer owned hardware co-ops and its innovative merchandising programs that enabled these co-ops to tap into the booming Do It Yourself Market, this was the same market that Wahl's consumer division was pursuing.

These two family-owned business would become the leading employers in the Twin Cities.

Wahl Clipper, with its prudent, enlightened management and skilled, dedicated workforce was a local example of the persistence of the small manufacturer in American economic life. Even though, for more than a century, the trend of American business was toward consolidation into larger and larger corporate units, small manufacturing firms continued to play a key role in the world's largest economy. In the world of multi-national corporations, these small companies, taken as a whole, remained America's largest employers. And some of them, such as Wahl were among the most effective and innovative companies anywhere.

Wahl Clipper was a participant in America's industrial revival that was beginning in the mid-eighties. After almost two decades of stagnation and decline, American manufacturing had begun to arrest the slide that threatened to make the nation a second rate power in the global marketplace. To meet rising foreign competition and to provide better customer service, many American companies had restructured themselves, and adopted new methods of management. They invested in technology and training and gave more decision making responsibilities to workers in the office and shop. The results were breathtaking. Between 1985 and 1994, the annual increase in productivity in the non-agricultural business sector was .98%; in manufacturing, though, it was a robust 3.04.%. It was an amazing turnabout. By the '90s America had the highest productivity in the world. [22]

The performance of Wahl Clipper in the early 1980s was clear proof that prudent, timely investment in machinery and technology was money well spent. For Wahl Clipper, the return on investment was huge and almost immediate. Acting on its consultant's recommendation to pour more profits back into the company, Wahl Clipper began to modernize in 1982 and 1983. After averaging $225,000 in capital investments in 1980 and 1981, Wahl more than doubled that amount in 1982 and 1983, spending 600,000 and $550,000, respectively. In these two years, Wahl not only grew but also became more productive and profitable. Net sales increased 31%, but net profits after taxes jumped even more—46%. It was the kind of growth Jack Wahl had envisioned, and it was only the beginning.

In the next year, 1984, Wahl Clipper upped the ante, increasing its capital investment to $950,000. Because of new products and sales growth, Wahl devoted most of these funds to a 30,000 square foot expansion of its office and factory. This project was actually the second expansion in what was to become an almost annual activity for Wahl Clipper in the '80s. In 1983, Wahl had purchased Jordan School, a 17,500 sq. ft. facility north of Sterling and used the gym as a recreation center for employees and the rest of the building as a warehouse. In

1986, Wahl bought a 12,600 sq. ft. Annex Building and built a 6,150 sq. ft. addition to it. In 1988, a 5,000 sq. ft. addition to its main plant was a good warm-up for projects which tacked on 41,000 sq. ft in 1989 and 40,000 sq. ft in 1992.

In the early '80s, Wahl Clipper had begun weaving capital investment, product development, and sales growth into a very strong, very golden braid. In 1984, it had more than quadrupled its capital investment over that of 1981 and achieved an 82% increase in net sales and almost a 100% increase in after tax net earnings. These might have been even higher were it not for a decrease in investment credits and a one-time charge of $121,000 against earnings due to the tax accounting dissolution of Wahl's Disc. As for stockholders, they had been asked to forego the instant gratification of dividends for the more substantial wealth accumulation of long-term growth, they had their cake and got to eat it too. Dividends per share rose from $.80 in 1981 to $1.00 in 1983 and $1.06 in 1984. This growth was all the more remarkable because Wahl had achieved it while the nation was struggling through a recession that began in 1982 and led "to higher unemployment and difficult times in many regions and industries."[23]

Here is an early indication that the personal care industry contained certain hedges against moderate economic slumps and that Wahl Clipper had tapped into them. With the exception of the Great Depression, which spared no one. Wahl Clipper was able to profit from fundamental things. Hair, as Jack Wahl liked to point out, grows 24 hours a day, and people always like to look good. In the age of instant communication, they like to look good according to the latest fashion. When things get tough parents look at buying a clipper and cutting their own kids hair.

Wahl had three major markets, and a fourth that added a little icing to the corporate cake. Between 1981 and 1984, all four visions had increased their sales, but the two largest had grown the most. Export and Electronics, Wahl's two smallest divisions, had increased 10% and 20% respectively. The different rates of growth led to a shift in the distribution of corporate sales.

DOMESTIC SALES BY DIVISION

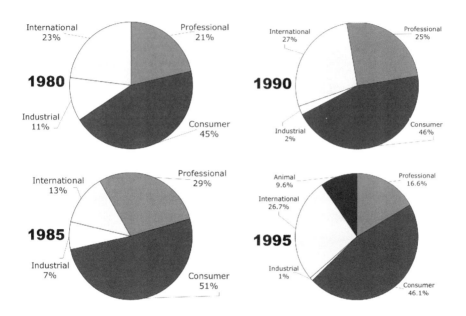

Hindsight now shows that two key indicators for the rest of the decade were the huge growth in the professional division and the reduction of growth in electronics. While Wahl had carved out a niche in the industrial market with breakthroughs in soldering tools, its traditional strength was in clippers and it would continue to lead with them. While the other four divisions boomed, Electronics was stagnate but profitable, not growing because the world was changing from Solder Connections to Solid State Circuitry. Most of the division's growth had come in 1984, with the hiring of Marion Halley, as new sales manager to assist division head, Noel Wallen. In the rest of the decade, the company did not exactly forget about its smallest division, but built on its gains by applying rechargeable technology to the creation of personal care consumer products for the other divisions. Clippers and trimmers, the mainstays of the other four divisions, had always been Wahl's strength, and with the introduction of rechargeable battery operated trimmers in 1984, they only became more important. All told, they accounted for almost 73% of all sales.

A High Flying Conservative Company

After five straight years of steady growth, the Professional Division, under Warren Wahl's son James, assisted by sales manager Ruth Heflebower, had become a national leader in clipper sales to Barbers and especially Cosmetologists. One factor contributing to the success of the Professional Division was the close working relationship it had developed with leading American hair designers. With the industry's movers and shakers as advisors, Wahl was developing products that fit the latest styles and techniques in the industry. The number of barbers decreased while the number of cosmetologist expanded rapidly. A new addition to the Professional line, Bravo, was something of a departure for Wahl, which usually manufactured the products it took to market. This Japanese-made cordless trimmer was small, easy to handle, and sported a powerful motor. It was a wake-up call for Wahl engineering to get back to designing clippers and trimmers.

Growth for the Professional Division was good news for Consumer and Export as well. The Professional Division continued to be the laboratory for new consumer products. Wahl's rookie product of the year and of the decade, the battery-operated Groomsman, had begun in the Professional Division as the 8900 rechargeable trimmer designed for professional Barbers and Cosmetologists. As Wahl began devoting more attention to foreign sales, products crossovers from the Professional Division gave Wahl a double boost. Professionals and consumers all over the world were finding the excellence of Wahl products irresistible. Because the same factory made products for all five divisions, Wahl Clipper could say with complete justification, "We build professional quality into our consumer products."[24]

After three years of hovering at the $5M mark in sales, Wahl's Consumer Division, under the direction of Sales Manager Robert J. Thurber, broke out in 1984 with a 56% leap in sales. A public relations consultant the company had hired proved especially helpful with this division. The product line packaging was updated with Wahl's new corporate colors. To build on these initiatives, the company created a new position, Director of Consumer Sales and Marketing, and hired an experienced sales and marketing executive, B. J. Cornstubble. As with so many other Wahl successes in this year, the Consumer Division's growth was the sign of bigger things to come. Throughout the 1980s, the company continued to build strength in its management teams. Marketing and research had pointed out the fact that men in sizable quantities were wearing beards and mustaches. Wahl's intention was to develop the world's best tool to groom facial hair.

Yes, the big story for Wahl and the Consumer Division during this period was Groomsman. This new line of battery-powered trimmers, the product of extensive consumer research created a huge stir. It was something new under the sun, the world's first battery operated hair trimmer. Powered by three long life alkaline batteries, the Groomsman featured an innovative trimming guide attachment that could trim the mustache and beard at five different settings. It could also shave and shape the neckline and side burns. Wahl had introduced the Groomsman at the Cologne, West Germany show in the fall of 1983. We began marketing it in the first quarter of 1984, but did not reach full production until the last quarter. Sales of almost 100,000 units in those three months were six times that of Wahl's 9243 Consumer Hair Clipper, Wahl's best selling clipper for the last five years. The impact of this new product led the trade publication, *Catalog Showroom Merchandiser*, to name Wahl supplier of the year in a brand-new product category, the facial hair trimmer.

Wahl Clipper, which only a few years before was innocent of such niceties as end caps, had now found a knack for new products. The Groomsman provided Wahl with the model for growth through product development and market penetration. The *Wahl Annual Report for 1984* summarized the lessons the company had learned. "By recognizing the need, developing the right product at the right time, positioning it correctly, purchasing and manufacturing it in large volume, and then going out with a bold advertising program, we have succeeded in creating a whole new Personal Care Product Category." Significantly, Wahl Clipper did not rest on its new won laurels. In the coming year, it introduced the Groomsman II, which offered an adjustable cutting length guide for beards as well as mustaches. Leo Wahl, Thomas Edison, and generations and generations of Midwest tinkerers would have approved: there was always room for improvement, and a little success was no cause to stop trying to get better.

Wahl Clipper was certainly bringing this mentality to its international trade, which could offer a confusing picture for all but the hardiest Illinois Yankee. Since 1980, Wahl's Export Division had grown at a rate only half again higher than Electronics, Wahl's smallest and slowest growing division. The personal care business, highly competitive and volatile, became even more so across the water. South Africa, for example, had Noel Wallen, VP of International Sales, shaking his head. Inflation and an unfavorable rate of exchange had priced Wahl out of a market that it had dominated until very recently. Asia, on the other hand, had a happier story. There, a stable currency was allowing Wahl to expand its business quite nicely. In 1984, a strong dollar had caused Wahl's international sales to drop by 14.3%, with consumer sales suffering the biggest hit. Three of Wahl's four leading foreign markets, Canada, Netherlands, and South Africa, all sagged after peaking in 1983.

This flatness was not dispiriting, because—God, save the Queen! —the United Kingdom had been following a steady, upward trajectory for four years. Wahl's sales since 1980 had nearly tripled from $101,430 then to almost $320,000. Just as the Groomsman had given the company a model for marketing a new product, so too, the United Kingdom was teaching Wahl Clipper what it could do elsewhere. A switch in distributors had provided a significant boost to business. The lesson was clear: it was essential to pick the right distributor, and equally important to build a close relationship with him that would provide support and guarantee accountability. Now that Wahl had the right Brits in place, Groomsman would give a healthy boost to international sales. The new trimmer had already generated much interest, and being battery powered, it did not require any modification to meet local specs. With its UK business growing steadily, Wahl was ready to enter into partnerships on the continent that would give them greater marketing, shipping, and service capabilities.

In 1984, Wahl management made one other key decision that helped spur the company's growth. It decided to invest in a campaign of advertising and publicity that would make the Wahl name better known among American consumers. The aim was to take the reputation for excellence that Wahl enjoyed in the professional market and extend it to the public. With advertisements, commercials, and articles in newspapers and trade journals, Wahl promoted its long-standing manufacturing excellence and its growing prowess as a creator of products for niche markets. It was great copy that was all the better because it was true and so typically American: a small, staid Midwestern company suddenly waxing dynamic by fusing old-fashioned excellence with new-found marketing savvy. It was like Pete Rose, chasing 4000 hits and along the way leading the Phillies to a world championship, or DePaul University's veteran basketball coach Ray Meyer, long known for developing George Mikan in the '40s, but now as he neared retirement, putting together a string of nationally ranked teams. Here, though the analogy breaks down, for Wahl Clipper, 65 years young and just beginning to make a name in the world.

6. New Departures
("Fare forward, Voyagers")

As Jack Wahl neared 60, he could look about and see the ranks of his contemporaries thinning noticeably. Within five years, Wahl's President and CEO would also be the Wahl employee with the longest years of service. This company that was getting better each year was also getting larger and younger. In 1984 its work force grew from 179 to 234, an increase of 31%. In remaining a non-union shop, Wahl Clipper was not only keeping manufacturing in Sterling, it was also increasing the jobs there.

Some of the milestones of 1984 involved farewells. On August 18, 1984, Donald A. Hennessey, who was a close friend of Warren's, retired as President and CEO of Wahl Clipper, Canada. Thirty years and five days before, Hennessey had joined Wahl Clipper after distinguishing himself as a teacher, coach, and athletic director at Newman High School in Sterling. He was hired by Leo Wahl to manage Wahl's new manufacturing plant in Windsor, Ontario. Though Wahl Clipper was expanding its business all over the world, particularly, in the United Kingdom, Canada remained its leading foreign market, accounting for 17.4% of all international sales in 1984.

In Wahl's Annual Report of 1984, Chairman of the Board Robert L. Wahl reported the retirement of another key Wahl executive: himself. "At the May 15, 1984 meeting of the Board," the Chairman begins solemnly, "Robert L. Wahl gave notice that on July 1, 1985 he planned to retire as Vice President and Treasurer of Wahl Clipper Corporation after completing 37 years of continuous service to the Corporation. As Chairman of the Board of Directors, I accepted his retirement plans." The prospect of retirement and more time for flying and travel might account for the playfulness from this veteran accountant and number cruncher. But then again, who could not be a bit high spirited given the way the corporation was performing? Chairman Wahl concludes, "All of our products are being accepted in the market place and we are continuing to make gains in all lines. I look forward to 1985, a very interesting year of growth for your corporation."

The Year of our Lord, 1985 would be a very interesting year indeed, and so too would those following it. In that same *Annual Report*, Jack Wahl offered this recap of his company's happy situation:

> The Sales History chart shows this as the largest yearly gain in at least the last 24 years. The Dividend Rate was increased and, we generated substantial funds to reinvest and renew ourselves for the future. That's the January 1, 1985 picture: a healthy, conservative, old-line company with a remarkable 66 year track record, now stepping ahead as an aggressive young upstart competitor.

Except that Wahl Clipper was a few years too young, Jack might have been describing Mr. Reagan, the current occupant of the White House, who was also "healthy, conservative, old line," but was "stepping ahead as an aggressive young upstart competitor." Here were two signs of the times, new evidence that American conservatism, like its British counterpart, had a splash of adventure to it, and that locally, Northern Illinois' Yankee heritage still had a lot of get up and go. While Dutch battled the lame duck vicissitudes of a second term and emerged more popular than ever, Wahl Clipper kept its growth going and then some. Indeed, "flexibility, diversification, new products, quality and continuous reassessment of the market," all enabled Wahl Clipper to accelerate that growth to record levels.[25]

Indeed, Wahl's sales curve and continuous growth performance compares favorably with Walgreens and Walmart, two of Wahl's very good customers. Many, many years of consecutive earnings and growth reflect Wahl's "fair and honest" business philosophy, a philosophy that served the company well as it took off with the cool spark of male fashion consciousness of the middle 1980s and into the '90's.

CHAPTER 6

SOMETHING THERE IS THAT LOVES A WAHL, 1985-1990

We are not just manufacturers; we are innovators;
We are always in search of a consumer need.

JACK WAHL, 1985

A few years ago we reached the conclusion that profitable
growth opportunities existed in great quantities all over
the world, if we could become a globally oriented
manufacturer and marketer. Since that time
we have been dedicated to this aggressive growth.

JACK WAHL, 1990

1. Wahl Through Veteran Eyes

Wahl Clipper had much to celebrate when it turned 70 in October 1989. In the last fifteen years, this small, conservative company, still family-owned and Midwest-based, had weathered the maelstrom of the '60s, the malaise of the '70s, and had emerged in the '80s as a manufacturing-marketing dynamo. One reason for its success was the company's long-time orientation to what became the primary corporate management focus of the 1980s and '90s: quality. Leo Wahl preached QUALITY to his sons, from the factory floor to the final product. He told his sons that the factory floor should be clean enough to eat off, and Jack recalls a time he proved it: "I remember when my Dad bought a brand-new pre-heater-thermo-set plastic molding machine. He cracked an egg in a dish, took it down to the factory, cooked it on the machine, and brought it back home for me to eat for breakfast. I still hate it when I order my eggs over easy and they come back well-done clear through."

As Wahl Clipper celebrated its tradition of excellence and its surging new strength in October 1989, it broke ground for a 41,000 sq ft main factory addition, with completion slated for that November. Demand for men's and women's grooming products boomed during the last half of the 1980s, resulting in the need for factory expansion. As the company looked both backward and forward, it turned to its two employees with the most seniority, Jack Wahl, President and CEO, and Reuben Bilbrey, General Foreman of the Assembly Department. Together, they both have been with the company for more than half of its existence. The views of these two veterans, whose combined experience totaled 77 years, were especially pertinent as the company both celebrated its past and prepared for its future. They could tell the rest of the workforce, half of which had only been with the company five years or less, how Wahl Clipper had become a world leader in the personal care industry and what it needed to do to maintain that position and improve on it.

SOMETHING THERE IS THAT LOVES A WAHL

During this time, Mr. Bilbrey, who had started with Wahl in the spring of 1952, exemplified the virtues of hard work, loyalty, and dedication. This general assembly department foreman, who directed the activities of five foremen and 165 other employees on the factory floor, had begun as a stock chaser but had too much drive and talent to remain one for long. Jack Wahl, who had joined the company in 1949, told a reporter that 70th anniversary week, "Reuben was very green but willing to learn, and I taught him the critical area of "tune" in electrical magnetic motor driven products. Wahl could not have become the world's largest manufacturer of electric hair clippers without a team of employees like Reuben. Very skilled department managers at one time were Jerry Hutsell, Laymond Miller, Ray Bable, Dave Garland, Dale Wiemken and Purchasing Manager Carl Nelson.

Reuben knew the business, he knew the people, and he knew how far Wahl had come since the early '50s. Everything about the company had grown, and as one who had participated in that growth and had contributed to it, Reuben could measure the magnitude of Wahl's recent achievements. "When I started in 1952, there were only 60 employees, and we were located in a small building in downtown Sterling. Now there are more than 350 employees. We have a large plant on the north side of town, and we'll soon be adding 41,000 square feet of factory space."

To the newest Wahl workers, many of whom were too young to know a world without computers, Reuben could testify that such achievements did not just happen. Wahl quality had been a constant throughout the years, but technology had changed the way Wahl Clipper made products. Because automation and high tech equipment achieved an extraordinary uniformity in components, Wahl could now manufacture products in quantity and with a quality far beyond the capacity of many factories in the '40s and '50s. Reuben recalled what it was like in a more labor intensive era. "I can remember many a day," he told the reporter, "when we would stay here until midnight, adjusting, correcting, and rebuilding defective hair clippers that had not passed muster. Our inspectors were dedicated to producing only perfect products." The company's consistent investment in cutting edge technology may have changed the way Wahl employees did their jobs, but their goals remained the same: quality products, satisfied customers.

Veteran though he was, Reuben was a good example of the new kind of American worker that was propelling the country's industrial revival in the '80s and '90s. Bright, articulate, motivated, he had adapted to new conditions and new demands. He was an expert on his job and in his department, but he also understood the Big Picture of what his company was doing in the market place and what it had to continue doing. His home was the shop floor but he could wax eloquent on Wahl's products, especially the Groomsman Beard and Mustache Trimmer which, said Reuben, was a "revolutionary new product. It hit the market about four years ago and continues to be a hot seller."

Though Wahl was experiencing phenomenal growth, Reuben made it clear that at Wahl Clipper fundamental things still applied. This family-owned company remained family-oriented. "It's not unusual to see a mother and her daughter or grandson working here," he explained. "It's company policy, though, for obvious reasons, that a supervisor can't directly supervise a relative. At Wahl, the wages and benefits are good, and you don't have to worry about losing your job. We operate pretty much like a big family. If you have a problem, you can sit down and work it out with the people involved." Having put the aberration of the union years behind it, Wahl restored its shops and offices to their original state as a worker's second home, his extended family where he spent a third of each week day. Such a place, said Wahl Clipper's second eldest elder statesman, "was a good place to be."

His long tenure at Wahl Clipper gave Reuben a clear view of the future. "I foresee even more company growth and expansion through the introduction of leading edge products." Wahl Clipper was a good place to be because it was a growing company and, if Reuben Bilbrey was any indication, a dedicated worker could do a whole lot of growing with such a company.

Wahl Clipper's eldest elder statesman, 40-year veteran Jack Wahl, saw things much as Reuben did and shared his vision with the workforce and their families. In an October newsletter, he recounted Wahl's achievements and its outstanding prospects.

Wahl Clipper's traditional strength in product design and development, he told his people, was only getting stronger. The Groomsman, a battery-powered, facial-hair trimmer introduced in late 1984 had become a spectacular success story, creating a whole new product category which many competitors had rushed to fill, but none had been able to dislodge Wahl from its position of dominance of this product. As sales clearly indicated, Wahl, which had first produced the Groomsman, still did it best. Another new product, the E-Z Trimmer, affectionately known as the nose-picker, was the first battery operated trimmer designed specially for removing hair from the nose, ears, and eyebrows. A third new product, the Euroflex Electric Shaver, helped fill out Wahl's consumer grooming line. Wahl's innovations were not limited to clippers, its traditional strength. It had developed the first flat curling iron for Z-shaped curls, which was a brand new styling tool for salons. Going from strength to strength and doing what had long been natural, Wahl had adapted this product to the consumer market and come out with FrenZee, a comparable product for the consumer market which gave hair the perm look without giving it an actual perm. From here, Wahl created Shapes of the Future, a 4 SKU line that included

1. The original Frenzee 7/8th inch-wide curling iron;
2. Wahl's exclusive Mini Angles, which created smaller, tighter, z-shaped curls for shorter hair;
3. Tri Angles, which created texture on texture to achieve fuller bodied hair style;
4. Spiral, an iron for bouncy spiral-shaped curls.

Jack pointed out, though, that these products were not Wahl's greatest cause for celebration. That honor, he said, went to Wahl's workforce, a group of "intelligent, loyal, working, and very dedicated employees," who for 70 years had been one of the chief reasons for Wahl's success. In the company's annual report, Jack gave fuller expression of the company's gratitude and commitment to its workers.

> As Chief Executive of Wahl Clipper Sterling, it was my responsibility not only to pursue profit, but also to create a community where those who are capable can complete their careers, be it 20 or more years, with a feeling that they have truly made a good life decision to be with this company. A company that does its best to avoid layoffs. As a privately owned family organization we should always keep this in mind. It is our responsibility, but it is also the basis of our strength.

These were no idle words but an official confirmation of what Reuben Bilbrey had told the reporter in October. By 1989, the strength of the Wahl community was most impressive indeed.

This septuagenarian company, which looked so young and strapping, was a curious hybrid in the new emerging global economy. It remained family-owned and operated; it still had its headquarters in the small Northern Illinois town where it started; and it still did what it had always done, make and invent clippers. And it did this in the heart of America, where, in the words of a recent Dylan song, "They don't make nothin' here no more."[26] Unlike so many companies which had resorted to outsourcing in order to remain competitive, Wahl Clipper was a vertically integrated manufacturer that produced almost all the components for its products in house. Though Wahl's growing international strength enabled it to source parts and products abroad, its greatest strength continued to be the self-sufficiency of its Sterling factory.

Wahl had roared through the 80's. While most of the nation was mired in recession during the first years of Ronald Reagan's presidency, Wahl was humming along at a fast clip. By the time the economy recovered, the company's growth was accelerating dramatically. To use a line from the Smith-Barney commercial of that period, "Wahl made money the old-fashioned way—it earned it!" To be exact, Wahl was increasing its profits by using the latest technology to improve productivity, developing new products to fit certain market niches, and opening new sales territories all over the world. Wahl Clipper had become a shrewd, formidable international manufacturer and marketer. Like the Ditka Bears of that era, Wahl Clipper was the corporate embodiment of its leader's skill and spirit. It demonstrated technical mastery, marketing sophistication, drive and delight in competition.

Under Jack Wahl, the company had learned how to win in a variety of ways and revel in new challenges. Like any champion unit, Wahl Clipper was tenacious, resilient, and so good at capitalizing on opportunities that it often seemed to manufacture them along with its products. A good example was its modified Groomsman, which had a special attachment that kept beards at a five day stubble. Though the producers of the TV series *Miami Vice* refused to let Wahl market it under the name *Miami Device*, Wahl nonetheless received a windfall of media coverage and free publicity when Don Johnson, the star of the series and a popularizer of the 5 -day stubble, let it be known that he used the product. By concentrating on excellence in all phases of its operations, Wahl put itself in the position to receive the gift of good luck, the very cultivated knack of being in the right place at the right time.

In October 1989, Jack Wahl invited his workers and their families to savor their achievements.

These he listed in a series of bullets that were not just silver but golden:

- We have world class products produced in a state of the art American factory with strong promotional marketing programs.

- Through the years our business has been GOOD, and in fact, all 70 of our years have been profitable.

- We have exactly doubled our employment in the last 5 years.

- In 1988 our corporate sales increased 25.8%.

- Our first quarter of '89 was 26.2% ahead of last year.

- It's a FACT, 1989 will be our 18th consecutive year of sales increases.

Jack Wahl, though, never stopped being a leader and motivator. He would not let the matter rest on past accomplishments, no matter how long and how sustained. He also invited Wahl employees to celebrate the future which they were now building. Jack's last two bullets were platinum:

- Wahl is investing approximately 3 million dollars to increase its capacity to serve our customers world-wide. This includes sizeable expansions to our plants.

- 41,000 sq. ft. addition is to be added to our main factory in Sterling, Illinois, with completion expected by mid November. A 20,000 sq. ft. facility in North Kent England has been acquired and is being renovated to expand our operations base in Europe.

Having come a long way, Wahl Clipper was not about to rest on its laurels. It was preparing to parley its most recent achievements into even more spectacular growth. Vigorous product development and a stronger foothold in Europe were helping Wahl Clipper attain a new critical mass, one which few other local companies had achieved. As it entered the '90s, Wahl Clipper, with a work force nearing 400 strong, was making the quantum leap to global manufacturing and marketing. Wahl was going to take its strong name recognition enjoyed among consumers in America and Canada and let it shine across the waters, to Europe and to Asia, to South America and to Africa.

2. Strong Divisions, Multiplying Profits, 1985-1989

During the last fifteen years of the 20th century, some of Wahl Clipper's most spectacular achievements were derived from overseas trade. Wahl was the little Illinois company that could and did. The reason it was even able to try, was its growing domestic strength. Selling abroad was costly and risky and required significant investment, not to mention patience and perseverance to see a return on that investment. Wahl Clipper, which has always been virtually debt-free, sallied forth to Britain and Europe and Asia on its own dollar, on the strength of the profits which its Professional and Consumer Divisions were generating. The little Illinois company that went abroad began its journey by doing all that it could at home and finding ways to do even more. Wahl's International divisions became more than a hedge against the volatility of the marketplace; they meshed to create one powerful engine of growth. Wahl had become a clipper ship that could go anywhere and, more importantly, its pilot and crew had learned and were continuing to learn where it should be going. It fared forward then like the Yankee clippers of old, with lightning bodacity.

The company was accumulating an impressive collection of consecutive streaks. Some went back to the beginning of Wahl Clipper: consecutive years of being profitable and consecutive years of paying dividends. These virtues testified to the prudence and foresight of Wahl's leadership, and these virtues were all the more remarkable because they had made the dangerous passage of generations. Handed down from father to sons, they formed a heritage that a third generation of Wahl's was preparing to receive and maintain. The streaks that were of more recent vintage were equally significant, for they revealed the direction of the clipper ship and its trajectory. Wahl had not had a layoff since 1974, when it was emerging from the trauma of the union. Its string of years with increasing sales went back to 1975. A few years later, after Jack Wahl had become president, Wahl Clipper began its string of consecutive years of profit sharing. The company had begun to get its mallards in a row in the '70s, with management and workforce pulling together in the same direction.

As proficient and consistent as Wahl Clipper had become, no one in the company regarded these consecutive streaks as automatic annual occurrences. Neither memory, nor the marketplace nor Jack Wahl would permit such complacency. The older hands could recall what the late '60s and early '70s were like. The challenges from Wahl's competitors were unrelenting, and the thrill of victory, of participating in a team effort to sell and service better than anyone in the world, was just the kind of intoxicant that every corporation needs. Besides, under Jack Wahl, the company had developed a host of incentives that provided tangible rewards for making the company more profitable.

One especially important incentive for the company and the workers was the perfect attendance award. Since approximately 40% of an employee's compensation consisted of benefits which the company had to pay whether the employee was at work or not, it was in the company's best interest that employees be on the job every day earning the other 60% of their wages and contributing to the productivity of the company. The company found that developing a tier of significant incentives for good attendance was an investment well worth making. Those employees with perfect attendance became eligible for awards each quarter. At year's end, those with one year's perfect attendance were entered in a drawing for a Caribbean cruise, a week in Florida, or a $1,000.00 (taxes paid) cash prize. Those with more than one year of perfect attendance were entered in the drawing for each year of perfect attendance. The company made sure that those who maintained their string of perfect attendance could not lose: after five straight years without missing work, an employee who had not yet won in a drawing, could automatically receive the grand prize.

Something There is That Loves A Wahl

As Wahl was beginning to consider new foreign initiatives, it was strengthening its base at home. The time was ripe for growth. Throughout the '80s, there was a rising demand for clippers throughout the personal care industry. Wahl's excellent reputation among barbers and hair stylists, as well as its increased name recognition among consumers, put it in an excellent position to capitalize on this boom in the industry. Wahl Clipper, though, balanced opportunism with prudential foresight. It looked the glittering gift horse in the mouth and recognized with some uneasiness that a major factor in rising sales was the expansion of large beauty supply store chains, whose cash and carry stores sold professional products to consumers as well as professionals. As in other areas of retailing in this period, these chains, with their multiple almost ubiquitous outlets, their enormous buying clout, and discount prices, were threatening independent full service dealers. One of Wahl's new product lines during this period, the Sterling family of deluxe professional hair clippers, was designed to give independents a strong, extremely profitable new product.

Wahl Clipper was responding to the decade's new opportunities by expanding its production capabilities and putting them to good use with a host of new products. The building expansion of 1985 increased the office space by 40%, doubled the tool room and maintenance department, and double decked the whole Sterling warehouse. At the same time, product development was getting up a head of steam. While Groomsman was claiming 90% of the market in 1985, Wahl also introduced two new lines of shavers, the Lady Wahl battery shaver and "What a Shaver," a battery operated shaver for black men. New products continued to roll out. 1986 was a big year, with the "Stubble Device," a variation of the Groomsman popularized by *Miami Vice* star Don Johnson; a battery operated pet trimmer and horse trimmer; a rod-less pin perm; a battery operated foot massage; and a makeover for the Vac-U-Klip, which was renamed and repackaged as the EZ Trimmer.

The next year was an even bigger year. In fact, 1987 was huge. The Z Curl professional curling iron, a Wahl invention that produced angular curls to add texture and body to the hair, headed a long list of new additions. Which included the Sterling line of professional hair clippers, a Sterling line of high quality electronic tools, the Designer line of professional hair clippers, a corded rechargeable Groomsman beard and mustache trimmer, the Homestyler battery operated home hair trimming kit; Comfort Curve, a massage cushion; Cordless Comfort, a rechargeable wand massager, Back Relaxer; and a Defuzzer-fabric shaver.

The rest of the decade was more of the same. In 1988, while the company was adding 4000 square feet to the Wahl annex, it was introducing a professional mini Z iron, a battery operated mustache trimmer, a close-up extension mirror line, and Frenzee, a Z curling iron for the Consumer Division. The following year, Wahl continued to introduce more curling irons, with the mini triangle and angle iron in the Consumer Division. It also came out with its first detachable blade professional trimmer. In 1990, Wahl introduced a new nose and brow trimmer, a rechargeable "What A Shaver," and a battery operated Cool Cuts for cutting designs in the hair. Even Electronics, Wahl's diminutive fourth division, got back in the act, building its first fiber optic splicing tool.

The two divisions which drove Wahl's growth in the '80s were Professional and Consumer Sales. The 1987 Annual Report's description of the Consumer Division can actually apply to both divisions: "Over the past five years this division has increased sales…changing from an unknown mediocre contributor with steady sales and low profit margins, to a well-known dynamic growth division with excellent profit margins." From 1983 to 1990, Professional increased its sales from $3.3M to $ 14.7M, while Consumer leaped even more spectacularly from $4.7M to $26.2M. Though the Consumer Division grew on a grander scale during this period, much of this growth actually began in Professional, which remained the proving ground for new products. There, Wahl developed clippers and curling irons that it was to adapt for the consumer market, creating the Groomsman battery operated trimmer and the FrenZee curling iron.

The catalog of new products and the sales figures are spectacular, but they do not indicate the extent of Wahl's achievement or how hard won it was. The personal care appliance market is enormously competitive, with major players from all over the world vying for market share. While the success of a company is reliant on huge amounts of time and expense spent on research and development, there is no assurance for victory in the market place. The next season, the next year, only bring with them a renewal of the battle for market share. Groomsman and the Zee Curling Irons showed that even when a company gets to market with an innovative new product, its success will not go unchallenged for long. Unless the innovative company is also savvy, tenacious, and resilient, it will soon be unseated. Once competitors see a successful new product, they do not waste time marveling at its ingenuity or despairing of the creativity of their own engineers. Within the year, they can be counted on to come out with their own versions. (Chances are they have already been working on something like that anyway). Sometimes their variations are an improvement or a different approach to design or operation. Some competitive importers become "category killers" because they drive the price down further and further as they eliminate advertising and other services provided by top quality manufactures. Sometimes, too, their version is a blatant copy, and the victimized company must weigh the merits of litigation. At any rate, the innovating company must respond: If an invention, the company will apply for patents and vigorously defend them, as Wahl did with Zee Curls. In other situations, the innovator can meet the competition by lowering its prices or upgrading its product and offering more value, as Wahl did with the Groomsman.

Wahl's big adventure with curling irons was enough to remind its people not to quit their day job, which was the manufacture and marketing of clippers, trimmers, and whatever other electrical cutting instrument Wahl ingenuity and marketing savvy could devise. The fortunes of Wahl's innovative curling iron zigged and zagged like the curls they created. Though it was not a clipper, the Zee Curling iron was like so many other Wahl products: Wahl Clipper developed and patented the iron; it started in the Professional Division and its success there led to its morphing over to the Consumer Division as did the home perm. What set it apart as a Wahl product—apart from the lack of vibrating, oscillating, or whirling blades was the way it got to market and what happened when it got there. Conceived and developed at Wahl engineering, the Zee curling iron was produced in China to keep its price competitive with the other curling irons on the market, most of which, since the mid-seventies, were made in Asia. Only the miracle of the fax machines, had permitted Wahl's engineering department to overcome the barriers of language and ocean. Engineering drawings were worth thousands of words, and a project which would have been impossible only a few years before, proved to be a rousing success—at least for awhile.

Introduced to the professional market in August 1987, the Zee Curl made an immediate impact that invited comparison with the Groomsman. Developed in collaboration with Nick Altamore, Wahl's Rockford based consultant in professional hair products, Zee Curl iron was something new under the sun, a styling tool that made angular curls which added texture and body to hair. "The product," the 1987 Wahl Annual Report noted, "shocked our curling iron competitors, created a huge amount of excitement with buyers, and generated an instant back order situation." Wahl acted quickly to build on its initial success. It made a series of instructional videos of the techniques in Clipper Cutting, Pin Perming, and Zee Curling. In 1988, Wahl introduced a smaller professional model, the Baby Zee to be used on shorter hair, and FrenZee a modification of the Zee Curling iron for the consumer market. At the 1988 National Housewares Show, Wahl's demonstration of its new line of curling irons was a resounding success. One major discount chain placed an order for a half million FrenZees.

Indeed, things were going well. After a relatively short time things went terribly wrong. The order for 500,000 irons was difficult to fill as quickly as needed. The number was huge, and Wahl's customers all demanded shipment immediately. Other companies rushed into the fray with low price knock-offs that Wahl's big customer could not and dared not resist. Determined to sell the product while, pardon the expression, it was hot, the big box backed out on its commitment to Wahl and began buying low-price knock-offs from Asia. It was a maddening situation. Wahl had applied for a patent on its curling iron but, until the patent office rendered its decision, it could do nothing to stop category killers who saw a golden opportunity to supplant heavily advertised Zee Curls and FrenZee with low-priced copycats. To make matters worse, the discount chain was selling both these copies and Wahl's FrenZee side by side in the stores. Racing to get its product to market ahead of the competition, Wahl labored to establish a production line in Sterling to supplement the FrenZees being turned out in China. Wahl incurred heavy air freight expenses flying the product over from China, invested heavily in ads in Seventeen and Teen Magazine, and with only half of its big order filled, wound up with a substantial inventory of curling irons.

The repercussions of this tumultuous venture continued into 1989. The market for curling irons had collapsed under the weight of low-priced knock-offs that had flooded the stores during the 1988 Christmas buying season. Wahl Clipper's sponsorship of Miss Teenage America, Miss Cathy Bliss, did not succeed in boosting curling iron sales. Wahl was forced to write-off its surplus of curling irons. Late in the year, Wahl finally received the first domestic and foreign patents on its curling iron and began patent infringement action. Its settlement in a suit against ConAir helped recoup some of its lost sales. After another long and diligent pursuit, we were able to enforce our Z-Curl patent against Vidal Sassoon, settling with their payment of $100,000 cash to Wahl and their destruction of 250,000 infringing Irons in their inventory.

Though the legal victory came far too late to salvage its curling iron trade, Wahl Clipper could still count the episode a success. The Zee Curl was Wahl's first significant business venture in China, and provided important experience for expansion there in the '90s. While Wahl had been bruised by the market stampede that its new products had unleashed, it emerged from the fray stronger than ever. These new curling irons had increased Wahl's name recognition with the public and solidified its reputation for innovation.

As interesting and instructive as the curling iron adventure was, neither its boom nor its bust could distract Wahl from its core business, which was the manufacturing and marketing of clippers. Even with the curling iron write-offs of 1989, the Consumer Division's sales only dropped off 6%. Here, the Groomsman cordless trimmer sparkled as a new product with remarkable staying power. In 1985, its first full year of sales it had claimed a market share of 90%, and it retained its leadership even though other competitors joined the field. Wahl found Windmere infringing one of its Groomsman patents and was happy to negotiate an out of court settlement. By 1990, though its market share was only 40%, Groomsman continued to be the leading seller in the product category that it had created just five years earlier. Of course, with the market now much larger than it was then, two-fifth's of the pie remained a sizeable piece indeed. Indeed, a little competition, excluding the cut-rate knock-offs of category killers, could be a helpful, healthy thing for a category leader like Groomsman. Armed with the Wahl name and its own reputation for excellence, Groomsman benefited from the advertising campaigns of Norelco, a leading rival which expanded the market and boosted demand for a product that the public associated with Wahl Clipper. When John Q. Public went to get a cordless trimmer, he was more than likely to find and buy a Wahl cordless trimmer.

It was clear that consumers were no longer shopping at many of their old haunts. Wahl's Annual Report of 1990 notes that that year "will also be remembered as an extremely rough year for retail merchants. Wahl suffered our largest ever bad debts. Bankruptcies were declared by a number of large long standing customers such as Best Products and Hills Department Stores. The losses were not confined to the Consumer Division and totaled over $400,000." The Big Boxification of America had begun, and large private chains such as Wal-Mart, Home Depot, and Lowes were expanding rapidly and driving smaller, less efficient competitors out of business. In the new global economy, independents of every stripe were under siege. And so were big discounters. Wal-Mart, another mass retailer with whom Wahl had been doing business since 1980, was already overtaking K-Mart. The future belonged to Sam Walton and other mass retailers who could source their inventory globally, reduce unit costs by buying in quantity, and offer everyday low prices that drew people from twenty, thirty, or forty miles around. In a world that was becoming increasingly one market, it was very good that Wahl Clipper at this time was also developing an international reach.

3. Europa and Exports: A Contact Sport

Exporting," Jack Wahl was to say later, when the International Division began to account for more than 20% of Wahl Clipper's sales, "is a contact sport." This witty nugget of wisdom had come to him by way of both setback and success. In the mid-eighties, the company had decided, in the words of its 1985 Annual Report, "to become an aggressive global marketer." Rising sales in the United Kingdom indicated that there was opportunity abroad; the intense competitiveness of a global marketplace also indicated that there had better be such opportunities. Wahl's competitors often sought a price edge by sourcing products in Asia, where labor costs were radically lower. Though it was beginning to source some parts and certain products abroad, Wahl Clipper was still a family-owned company based in Sterling, Illinois that was committed to manufacturing in Sterling, Illinois. It looked for another solution. If Wahl Clipper could significantly boost its international sales, it could expand production, lower the unit cost of its products, and take them to market competitively priced.

It soon became apparent that Wahl quality alone could not crack a lucrative, intensively competitive market like Western Europe. The Groomsman, an innovative, superbly crafted product, was a case in point. In the first couple years after Wahl set out to become an aggressive global marketer, Groomsman had not even made a dent in Europe. Sales were soaring in the States but, across the water, Braun, Kuno Moser, Remington, Panasonic, Phillips, Hitachi, and Pifco battled for market share without worrying over an upstart from the frontiers of Northern Illinois. It was clear that Wahl needed trained sales people in Europe and more control over sales and distribution there. It was also becoming clear that History might be providing an opportunity for turning things around.

The beginnings of Wahl Europe Ltd. go back to my touring of the Domotechnica, the worlds largest Housewares and Domestic Appliance fair held yearly in Cologne Germany. I was surprised to find a company named Fernhurst manufacturing small electrical appliances in England. That is where I met Brian Hollands, President of Fernhurst. Since I was interested in Wahl Clippers growth, we talked about ways which we might form a partnership. I learned that Fernhurst was in trouble financially, and I reported that information back to the Board and Wahl Management. The conclusion was reached that we should have Bill Burke, Wahl's CFO go to Fernhurst, look at their financials, and make his recommendation. His report was that Wahl not bid on the corporation. I concurred and we decided to wait and see if they wouldn't just liquidate the company.

My Administrative Assistant, Linda Gieson, established a close relationship with Brian Hollands and his secretary and throughout the year kept me informed on the situation. I was particularity interested in hiring Brian Hollands. In the meantime, Marchant Hills, our exclusive Distributorship in the U.K., visited us in Sterling at the request of Nolen Wallen, VP of International Sales. I asked what their plans were for the future—Did they have family in the business etc. It seems they were already thinking about a possible sale of the business and I told them Wahl would be interested. Our next visit with Marchant Hills was in Birmingham, England at a consumer trade show. There we seriously discussed the acquisition of their distributorship by Wahl Clipper. If we were to acquire the business, there were two people who would be required to stay on for a short while—Owen Owens, the outside sales manager, for 18 months and Ken Reynolds, the inside manager, for 6 months. Meanwhile, back in Sterling at the October 28,1987 Board meeting my President's Strategic Plan regarding the formation of Wahl Europe Ltd. was reviewed and approved. Operations were scheduled to begin on January 1, 1988. There were to be 1000 shares issued with Wahl Clipper Corporation owning 998 shares; John F. Wahl owning 1 share; and Brian Hollands owning 1 share. The Board specifically approved a 25-year lease for a building in Herne Bay Kent, which is about 90 miles southeast of Central London, England. We leased a building of 5,000 square feet and expected it to be sufficient space for a year or two, but within 6 months the building was at capacity.

The three parts that had to fit together to make the venture a success were 1- we needed to obtain ownership of the Distributorship; 2-we would have to decide on a location and acquire a building; and, most important, 3-we needed to hire a motivated manager, specifically we needed to hire Brian Hollands. This being the first acquisition of an International operation negotiations were long and tedious but it would turn out to be fantastically successful.

Wahl Clipper Corporation had passed one of those quintessential Wahl turning points, the moment of the prudent gamble. Just as one hundred thirty years earlier Frederick Wahl chose to pack up and head for the New World, the company his grandson had founded and which his great grandson was running, now decided to invest in founding a subsidiary in the Old World. Western Europe itself was in the midst of a prudent gamble of its own, an epic attempt to do something absolutely new—achieving political and economic unity, not by force of arms, but by peaceful, politic negotiation, the rule of law, and mutual consent.

This new united, free-trading Europe had been a long time coming, and though it was not there yet, the goal was in view.[27] Europe had taken its first steps toward economic and political union way back in 1957, the year of Leo Wahl's death. The nations of Western Europe signed the Treaty of Rome, which established a European Customs Union for setting trade policy within the union and for breaking down and removing all internal tariffs that blocked the free flow of goods and services within Western Europe. It took almost three decades before the European Community actually began to dismantle these trade barriers. The decisive breakthrough came in 1985, when Western Europe approved a White Paper identifying almost 300 separate reforms necessary for making Europe a single market. Two years later, the member states signed the Single European Act which set December 31, 1992 as the deadline for establishing the single market. The ambitious goal of this act provoked a lively debate over how to establish a single European Banking System, which was absolutely necessary if such a market were to be sustained.

The difficulties were enormous, but the benefits were incalculable. From her vantage point in the British Isles, Prime Minister Margaret Thatcher had a pretty good view of this unprecedented historical situation. "What a prospect it is," said the Prime Minister, a plain speaker, not given to hyperbole, "A single market without barriers, visible or invisible, giving you direct and unhindered access to the purchasing power of over 300 million of the world's wealthiest and most prosperous people." Businesses all over the world were thinking of it, and not a few CEO's were salivating. Kazuo Chiba, Japanese ambassador to Britain observed, "With 1992 in mind, Britain has come to be regarded as the springboard for opportunity in Europe." Companies which had established manufacturing operations in Britain or on the continent by 1992 would have a competitive edge, being situated within the new market and free of import duties on its products.

With the support of his uncle Wayne, Jack persuaded the Board of Directors to expand the company's operations in Britain and Europe. Wayne was especially persuasive because he spoke from experience. He was an executive at IBM, a company that had profited enormously in Europe. He was especially enthusiastic about the prospects in the United Kingdom. "To grow," he told the board,(with the experience of Matthias Wahl, Frederick Wahl, and Leo Wahl supporting him), "we have to take risks." The United Kingdom was a natural base for Wahl Clipper. It had been selling in Britain for almost 50 years and its sales had been climbing steadily in recent years, making it the top market for Wahl's exports.

In fact, establishing a wholly-owned subsidiary there was not a new idea. Founder Leo Wahl had established a Wahl office in Britain prior to the First World War, run by a man named Oswald Hill. Oswald was a navigator on a plane that crashed during the war. He disappeared. Unbeknownst to Leo, Oswald had entrusted the business to another man, who ran it while Oswald was in the service and began to manufacturer clippers on his own. After a few years, Oswald, who had regained his health, reappeared to continue Wahl operations in Britain. Years later, Wahl learned of the manufacturing operations set up by Oswald's caretaker, when the British government liquidated the manufacturer's assets and sent Wahl its $15,000 share. Wahl Clipper got one of its first lessons in the importance of the need to carefully watch overseas assets.

To begin meeting the Euro Union's 1992 deadline, Wahl Clipper had to gain control over the sales and distribution of Wahl products in Britain and Europe. In 1987 and 1988, it founded a British subsidiary, Wahl, Europe, Ltd., with headquarters in Herne Bay. Jack Wahl was its Chairman and Brian Hollands its Director. There it established a bond-ed warehouse where products could go in and out free of duties and V.A.T. charges. Wahl then bought out its very successful British distributor, Marchant Hills, and also Throssle Suppliers, Ltd.

Herne Bay was a good location in several ways. It was a two hour drive from London's Heathrow Airport, and once the tunnel under the English Channel was completed, it was also a two hour drive from France. Herne Bay had another thing going for it. It was the home town of Wahl Europe's general manager, Brian Hollands, characterized in Wahl's annual report in pip-pip jolly good British fashion as "a pleasant chap" with "a strong manufacturing and sales background." Indeed, under Holland, Wahl Europe expanded rapidly.

Wahl began its new European venture with prudence and caution. For the first 6 months, Holland's home also served as his office and showroom. Because land and construction costs were high, Wahl leased a small warehouse, but that "pleasant chap" Holland was also a sales dynamo. Within six months, Wahl Europe was looking for a larger warehouse. By 1988, Wahl Europe employed 9 people at Herne Bay, and in another three years, its work force there had risen to 25 and was handling all distribution and invoicing to Europe as well as offering service in seven languages. In 1990, Wahl Europe moved into a 20,000 square foot facility which it still occupies. With its base in Herne Bay, its vigorous sales efforts directed by Hollands, and regular participation in major trade shows, Wahl Europe has steadily increased its sales and established the Wahl name among European professionals and consumers both.

Brian took the lead and presented the first home hair cutting kit to a catalog house, and opened the United Kingdom to the use of home hair clippers. As Brian had guaranteed, sales were extremely good.

With Wahl Europe leading the way, Wahl's International Division made a quantum leap in the last half of the 1980s. In 1985, International accounted for 13% of Wahl's sales. By 1990, its piece of the pie had risen to 27.4%. This upsurge is all the more remarkable because in those five years, the Wahl pie had more than doubled, from $22MM in total sales in 1985 to more than $58MM in 1990. By the early '90s Wahl was exporting to more than 70 countries and, in many of these, Wahl had a market share of 80% or more. In South Africa and Nigeria, the market share exceeded 95%. The Asian and Pacific sales region, under the direction of Robert Wahl's son, Lee, realized significant growth in this period, and in 1992, Lee Wahl helped the company secure 25% ownership of Unity Distributors, a profitable sales agency in Australia.

In a 1994 speech, "How to Market Around the World," Jack cited three reasons for his company's success in exporting: it used its domestic strength as a foundation for overseas trade; it established a presence in foreign markets; and it adapted its products and sales strategies to individual countries. Wahl's great domestic strength has been its professional division, which is the laboratory and proving ground for new products. The profits and products for this division fueled the growth of the consumer division, which by the 1980s had become sales leader among Wahl's four divisions. Together, the professional and consumer divisions provided the foundation for building up Wahl's international trade. Their profits provided the capital for foreign ventures, and their leading products were the ones that Wahl generally took overseas.

From its experience in the U. K., Wahl learned that the way to build foreign sales was to establish a strong presence in foreign countries. Just as the Groomsman taught the company how to develop and market a new product, Wahl Europe provided the model for foreign expansion. Without a strong presence, Wahl could not impress the virtues of its product upon the consumer and the professional hair stylist. Languages and customs may vary, but customers are customers everywhere: they require order fill, quality products, and strong customer service, including repairs and merchandising support. Wahl learned that when it went into a new market, it needed to establish close working partnerships with local importers and distributors. As Wahl's international reputation grew in these years, it found that its exceptional service sealed deals and guaranteed more business in the future.

With a strong overseas presence, Wahl was able to adapt its products and sales strategy to local markets. Flexibility and attention to detail proved to be key virtues. In South Africa in the 1980s, Wahl's distributor developed blister packaging for a home clipper kit and added as a personal touch, a picture of his family. Sales took off. While American shoppers were used to see-through packaging, European consumers in the early '90s only expected boxes with the product's picture on them. Another crucial adjustment to local markets came in setting the product to the local electrical standards. Wahl had to adjust its clippers to various voltages—105/240 AC and either 50 or 60 cycles. Wahl also had to fit its product with cord and plugs used in that particular market and it then had to have the product tested at international testing laboratories, which were like the Underwriters Laboratory but were far more rigorous. While electrical standards were becoming more uniform from country to country, there were still variations, and these were among those unofficial trade barriers that added cost to the Wahl product.

Wahl Clipper's growing international business widened the horizons of many of its employees and sent new ideas flowing through the company. While Jack Wahl was vigilant in keeping Wahl Clipper lean and mean and free of needless frills and expenses, he also recognized that international business required a great deal of travel and secured the board's approval for its funding. Here again, Wayne Wahl and William J. Gearns were progressive forces on the board, supporting the international initiative and the cost that went with it. After the lightning success of the U.K. venture, overseas travel became a necessity, and the board granted Jack full discretion in the regulation of trips abroad. Is Wahl Clipper still a family peanut operation?

Jack did not take this concession lightly. As the expansion of foreign business required more key employees to venture overseas, he set guidelines that controlled travel expenses and made sure foreign trips stuck to business. In the early days, many of Wahl's Asian contacts worked a 6 and 7 day week. The company scheduled foreign air travel in economy or business class, usually in mid week at off hours, when rates were lower and flights were less booked. Wahl travelers might then have more room even in economy class, and could fold up the arm rests and lay down on five seats. If they wished to travel in a little more style, they were allowed to use their free mileage to upgrade their accommodations. As a check on the lure of sight-seeing, Wahl's emissaries were required to phone in their schedules and do call reports every other day. In this way, employees were able to serve the company and be also enriched by foreign contacts and new experiences.

Business travel, if it were at all worthwhile, was not an activity for sissies. Apart from the jet lag, the layovers, the adventure of strange cuisine, and the awareness of terrorist attacks, the days were long and hard, filled with meetings and visits to customers and prospects. Political terrorism, even before the U.S. had its awareness heightened by 9/11, was always a concern to Wahl's increasing number of overseas visitors. On one visit to the Philippines, Jack and his executive assistant Donna Rosenthal were staying at the Sheridan Hotel when terrorists set off a bomb that blew a dozen windows out of a neighboring hotel. Donna called from her room, which overlooked a small commercial area of Manila Bay, wanting to know what a "coup" was. Using old World War II planes, terrorists were dive bombing Corazon Aquino's castle. She was the President of the Philippines at the time, and the U.S. government stepped in and sent a half dozen military jets screaming over the roof tops. Another such incident occurred when Jack and his wife Margaret were in Buenos Aires Argentina with a customer when a car bomb went off in front of Israeli Embassy, killing a dozen and half people and scaring the day lights out of Jack and Margaret. Despite the risks, however, these days of hard work were important investments in the future, for they built a bank of knowledge, especially in the Far East, where Wahl's competition was very active.

Wahl's success in foreign markets attracted attention at home. In 1989 and 1990, the Small Business Administration gave Wahl employees the Illinois Exporter of the Year Award. In August 1991, the United States Department of Commerce awarded Wahl Clipper the prestigious President's E Award for success in exporting. Wahl was only the eighth Illinois company to receive this award since its inception in 1961. The coveted award included commendations from President George Bush and Illinois Secretary of State, George Ryan, and a flag which Wahl flew proudly at its Sterling plant. It was a sign of how far Wahl Clipper had come in just a short time, and also a good reminder to a rust belt community that local talent could still hold its own anywhere in the wide world.

4. Engineering: Tasked With Growth

We always look to design better quality into our products. That's the only answer to international manufacturing. Costs go down and productivity goes up as quality improvements are accomplished.

THE 1987 WAHL ANNUAL REPORT

Wahl Clipper is a company that runs on engineering. An engineer, Leo Wahl, started it with an invention, validated that invention at the patent office and in courts of law, and with wisdom and care built a company and made it a success. His offspring, sons Warren and Jack and grandson Greg—engineers one and all—succeeded him at the helm and have turned his example into a tradition. Wahl and engineering: after 80 years of quality electrical products at competitive prices, customers have come to associate the two. The Wahl name on a product tells them that it is elegant in design, superior in performance, and good for the long haul.

It was in the eighties that Wahl and engineering received an even tighter seal. While Wahl invested in increasing the company's name recognition, it was also producing an annual crop of innovative new products and selling them to more and more customers throughout the world. Product, production, and promotion were in perfect sync. Sales took off; the company expanded rapidly to meet new production demands, and did it without sacrificing its time-honored standard of excellence. The Engineering Department was largely responsible for enabling Wahl Clipper to combine quantity of production with quality of workmanship. Indeed, this department showed a marvelous knack for making more and more work for itself: its effectiveness in product development led to the rollout of exciting new products which boosted company sales and required more machinery, tooling, and refinement of manufacturing processes. By the late '80s, Engineering's crucial role in creative product development, factory productivity, quality control and manufacturing upgrades made it the focus of major reinvestments in the factory. This enabled Wahl Clipper to handle the new business generated by its five major sales and marketing divisions, now that the animal division was stand alone.

In some ways, it was a case of the more things change, the more they stay the same. As Wahl Clipper approached its 70th birthday, the Engineering Department numbered 28 people, who were equipped with computers and cad-corders and other weapons of high tech mastery. Even so, their task remained essentially the same as it was in the company's first three decades, when Leo Wahl was the engineering department, or in that transitional fourth decade, when Jack succeeded his father as head of engineering and doubled the department by hiring a draughtsman. However few or many, the engineering staff was there to design superior personal care electric appliances and develop the tooling and the processes that could get them to market on time and at a competitive price. And now in the age of Reagan, a Wahl still led them: Greg Wahl, Jack's son, had managed Engineering since 1979, and in 1985 was made Vice-President of Engineering.

To support Wahl Clipper's efforts to handle rapid growth and increase productivity, Greg Wahl had to make Engineering an ever more efficient engine of Wahl Clipper's accelerating growth, and he had to do it immediately. This he did by computerizing its operations and expanding the Tool Room and Maintenance Department. Those modernization initiatives came none too soon. During Greg Wahl's first year, the department was tasked with such jobs as building back-up molds for Professional clippers and the brand new Groomsman rechargeable trimmer; installing new Arburg injection molders, which maximized the productivity of the Molding Department; setting up a special blade polishing machine, without which Wahl Clipper would have had difficulty keeping up with its growing volume of cutting blades; and revamping the production area for the Groomsman, Wahl's new star performer. This job was only beginning, for Wahl was beginning to automate every part of Groomsman's production, so that it could lower unit production costs and fight off competitors who were reaching for their share in the new market category that Groomsman had created. Wahl Clipper was growing so fast that its warehouse, which had been expanded by 30,000 square feet the year before, was almost full by the end of 1985. Engineering had to install decking to make the most effective use of the new and soon to be antiquated addition.

New technology helped the department handle its work load that was growing on all three fronts: product development, tooling and plant maintenance, and the installation of new machinery and processes. Product development was a two-edged sword. Engineering not only had to make "something new under the sun," it also had to develop the manufacturing capability that could satisfy the market's demand for Wahl's new products. The Zee Curl project was a good test of Engineering's effectiveness in the designing and tooling of this product. The curling iron project was a huge operation that transported Wahl Clipper well out of any previous comfort zone. It took place on both sides of the Pacific, involved a product that did not use blades, and it provoked early on (pardon the expression) a "frenzy" of competition from well established Asian curling iron companies. Boldly going where Wahl engineering had not gone before, the

Engineering Department learned on the job, working with the Cad screen at home and Asian engineers 13 hours and 8000 miles away. When the venture failed, it was not for lack of innovation or resourcefulness or productivity. It would have been a different story if Wahl Clipper could have held production or any information to the trade until it had a patent ready to issue. A couple of "what if" sessions could have been held with the professional and consumer division.

Interestingly, the company drew a most unexpected moral from its Zee Curl adventure. As expensive and time consuming as it was, it contributed only a 20% increase to Wahl's research and development expenditure in 1987. The total outlay of $724,000 was not quite 2.2% of sales. Such economies, concluded the 1987 Annual Report, did not square with the company's goal of maintaining its leadership in the development of bold, innovative new products. Rather than causing Wahl Clipper to recoil from new ventures, Zee Curls only prodded it to intensify its efforts to find new products for particular market niches. Wahl's Zee Curl and FrenZee lines had offered buyers and consumers new proof of Wahl Engineering's gift for producing hip new products. The company was not going to retreat from this victory; it was going to learn from it and build on it.

Meanwhile back in the factory, Engineering had to keep up the twin demands of expanding production and increasing productivity. The biggest single capital improvement of that year was the $224,000 Brudere High Speed Punch Press. A triumph of the engineer's art, the Brudere was in the words of the Annual Report, "one of the world's finest machines." Variable in speed and stroke, it could reach a maximum punching speed of 1200 strokes per minute.

As Wahl Clipper roared through the '80s into the '90s, the demands on Engineering intensified. These were years of challenge and achievement followed by more challenges. In addition to developing new products, Engineering was also constantly upgrading its designing technology and streamlining manufacturing operations. In 1989, the department replaced its CAD CPU and added two work stations. Wahl was now producing almost all of its engineering drawings as well as much of its tooling by computer. The following year it moved into brand new offices but was too busy to appreciate the new furnishings. "Engineering," said that year's Annual Report, "was immediately swallowed up by demands for new and better tooling and production machinery. There was no time to shut a machine down nor was it possible to plan for redesigned improvements." There was truly no rest for the winning. In 1989, Engineering produced tooling for making a low cost perm rod and redesigned a solder station and put it into operation. Every year Wahl added another new Arburg Molding Machine and new material dryer in the Plastics Department. It debugged a new surface grinder, increasing productivity. That was 1989; this was 1990: installation of another new rotary assembly line, more Arburg molding machines, and four new machines for the tool room.

The more things changed, the more they stayed the same for Wahl Clipper. In an age of outsourcing, this most sprightly of septuagenarians remained a vertically integrated manufacturer and, more than ever, depended on superior engineering to take it to market and to take that market by storm.

3. The Next Generation: The Fun Continues

Under Jack Wahl's direction, Wahl Clipper had re-invented itself. Building on its tradition of superior workmanship, it had also learned new skills in employee relations, manufacturing, marketing, and public relations . It had grown dramatically throughout the '80s and now that growth was accelerating even more. This family-owned company could look forward to the last decade of the 20th century. Business prospects were good, the prospects were also good for a smooth transition of leadership among the third generation of Wahls. This younger generation was already distinguishing itself. James Wahl in Professional Sales, Lee Wahl in Asian Sales, Greg Wahl in Engineering/Manufacturing, and Mark Wahl in Animal Sales.

David Wahl in Scheduling and Production Control—all in their late thirties or early forties—already exercised key leadership positions in the company and promised to play even more significant roles in the future. One of the most successful ways to navigate nepotism is to assign a clear cut responsibility to each family member and then to evaluate performance and set salaries accordingly.

James Wahl, born in 1949 to Warren and Mary McKenney Wahl, graduated from Creighton in 1971 with a degree in business management. After a year in the Army Reserve, he joined Wahl Clipper in January 1973, working 8 years for Bob Thuber in the Home Line. Within a few years he became manager of Professional Sales, and in 1982 was elected to the Board of Directors of Wahl Clipper. Under his direction, Professional Sales grew from $2.1M in 1980 to $14.7M in 1990.

Mark Carter Wahl, born in 1962 to John and Margaret Keefe Wahl, the youngest son, graduated from Marquette University with a degree in BioMedical Engineering.

Leo (Lee) T. Wahl, born in 1948 to Robert and Mary Drew Wahl, graduated from St. Ambrose College in Davenport, Iowa, receiving both his bachelor's and master's degrees, and joined Wahl Clipper on February 5, 1973. In 1983, the Board of Directors chose him to be assistant secretary. Under his direction, International Sales for Asia and Canada rose from $1.1M in 1985 to $2.7M in 1990.

Greg Wahl, born in 1951 to John and Margaret Keefe Wahl, received a degree in mechanical engineering from The University of Notre Dame in 1973 and an M.B.A. from the University of Illinois. Greg's application was received at Notre Dame, accepted all of his credentials and awarded him "a Notre Dame Scholar." During three years with Hamlin Corporation in Lake Mills, Wisconsin, he worked in their engineering department and made frequent trips to Mexico to debug some of their precision switches. Julius Sandy was engineering manager at Wahl Clipper and, when he decided to leave Wahl and go to one of the major toy companies in California, Jack started to interview for a replacement. Then he decided that it was time to offer the engineering job to Greg. Greg joined Wahl in 1978, and the following year was appointed manager of Engineering. Four years later, the Board of Directors elected him secretary, and in 1985 he was named V.P. of Engineering. In this capacity, Greg was already demonstrating the temperament and talents that Jack Wahl's successor would have to have. Like his father, he brought to product development and manufacturing a sense of creativity and design. However, while Jack liked to follow his instincts, Greg was more inclined to crunch numbers, analyze data, and eventually make decisions based on key measurements. Not surprisingly for one of his generation, he was at home with computers, while Jack studiously left keyboard work to his executive assistant. In the coming decade, Greg would assume more leadership responsibilities. In 1991, he was made VP and COO of Wahl Clipper. In June, 1997, he became President of the company and worked with his father Jack sharing responsibilities. Father and son each had his areas of special interest. Jack focused on the shaver business and developing the Chinese factory, while Greg took over other areas of the company and was especially involved in managing Wahl's business in the U.K., Germany and Hungary.

David Wahl, born in 1951 to Bob and Mary Drew Wahl, went to Sauk Valley College for two years and on to the University of Wisconsin at Oskosh. For many years he was head of the Repair Department and is currently in Scheduling and Production Control, and was elected in 1999 to serve on the Board of Directors of Wahl Clipper Corporation.

The picture of Jack Wahl at the Berlin Wall shows a vigorous white-haired gentleman standing before a huge diamond-shaped hole in the wall. He is looking back over his shoulder and he is smiling. As the caption in the Annual Report suggests, he is contemplating the opportunities for growth waiting on the other side. What really gives him pleasure, though, is the knowledge that he and his son and his company will be stepping through that passage together to find fun and profit on the other side. After all, *who has more fun than people*? And it is this story, Jack and Greg's and Wahl Clipper's Great Adventure, that continues in the history's concluding chapter.

CHAPTER 7
THE GREAT WAHL, 1991-2001

As long as hair keeps growing, so should we.
1994 WAHL CLIPPER ANNUAL REPORT

*It's a people business, and we've made it our business
to create products that people buy.*
WAHL AD, 1991

*The whole world is out there and it has risks,
but everything has risks...I would not rely on the
U. S. Government to be helpful; rely on
your own resources.*
DONALD RUMSFELD,
then Chairman of the Rand Corporation,
QUOTED IN THE 1995 WAHL CLIPPER ANNUAL REPORT

1. Wahl: Turning the Corner

The 1998 Wahl Clipper Annual Report presented Wahl stockholders with a sight that they had not seen in 27 years: a net sales history bar graph in which the last bar, signifying the net sales for the year just past, was not higher than all other bars on the graph.

WAHL CLIPPER NET SALES 1990-1998
(in $ Millions)

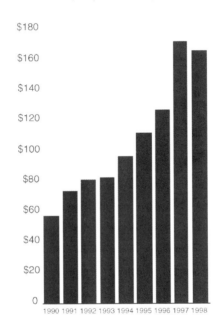

While everyone at Wahl hated to see the company's streak of rising sales come to an end at 26 years, they had good reasons not to get too worried. The drop off from 1997, $174.1 Million to $169.9 M, had been slight, less than 2%, and 1997 had been a smashing record breaking year with net sales up 37% over 1996. A more significant statistic for the company was the number 74, which was the number of consecutive years that Wahl had paid a dividend. Not only that, the dividend per share had climbed and, even better, the total payout was a new record. While after tax net earnings dropped, this mark was still the third highest in Wahl history and not far short of 1996, Wahl's second best year for net income.

Given the market conditions, Wahl had made a very strong showing. On one hand, Europe and Asia were both struggling with recession; on the other, global competition continued to intensify. The Wahl Annual Report estimated that there were at least 108 companies throughout the world competing in the clipper and trimmer market. With so many of them from developing countries with low labor costs, there was a consistent downward pressure on prices. Wahl Clipper, though, continued to be a leader in the manufacture and marketing of electrical clippers, trimmers, and other personal care products. With a 20.8% before taxes return on assets, Wahl was still on a growth path. It prudently invested in computer technology, new machinery, and product development. The company also concentrated on squeezing waste out of its operation, developing a cohesive leadership team for its global operations, and offering superior quality and service in every market it entered.

By 1998 Wahl Clipper was a very different company than the one that had entered the '90s as the whiz kid exporter from Corn Country, Illinois. In 1991 it had 550 employees in Sterling and 35 more at subsidiaries in Canada and England. In a mere seven years, Wahl Clipper had transmogrified into a multi-national corporation, still headquartered in Sterling but now owning subsidiaries on four continents, including major manufacturing plants in China, Hungary, and Germany. It now had 1600 employees, and less than half of them, (750), were in the United States. Early in the decade, Jack Wahl and his management team had recognized that they would have to expand their overseas operations if they were to remain competitive. Once they worked out a strategy, they acted upon it with dispatch, buying a small Chinese company in 1995 and, the following year, acquiring a clipper/shaver manufacturer with plants in Germany and Hungary Wahl's strong performance in 1996, 1997, and 1998 came in the face of substantial costs of absorbing its acquisitions and upgrading their operations.

A visual from the 1996 Annual Report, "The Divisional Pie Charts," demonstrates what these acquisitions meant for Wahl's business. Wahl Clipper's business in 1997 was about 140% larger than it was in 1991: $172M to $72 million. The pie now was huge, and the proportions had changed. In 1991, the American Consumer Division accounted for 53.7% of total sales, while Foreign sales were 24.1%, Professional Sales were 20.5%, and Industrial was 1.7%.

The Electric Shaver business is unique. Jack was interested from the moment his Father showed him his early prototype and, from that day on, he tested all new shavers and studied the weekly patent Gazettes on shavers as well as clippers. In many ways shavers are similar to trimmers. They both cut hair, but the shaver must cut much closer and stand up to daily use. Years later, when the opportunity arose to purchase the tooling and the technology for a line of Porsche design shavers from Payer Corporation in Graz, Austria, Jack grabbed it. We sent a team to observe a production run in Austria. Then we brought the tooling to our U.S. plant and proceeded to improve the cutting with my newly patented dynaflex blade drive. Our research has taught us that skin and whiskers are very much different from one person to the next. Whiskers vary in diameter, number per square inch, straight or curly etc. There is no one perfect shaving head. At the suggestion of Mark Wahl, they went to market with a "custom" shaver having the choice of using any one of three included cutting foils. They are Sensitive, Close, and Super Close. Usually the buyer is the same one who purchases clippers and groomsmen products. Big advertising dollars of $5 to $20 million were spent annually by Wahl's competitors to keep their product on the shelf. Advertising was modest but did create a demand for Wahl shavers. We joined Norelco, Remington, Braun and Panasonic. They had some great years and some good years with annual production runs exceeding 330,000 units. Over a 5 year period from 1996 to 2000 Wahl had a total of $50 million in sales of shavers and accessories. We all knew the competition would be tough and right now we had plenty of orders for clippers and trimmers. Some of my senior managers thought the competition was just too tough. I'd say, "If it was easy, everybody would be doing it."

An introduction by Mark Grand at Sears Annual Awards Banquet: Paul Harvey does a fabulous job of building Wahl brand awareness, and especially creating demand for the Wahl Customs Shavers. Yes, we are beginning to reach critical mass.

Our shaver SKU was rated by Sears their number one selling shaver for 1996 in both Sales $ and in units. By the year end we were on the shelf at most major outlets, including Wal-Mart, and Service Merchandise.

2. Critical Mass and Synergy: Toward the New Millennium

We seem to have gotten to a critical mass. It takes some size to be able to hold your own against the Big Boys who have been attracted to the the growing hair clipper/trimmer business.

1994 WAHL CLIPPER ANNUAL REPORT

Wahl roared into the '90s. The market for clippers and trimmers was booming, and Wahl's manufacturing and marketing expertise enabled it to capitalize on the opportunities all across the globe. Wahl was following and refining a proven strategy for growth: reducing production costs, improving quality of product and service, and adding innovative new products to fit particular market niches. Almost two decades of steadily growing sales had taught the company how to win in a global economy. Between 1988 and 1992, its net sales had almost doubled, climbing from $42M to a little over $80M. During these years the company far outperformed the U.S. economy, whose sluggish performance had undone the merits that George Bush, Sr. had gained from victory in Iraq, doomed his re-election bid, and confirmed the bottom line of American politics, so baldly expressed by the Clinton Doctrine, "It's the economy, stupid."

Wahl was suffering no such rebuff. With the success of the Wahl subsidiary in the United Kingdom and its penetration of the market in Western Europe, the International Division now joined Wahl's Professional and Consumer Division to give the company a one-two-three punch. Parlaying booming sales into increased recognition of the Wahl name and its association with innovative and dependable products, Wahl had established a momentum of growth that only accelerated during the dot com boom of the Clinton years. Capitalizing on boom times without being captive to them, Wahl was still going strong even after the bubble burst in the first year of the 21st century. Wahl was, by then, bigger, stronger, and more global than ever before.

For a concise description of Wahl's strength at the start of the '90s, one need look no further than a 1991 ad,

> It's a people business, and we've made it our business to create the products that people buy…like the Groomsman Collection of Trimmers and Shavers; the Comfort Collection of Massagers; home haircutting products and much more. All supported by national advertising; well designed point-of-purchase materials; dynamic versatile packaging; and supportive co-op advertising.

> To get your piece of this people business contact the People from Wahl for our complete promotional program.

Here indeed was truth in advertising. Without boasting, Wahl was offering a fair summation of the things that made it successful and would help its customers prosper. This idea of a people business was not a new truth. Any business is people business but, in this case, truism is also truth. By the '90s, the most successful American companies were tapping into this principle and applying it more conscientiously and completely than ever before. Businessmen and women realized that in highly competitive global markets the way to get business and keep it was to establish lasting personal relationships built on value, honesty, dependability, quality production, and superior service. These benefits delighted customers and created new opportunities. It was no accident that Wahl counted among its best customers companies like Wal-Mart and Walgreens. All were long-standing, highly successful companies who did business with excellence and integrity. The success of such companies demonstrated the union of the Midwest's two great patriarchs, Lincoln and Edison, the synergistic virtues of honesty and know-how, of integrity and innovation. Of course, virtue and virtuosity were not the sole possession of the Midwest. Indeed, that was the point, of which Wahl was a brilliant example: these were universal values, which, when built into products and services, could sell anywhere on the globe.

Necessary though they were, integrity and excellence were not in themselves sufficient to guarantee continued business success. Competition and unforeseen consequences were everywhere to undo the best laid plans. Any number of American companies, including many in Sterling and Rock Falls, were proof enough of this point. Locally, Wahl was not only outperforming most factories, its fortunes were in some instances going in a diametrically opposite direction. The October 30, 1991 issue of *The Greater Sterling Development Corporation Newsletter* reported that in the decade from 1979 to 1989 wages in Twin City factories grew annually by 1.9%, rising from $482.5 M at the start of the period to $584.9 M a decade later. Typical of the difficulties faced by American manufacturers in this period, the portion of these wages that came from the production of durable goods dropped from 52.5% to 39.1%. Both automation and foreign competition both contributed to a reduction in the number of people employed in local factories. "The County Business Patterns," a report by The Illinois Department of Employment Services, showed that in March 1979 local industries employed 10,810 people, but by March 1989 that number had dropped to 7668.[28] While Dylan's line, "They don't make nothin' here anymore," was not exactly true, another one was: "It's not dark yet, but it's getting there."[29]

During this period, American manufacturers found that rising health care costs made their battle against low-cost Asian imports increasingly difficult. Even a stellar performer like Wahl, which entered the decade with a string of 16 years without a layoff, found itself challenged. By 1994, group medical expenses and workers compensation plans had become Wahl's third largest expense, exceeded only by wages and purchased material.[30] In 1993, Wahl entered into a consortium with 17 other local companies. The River Valley Health Care Council, in an effort to keep the cost of health care under control, had some success in educating employees to be more knowledgeable users of health care. However, by the end of the decade Wahl reported to its employees that local health care costs were rising faster in the Twin Cities than anywhere in northern Illinois.[31]

This sudden rise in overhead could not have come at a worse time. Globalization had pitched American manufacturing into the economic equivalent of the Cold War. It was a long twilight struggle with foes that were if anything more formidable, being Asian capitalists without the onus of high wages, health benefits, pension plans, or exacting government standards for safety and pollution. Even the dot-com boom, as bracing as it was, did not provide any lasting deliverance for American industry, which like the rest of American society found the new century a far more dangerous place than what was promised by the fall of the Berlin Wall. It was not the end of history by any means, but it sometimes looked like the end of the American Dream of prosperity and opportunity. Eighteen months after the September 11, 2001 attack, a survey of 300 members of the National Association of Manufacturers showed that almost 75% of them thought the U.S. was in crisis. Those polled cited rising costs of health care and energy, as well as imports from China, as prime threats.[32] By this time, the economic woes in the Twin Cities had also intensified with the bankruptcies of Northwestern Steel and Wire and Lawrence Brothers and saw the sale of their companies and survival with smaller workforces. The closing of Reliant Manufacturing, formerly RB&W, was woe on woe.

Wahl Clipper, too, faced serious challenges, but unlike other local firms, it did so from a position of strength, a confidence borne of success, and conviction about what it needed to do.

Wahl's very favorable position at the start of the '90s was not something it could maintain without continued growth. Here another Dylan line suggests itself, "He not busy being born, is busy dying."[33] Jack Wahl and his management team could see the handwriting on the Wahl. The 1991 Annual Report predicted that low cost clippers from China and Russia would pose a major threat in 1992. Sure enough, the next year's report noted that the 4% drop off in trimmer sales that year was no temporary dip and offered this historical perspective: "After a 1988 sales drop, 1989,1990, and 1991 all showed growth but now we are in a losing battle with numerous low cost Asian imports, (which are) chipping away at our dominant market share. International was the only growth area for this product." Wahl's own success had made it a target. The booming market for clippers, trimmers, and shavers had attracted companies from all over the world. The Trimmer product category, which Wahl itself had created, had in a few short years assumed a very important position in the Wahl line. The high profit margins on trimmers in those days made them engines of growth. "While magnetic hair clippers amount to over 62% of total unit sales," the report explained, "total trimmers amount to more than half the profits." A decline in trimmer sales or the downward pressure on prices would reduce profits and diminish Wahl's capacity to invest in R&D and automation. Wahl would, then, find it harder to compete.

Though this threat was real, Wahl had the resources and the will to meet it. To put it another way, Wahl Clipper was ready to make some more right choices. It continued doing what it had been doing. It continued to diversify and develop new products and new markets. For example, the Peanut developed by its Engineering Department, was a very powerful compact professional trimmer/clipper which combined power and finesse. Charlie Struck, an inventor from California, developed the nose trimmer and brought it to Wahl. He was the original inventor and sold them to customers through Barber Shops. Wahl manufactured the product in its Sterling factory and introduced it at the Housewares Show. It was a brand new product and initially hard to sell to consumers. Eventually Remington entered the market with a similar but smaller single cell battery operated product. With Wahl and Remington both advertising the trimmer, sales took off and it became a standard product. It wasn't long before Wahl introduced its washable single cell trimmer.

To develop more new business, Wahl created a fifth sales division in 1994, Animal Product Sales. Wahl management believed that it could increase its animal product sales by separating them from the consumer division and creating a new separate sales and marketing manager devoted to developing animal products. In time, animal sales revealed itself as five distinct smaller markets: consumer, professional grooming, large animal and equine, and the ethical veterinarian trade.

The new Animal Products Division, under the direction of General Manager Mark Wahl, started in 1994 with a total net sales of $3.6 million and got off to an excellent start. Net sales jumped to $5.4 million in 1995, a full 50% increase. An accomplishment like this doesn't happen without a tremendous amount of effort. The success story is Mark's culmination of efforts to improve and repackage the product, reorganize the sales force, rework the pricing and distribution structure, and administer a meaningful advertising program.

Mark's Animal products division had another good year in 1996, even though Wahl made an executive decision to temporarily drop out of K-Mart rather than meet their unrealistic demands. The temporary loss of the K-Mart account caused a reduction in net sales of Mark's division to $4 million for the year. A highlight of the year was the introduction of the new rotary motor clipper (KM 1) from Moser. This product was designed to have a full line of detachable blades, which would be interchangeable to fit Oster animal clippers. Late in the year Wahl also received its initial production samples of another product from Moser, the "Electric Detangler Comb." The company saw a sizable amount of growth world wide for this division.

Mark Wahl's 1997 U.S. Animal Products Division had another good year, experiencing a 42.5% gain over 1996 net sales for a total of $5.7 million.

In 1997 Wahl began supplying the 9281-601 pet clipper to Wal-Mart, with net sales of almost $1 million. Securing Wal-Mart's business went a long way toward making up for the loss of sales suffered from the previous year's decision to temporarily cease doing business with K-Mart.

The 1995 charts have the animal division at 9.6% which reduced the other percentages proportionally. Fifteen years of charts show the slow decreasing of the industrial product line from 11% in 1990 to 1% in 1995.

Rapid growth was seen by the foreign and animal divisions. The division with the largest profit margin, the professional, was relinquishing a bit of its share, but all was well with such a large pie and with the prospects of an even larger pie in the future. Wahl's new foreign operations were already making a profit and could expect to become more profitable in the future as the company was dedicated to bringing its operations up to the standards of its home base in Sterling. The story of how Wahl Clipper got to this position and planned to go even further, is but the latest and most thoroughly modern instance of the Wahl gift for choosing wisely and well.

The company's growing strength, though, and the competition that it attracted, encouraged Jack and the management team to make a more dramatic move. It was a case of "going for it," without at the same time "betting the farm." Sales, profits, and years of adroit marketing, which had made Wahl a brand name that consumers equated with personal care products, now gave Wahl the critical mass, which would enable it to make the leap from a successful exporter to a large multinational corporation. It would remain based in Sterling and continue to do most of its manufacturing there, but Wahl Clipper was looking to create new divisions overseas, especially in Asia, which would give the company a truly global reach, new flexibility and new leverage to enter and command markets—indeed a synergy, which, as the dictionary defines it, is "the interaction of discrete agencies, agents, (and) conditions such that the total effect is greater than the sum of the individual effects."[34] Wahl's capacity to combat imports by adding value to its product had its limits. An Asian factory, would give Wahl access to parts and products that could compete at the low end of the price spectrum. Then too, a company with a complementary product line and factory in Europe would be strengthened in that market and perhaps create new possibilities up and down the spectrum in both the professional and consumer trade in North America. These would be bold enterprises, but not out of character for Jack Wahl or the company his father founded. In pursuing them, Wahl Clipper was taking Jack's strategy of diversification and giving it a truly global application.

3. The Great Leap Forward

The major drive of change for Wahl Clipper Corporation today
is the same as for most companies: it's globalization. Advances
In technology and communications are making the small world
a reality, and the world will get smaller and smaller in coming
years. The real growth markets of the 21st century are outside
North America and Western Europe. It is easier than ever
for global companies to manufacture virtually any product in
virtually any region. The trend toward global integration should
be viewed as an opportunity not a problem.

1994 WAHL CLIPPER ANNUAL REPORT

An old adage among baseball general managers is that sometimes your best deal is the one you don't make. Jack Wahl found that to be the case after the fall of the Berlin Wall, when Wahl Clipper entered into negotiations to form a partnership with a Russian clipper manufacturer. In 1991, he visited Russia, and found a factory making a copy of Wahl's 1947 hair clipper that was for sale, or so it seemed at first. Jack had a full tour of the factory which was decrepit by Western standards, but it had possibilities that Wahl know how could transform— that is, of course, if Jack and his team could work out a deal with the Russian team of negotiators that included a former Communist official, an engineer, a couple sales people, and a Swiss businessman. We wanted an option for controlling interest, they wanted to see all of our factory. They came to Sterling but without an agreement they were not allowed to see the entire factory. The parties talked about it and talked about it. The Russians attitude seemed more like a pretext for jump starting their factory with a little raid on Wahl technology. Even if Wahl Clipper had gained controlling interest in the Russian plant, it would not have been able to control the turbulence that accompanied the fall of Communism. As the 1990s unfolded, it was clear that Russia lacked the institutions and infrastructure to support a venture that Wahl was seeking.

Because it was our core business we had to keep control. Their factory was approximately the same as our factory was in 1947. As the worlds best, Wahl Clipper could not allow these fine gentlemen an opportunity to study our manufacturing methods until we were sure they would be a partner and not a competitor. It seems we would have made a deal except for the position taken by the Swiss Businessman who helped them make a hair clipper many years before.

It was a wide world, though, and Wahl Clipper by now was a global player. Russia may have had possibilities, but the real growth potential was in Asia, where Japan and the Asian tigers had already made their mark, and sleeping giants were starting to awake. The question was: should Wahl try India or China? India had much to recommend it. It was a giant country, with a huge population and genuine market potential. Its long tutelage in the British Empire, the presence of the English language and its democratic institutions, made it a little more familiar than the rest of Asia and perhaps more congenial.

China, though, was impossible to ignore. With a population of 1.2

billion people, it was the largest market in the world, and after Mao's passing, the Communist party had undertaken a capitalist experiment that was making China the world's fastest growing economy, and as Wahl and every other western manufacturer could testify, its formidable exporter.

Wahl Clipper already had familiarity with the country. Jack had many trips to the Far East attending Electronics exhibits and touring factories already producing all types of small electric appliances, including hair clippers, some quality, some not. Then there was the great Zee-Curl adventure: the curling irons that almost conquered America were made in China. In fact, for a number of years now, other Wahl executives had made visits there to source components and products. Early on Jack had established a reliable contact in China, a Mr. Uchida, a solid Japanese businessman who understood product design and production, and also had a passable command of English. He was especially expert in new product development and the techniques of heat treatment and grinding as in making hair clippers/trimmer/shaver blades. Mr. Uchida produced a wet/dry ladies shaver and scouted parts and products for Wahl, and the company came to rely on him. On his own initiative he built a new style single cell washable nose trimmer and presented it to Wahl, for exclusive sales, his own version of the wet-dry nose trimmer. This was the first ever washable wet/dry nose trimmer on the market. The product was excellent and sold well but, a few months later delivery became a terrible problem with the moving of the plant from Taiwan to mainland China.

However, Mr. Uchida embodied some of the hazards of the Asian marketplace. He had operated his own factory in Taiwan, but when he found his costs going up he began moving his operations to the mainland. His employees, lacking the means to move with him or a safety net to catch them when he was gone, wreaked havoc on his factory by loosing a truckload of molds and dyes. Mr. Uchida, like so many Asian manufacturers, was the sole proprietor on his plant and operated it beyond the pale of accountability. He and so many others took great risks purchasing large volumes of material at the best price.

So many Asian entrepreneurs were buccaneers and gamblers. They were good at low cost product development and production. Others like Richard Lun of Tune Great Ltd. and, Joe Wong of Fairform would source products on a cost plus basis.

As Jack calculated things, China offered worlds of potential and enormous pitfalls too. Establishing a foothold there was like laying a foundation in a minefield. There was not one Chinese wall but many: language, culture, customs, and a Communist dictatorship that could shut down the budding free market system anytime it chose. The 1994 Wahl Annual Report was only joking, when it observed, "Of course, there is a risk; it is Red China…We could be at war next year!!!"

Jack and his management team, though, knew that inaction was an even greater risk. Asian plants, untrammeled by Western copyright laws or labor costs, were copying Wahl products and flooding Western markets with low-priced knock-offs. Jack decided that Wahl Clipper needed to start operations in the Far East. After dodging the Russian bullet, Jack also knew the company did not want to source our core products in an uncontrollable Asian factory and teach it Wahl's secrets for making the best quality products in the world. While manufacturing in Asia was imperative, it was equally imperative that Wahl do so on its own terms. It had to have full ownership or the next thing to it. The only way to know where to start was to go and see. In early 1994, a Wahl team headed by Jack Wahl and Executive Assistant, Sandy Conley sallied forth to Asia in search of a clipper factory. They were not innocents abroad, by any means, but they were explorers, and in this old inscrutable world now made suddenly new, they did not exactly know what they were to find.

Fate helped narrow the choices, though. Their first stop was to be Bombay. But ten days before they left, their reservations there were canceled. Plague warnings had driven people from outlying areas to flee to Bombay. The hotels were soon filled, and airlines began canceling flights. That decided it. Forget the passage to India. Bring on Cathay.

In China, the Wahl team met with Mr. Uchida at his China based factory in Xiamen, China. They had some serious talks about buying him out, but nothing came of them. Instead, they learned from him about other quality manufacturers in China. Jack was looking for a company that made hair clippers and trimmers and, most important of all, shavers. He was hoping to find somebody with the technology for foils and inside cutters. He believed there was great potential in the shaver line, which Wahl had only entered a few years before. Having bought a shaver from Austria and marketed it in America as the Euroflex, Jack was looking to augment the line with a competitively priced rechargeable Asian product. Among the companies and products that they checked out at trade shows, Jack found a company that made a round shaver that sat on a stand and looked like a globe of the world. Rechargeable battery operated, it turned on when it was picked up and provided a fairly good shave. It might have real possibilities. Jack could see selling it in the U.S. to guys with four o'clock shadows. It could sit on a desk and be available for a quick touch up.

As a fact-finding mission, the trip was proving to be a great success but, as the days wore on, the team was no nearer to its goal of making a major acquisition. The frustration came to a head in a meeting in Shanghai. Jack and Sandy Conley had real difficulty with the interpreter. All they could understand was that their Chinese counterparts wanted an order for 100,000 or 250,000 pieces. It was a huge amount, but with their go-for-broke style of capitalism, the Chinese manufacturers did not understand why Wahl would want to buy a mere 500, package them, and do a market test. Their incomprehension only grew when the Americans tried to explain what had to be done to make their product acceptable to Underwriters Laboratory.

At some point two other Chinese joined our meeting. One of them asked us many, many questions about Wahl Clipper and suggested we visit a PuDong area factory and also Xikou. Question, Where is PuDong-Xikou? We told them we were very much interested in seeing these factories.

Early the next morning, we were to taxi to a port where we were to take a ship to Ningbo, but the translator said he would take us in his car instead. Bad Idea! He drove from 8:00 am to 12:30 pm before he found a Port but it was the wrong Port. After 3 hours of waiting, finally a hydro foil showed up at the end of the pier which was at least 200 yards from the shore. With our bags, Sandy and Jack piled into the back end of one of those little three wheeled trucks. We bounced all the way out to the boat. It was dark by the time we reached Ningbo Port and taken to a nice hotel. After dinner and further discussion, we were told that they would pick us up at 9:00 am the next morning for the trip to Xikou, which is about 100 miles from Shanghai, and see a factory where Double Arrow Clippers were manufactured. We dreaded the trip because the translator was terrible and it was so frustratingly difficult for us to understand his English.

The envoys from Sterling had reached a strange fork in the road. They had not been able to do any business and they had little reason to expect that they would be able to do so soon, and yet more than ever before, they were convinced that they needed to start their own Chinese company or purchase one that made a comparable line of clippers and trimmers. That night Jack went to bed disgusted. Our trip was drawing to a close and we had gotten nowhere. The next day, though, was indeed another day. Jack woke up at 5:00 a.m. and looked at the situation. Arriving at the conclusion that the translator was so poor that neither he nor Sandy knew the true situation. Jack called the concierge and told him that he urgently needed the best English speaking translator he could find; he then dressed and went to the next hotel to ask the concierge the same, and that the person would have to go to work today. Back at our hotel, the concierge said he had gotten in touch with a professor at Ningbo University who might be suitable. The concierge introduced them to William Xu Shi Yong. They were thrilled at his grasp of the English language. It could not have been a wiser choice as this fine young gentleman would in the future grow in knowledge and receive the respect of those in Sterling as well as those he supervised in China. Plague had kept us out of India, and now impediment upon impediment was closing China. "I want to tell you, " Jack would say when he got back to Sterling, "If you go to the Far East for business, you have to have a really good translator."

We were scheduled to fly home the next day, and had accomplished nothing. The meeting with William Yu Shi Yung in Ningbo was my first encounter with the man who was to eventually become General Manager of Wahl's Chinese subsidiary. Teacher, businessman, and translator, William Xu was a man of many talents and broad experience, including a job doing translations at headquarters for a Swiss company that exported all over the world. A small man with a large command of English, Mr. Xu agreed to a fee of $30 a day and accompanied the Wahl group. It was the beginning of a very long journey together.

The journey this day however, was not easy. Shanghai had excellent internal transportation, but here they were out in the provinces, (the boonies, in Americanese) and the trip from Ningbo to the factory was over roads still under construction. It was a rocky terrible ride, mostly at speeds of 15 to 20 mph. One time they even had to stop and get out of the vehicle to move a rock.

Xikou, where the factory was located, was a small town kind of like Sterling, with a fairly decent hotel. As the birthplace and childhood home of Chiang Kai Shek, Xikou aspired to be a tourist center. The officials wanted good roads and a good hotel. They came close with the latter, but the roads had a long way to go. Anyone riding on them inevitably thought the journey much longer than it really was.

The plant looked workable. Unlike the run down factory they had toured in Shanghai, this one had possibilities. In one of his early trips through the factory, Jack observed the equipment and came away with an estimate of $2 to 3 million. His host asked if Wahl would be interested in selling any of its products. There was one product, a pivot motor hair clipper, that particularly interested Jack. Wahl did not have anything like it, although Oster had something similar. Jack could see where that might be an asset to bring to the American market.

All in all, the company was very desirable. Its machinery had been appraised fairly recently—less than six months before, in a buy out from the government. Its general manager, Mr Xia Jia Ping, was a very bright self-made engineer. Jack took a liking to him immediately. As a businessman and engineer he appreciated the job Mr. Xia was doing. He liked his practicality and resourcefulness. Under his direction, the factory was building a grinder from scratch using no more than a catalog picture of the machine. Jack was very impressed with how much they did with so little. They did not use progressive dies to stamp their laminations, but did them by hand feeding small parts. On the other hand they also ran 20 to 30 milling machines with one man operating as many as five machines. He would load one magazine and move on to the next machine and just kept circulating, moving finished parts from one machine to the next. It was not high accuracy, but technically it was a good way of getting low cost milling. "It was a shock," he later explained, "to see what improvements we could make almost immediately."

It soon became apparent that this company, an independent corporation with stockholders, was available. When the Wahl party expressed their intention to make an offer, the Chinese indicated their willingness to entertain an offer. Here was Wahl's opportunity for a joint venture in which Wahl could obtain controlling interest. Back in the states, the Board of Directors read my report with enthusiasm. They agreed with me. This company was just what Wahl had wanted. The growing profitability of the U.K. operation encouraged them to duplicate this success elsewhere, and here in China they would have a foothold in the world's largest market as well as a brand new resource, and an Asian resource at that, for stopping the inroads of Asian competition.

Jack had found what he was looking for, but acquiring it was another matter. Chinese ways of doing business were new to Wahl

Clipper. Part of the fault lines separating American and Chinese culture lay in the area of business practices. Jack and his team worked diligently to come up with a fair purchase price, but at the first meetings it was hard to tell what was going on. There were many discussions among the Chinese at the table—the owners, Chinese government officials, economic development experts—and it was all in Chinese. Even with a good translator like Mr. Xu, it was hard to make headway. The Chinese had the habit of ordering champagne at the noon luncheon. The Americans soon learned that once the bubbly reached the table and started flowing, the negotiations that day were over. When the parlay took two steps forward, it was never clear how many steps back it would take, for the Chinese had the vexing habit of returning to points that the Americans thought they had agreed on the day before. Even so, the talks continued, with meetings in China and America, and much good, hard negotiating. On October 10, 1994, John F. Wahl signed a letter of intent for Wahl Clipper Corporation U.S.A. to form a joint stock venture with the company in Xikou. A letter of intent and a full blown business plan had to be submitted. Six months later, on April 1, 1995, with plans approved Wahl organized our new subsidiary, Ningbo Wahl Knives and Scissors Company, a joint venture in which it owned 90% of the company and ten Chinese investors owned the other 10%. Within the next year at their request, Wahl Clipper bought out nine of these gentleman and owned all but Mr. Xia's 3.2%.

4. Toehold and Foothold

One striking thing about Wahl Clipper's growth in the '90s was the way it proceeded by leaps and bounds. The huge spurts of growth that came with Asian and German acquisitions were quantum leaps born of the critical mass that Wahl achieved early in this decade: ingenious and timely product development, steady diversification of its sales & marketing divisions and mutual support they gave each other, and the adroit promotion of the Wahl name all over the world. All these combined with the company's prudential leadership and highly productive workforce gave Wahl Clipper a winning edge comparable to that which Michael Jordan and the Bulls exhibited during these years. The company was growing without any loss to its cohesion. Indeed, success was breeding success. It knew how to win and could also make its own breaks. It could also withstand the shocks of setbacks and play to its strength.

In 1995, Wahl Clipper actually expanded into Asia on two fronts, in Japan as well as China. That year, Wahl spent $.75 M to establish Nippon Wahl, a wholly owned sales & service distribution office in Tokyo, Japan. With hair cuts running at $40 a clip, Wahl thought there was a great opportunity for its professional and consumer clippers. Ironically, Japan with its well-developed capitalist and democratic institutions, proved inhospitable to the Wahl venture, while Communist China, post-Tiananmen Square and all, supplied Wahl with a thriving base for its Asian operations. Japan, with its high yen and strong local competition—Panasonic has its home base there—has been a very tough market to crack. Wahl's first year in Asia was a good indicator of things to come. Nippon Wahl lost $79,000, while Ningbo Wahl made $5,000. True, it was a very slender profit, but it was an encouraging start, and Wahl wasted little time in building on it.

The challenges in China were enormous, but so too were the opportunities. The plant, with its 300 employees, was productive by Chinese standards, but it required major improvements to become a world class operation that could expand its market share in China and export parts and finished products to America and Europe through Wahl's existing international sales forces. Wahl's efforts in 1996 were directed toward upgrading manufacturing operations and improving the quality of Ningbo's finished product. Both language and distance made it difficult but did not stop Jack from the kinds of hands-on involvement that he was used to in new projects. It was frustrating, because he knew that more visits there would hasten the factory's modernization and he averaged over three trips a year to the China Factory. It was hard work, but fun too.

Even so, the new management and Wahl know-how were having an impact. In 1996, the Chinese plant began turning out hand and electric hair clippers that approached Wahl standards. The next year continued the company's slow but steady growth. With net sales of $3.5 M, Ningbo Wahl realized a 12% increase in net profits. With 81% of its sales going overseas, it was becoming a much more effective exporter.

Key to Wahl's success was its strict policy of straight and sound business practices, especially with financial reports and product quality. In contrast with typical Chinese practice, Wahl paid its taxes accurately and on time.

The relationship between the people of China and our company is mutually strong. We work hard to keep a high level of respect between our organizations. "We gave assistance to a small group of businessmen from China with a chance to come to the U.S. and tell their story to the industrialists."

As recognition, the town presented a special award to Jack. "William Xu called early one morning to give him the news that he had been awarded an 'Ornery' Citizen Award. He was baffled and asked him to repeat. It turns out he was to be an 'Honorary Citizen of Fenghua.' "

That year the corporate office took additional measures to over-come the language barrier. It hired an English-speaking Chinese engineer and an accountant. Bill Burke was the first American financial guy to go over to China. He was followed by Tom Davis, who the year before had spent 80% of his time in China and 20% in Sterling. Wahl was hiring people who had a fair knowledge of English and began giving English lessons to 30 key Ningbo Wahl employees. Engineers were regularly exchanged between Sterling and Ningbo.

In 1998, the Chinese operation continued to change for the better. The quality of the Work Force improved rapidly and sales and profits were up: 11% and 38%, respectively. The plant's efforts to improve quality were helping boost its sales in China. Wahl continued to bolster its Chinese management team. On Saturday Morning early, we made arrangements to visit our Shanghai distributor by way of lunch and a visit to the Great Wall. On the return trip, moving rapidly on a 4 lane highway, a car crossed over the center line and crashed into the second car in front of us, a small taxi and then into the van in front of us. The door of the van burst open and a man fell out onto the highway. All traffic stopped. Sandy Conley shouted from the back seat, "Mr. Xia was in that taxi." Jack jumped out and ran up and found Mr.Xia with his head bleeding and pinned under the taxi which was on its side and giving off a strong smell of gasoline. Jack tried to roll the taxi off of him, and other people helped to move the taxi. Also in the taxi was our National Sales Manager. Without thinking Jack followed the direction of a military man in a military van who motioned to bring Mr. Xia and put him in his van. Sandy went with our Distributor and they brought our sales manager to the hospital. The driver of the Military Van kept saying hospital and drove us about 2 miles to a hospital. The hospital had dark hallways and we had to wait for a gurney until our sales manager was taken off for x-rays and Mr. Xia could use the gurney. Surprisingly, very soon a doctor walked out with x-rays. He held them for us to see and Jack was shocked to see two broken legs. After about an hour of waiting, they learned that the sales manager, not Mr. Xia, had the broken legs. Mr. Xia was wheeled out with all the hair shaved off his head, bandaged up with a concussion that probably would be okay after a week of bed rest. Somehow we got back to our hotel for a few hours sleep before the 20 hour flights heading home the next morning. Most taxis in China are normally very light weight, small, flimsy, and have poor to no protection in an accident.

At different times management problems would come up and it became clear that Mr. Xia's, the Chinese way, was somewhat different from ours. The lax management practices of Mr. Xia forced Jack as

Chairman to discharge him. A questionable incident attracted the Government People who were the ones who recommended to fire Mr. Xia Jia Ping.

After all the camaraderie we had, it was very difficult for me to let Mr. Xia go. At the direction of our Best Legal Advice, Wahl had to terminate him. Eventuality the able translator, William Xu, was selected as his replacement. Cherry Yue Ke Hong took over as controller, replacing Tom Davis. Our long-term objective was to give Wahl a low cost, high quality manufacturing base for exports all over the world. Another objective was to make Wahl #1 in sales to the huge Chinese market.

Jack and Sue married on May 22, 1999 at St. Mary's Catholic Church, Sterling, IL. Sue's children are: Gene Jr., Mark, Melanie and Rob.

Jack had made many trips to the Far East, working as an engineer in the factory and also attempting to develop a team to sell Wahl's China made products to the Chinese people. In order to expand the professional business in China, we began exhibiting at the main professional Barber and Beauty Trade Shows. An educator from the U.S. , Sue Wahl, Jacks wife introduced the finest clippers made by Wahl to an audience of licensed Chinese barbers and hairdressers. She used the hair clipper to cut the latest ladies and men's hairstyles on the Chinese. Three days demonstrating the Wahl Razor Blade cuts on stage introduced Wahl Quality to thousands. They were able to set up and train a traveling Wahl Educational team to work with our distributors and teach in other areas of China. This was the first Hairstyling Educational team set up and trained by a manufacture to teach within China. One of the most interesting hair clipper presentations was tied to a beauty pageant, with 6' tall gorgeous Chinese ladies, exceptionally strong in Harbin, Northern China. It was hard work but still a lot of fun. In all of the trips and working in China, the only problem came when Jack got on stage for a hair cut and his sport coat was taken, which had his passport in the pocket. Believe me, it is tough to get a passport and visa while you're in China. If it was not for William Xu, Jack would still be there.

By 1998, Wahl's outlook in Asia was very good. Though the Asian economic downturn that year had put a crimp on Wahl's exports to the Far East, its subsidiaries and affiliates there had much good news to report. Unity Agency, the Australian affiliate in which Wahl owned a quarter share, was enjoying excellent growth under the direction of another go-getter, George Davie assisted by Richard Gresham. The struggling Japanese subsidiary, Nippon Wahl, seemed to have turned a corner in 1998. Hiring two respected professional barber and hair stylists, Nippon Wahl intensified its marketing efforts, staged several workshops and seminars, and broke into the black for the first time with profits of $132,000. As it was doing in Europe, Wahl was establishing a network of operations in Asia that could expand into local markets and also advance the international interests of the company. During these years, Wahl was growing in the European and Asian theaters. Indeed, while Jack was overseeing China's growth, his son Greg was directing Wahl's return to the Fatherland.

5. Going Home Again: Die Gute Wahl
Last year we said we were going to "Go For It."
With 850 full time Employees outside the USA,
we do have a full plate.

1996 WAHL CLIPPER ANNUAL REPORT

In 1996 Wahl made a decisive move to strengthen its position in Europe. With COO Greg Wahl, VP-Finance William B. Burke, and Administrative Assistant Donna Rosenthal heading the acquisition team, Wahl Clipper purchased a leading European competitor, Moser Elektogerate GMB Moser. This move should be good business. On October 16, 1996, when Greg Wahl and Moser owner, Albert Esner, signed the papers making Moser a Wahl subsidiary, the German company immediately gave Wahl a 25% boost in sales and a solid position in central Europe. With Wahl-Europe based in the United Kingdom, a warehouse in Holland, and Moser, which included a subsidiary in Hungary, Wahl now had the lucrative and highly competitive European market well covered.

The acquisition was also a triumphant homecoming for the Wahl family. Moser's headquarters were in Unterkirnach, in Baden-Wurtemberg, Germany, about 105 miles southwest of Oppenweiler, the birthplace of Greg's great-great-great grandfather, Frederich Wahl, the enterprising young man who led the Wahl family to America 143 years earlier.

Like the Chinese acquisition a year before, Moser presented Wahl with great opportunities and great challenges, although of a different order. Where the Chinese acquisition gave Wahl a foothold in the world's largest and fastest growing economy, Moser strengthened Wahl's hand in the world's wealthiest and most developed markets. The German company was one of the leading European manufacturers of personal care products. It was number one in the hair clipper category; however it was not profitable. The bottom line needed attention because it had not been in the black in 5 years. Moser's product line was comparable to Wahl's in clippers, electric shavers, massagers and animal grooming products. It also featured an intriguing new category, dental oral hygiene products. Wahl could now compete in Europe and North America with a larger line, more resources for product development, and the prospect of low-priced Chinese imports for added clout. "We have," said the 1996 Wahl Annual Report, "a large pollination of product lines."

At the outset, though, this new clout was still largely potential. It would take some hard, skillful work to make it a reality. Ningbo-Wahl was not the only factory that required a major makeover. The fifty-year old Moser had begun to flounder a few years before when its owner, Albert Esner, began to have health problems. Mr. Esner eventually hired Helmut Ronde to get the company ready for sale by restructuring it and boosting its market value. The company that

Esner and Ronde brought to market did turn out quality products and, like Wahl, had been trying to stay competitive through progressive management techniques, a skilled, motivated workforce, new technology and new product design. If the company had not been as successful in this program as Wahl, it at least knew some of the strategies of the new ownership and had the expectation of quickly becoming more profitable. They had a good solid base in Shaver Manufacturing.

Wahl's German subsidiary entered 1997 with two immediate challenges: correcting some mistakes by the previous management and integrating its operations with Wahl's global strategy. Under Managing Director Detlef Witte and Sales and Marketing GM Thomas Kammerer, Moser-Wahl began making headway. It introduced greater automation to make its blades of world-class quality and achieved greater savings by employing its Hungarian plant, with its lower labor costs, to assemble and ship its products. Many of the hurdles that first year were financial—redistributing the company for tax purposes and harmonizing its operations with the rest of Wahl. Though change, even for the better, is never easy, the Moser workforce responded well, and in that first year, the company had a net profit of $155,243.

In 1998, Moser continued to improve efficiency and quality and integrate its activities with Wahl's global operations. It had some notable successes. That year, Moser introduced three new professional clippers and redesigned a toothbrush for the consumer market. Witte boosted productivity by persuading union officials to increase the workweek from 37 to 40 hours. The success of these and other measures could be seen in the bottom line. In 1998, Moser had net sales of $41.5M and net profits of $.85 M, a 500% increase over the previous year.

In that first year under American ownership, a new slogan became popular among Moser employees: *"Die Gute Wahl: Moser,"* which, translates, "The Good Choice: Moser." It was a slogan that Wahl's American management could also adopt. Their German subsidiary was making steady progress. Historically, the situation had a certain elegance to it. Almost a century and a half earlier, Frederick Wahl had made a good choice by going to America; now Jack and Greg Wahl and company had completed the circle and brought the family business back to Germany, almost, as it were, to the old neighborhood.

6. Faring Forward

Wahl Clipper Corporation maintains a world leadership position because of an intimate knowledge of hair cutting tool design and manufacturing, a heritage that has been handed down through the Wahl family. A deep personal involvement and commitment continues into the third generation, providing both continuity and leadership.

1998 WAHL CLIPPER ANNUAL REPORT

Old men should be explorers.

T.S. ELIOT[35]

The Wahl management team now had the delicate task of interweaving the Senior management of the three companies so that their actions would be to the greater benefit of the group. The new size and geographical reach of Wahl did not automatically translate into real growth. The aim was synergy, to translate critical mass into productive, profitable energy at a level not reached before. There will be the sharing of production methods, trade secrets, ideas, successes and failures.

To have the continuous growth we have shown you must put major effort into a high number of projects. I believe Wahl Clipper has been unique in accepting the high risks which go along with new products and new projects. Some of the major projects we have been involved in over the past 50 years are listed on the next page, most of these projects didn't pass the test of time and are not in our product core line of business today. Their efforts are part of our History.

Electric Shear Sharpener   Commercial Beauty Salon Hair Dryer

Back Massagers	Agitator-Malted Milk Mixer
Curls–To-Go, rechargeable cordless curling brush	Self Styling Hair Trimmer
Cordless Rechargeable Soldering Iron, 16 detachable tips & Quick Charge Soldering Iron	Hand Clippers
Comfort Zone Foot Massager	Single Head Rotary Shaver
Wet Dry Ladies Shaver	Black Man's Shaver Shaper
Vac-U-Clip Nose Trimmer	Groomsmen Beard and Mustache Trimmer
Wahl Custom Shaver	Clip-Pet, small animal clipper
Clipper-Vac	Professional Animal Clippers
Vacuum Pick-up Hair Clipper	Fish Pump
Lather Maker	Magnifying Mirror
Hair Detangler	Facial Sauna
Solder Gun with Feeder-Rechargeable	Aluminum Case Professional Clippers
ISO Tip Soldering Iron	30 Minute Dryer
Z-Curling Iron	Frenzee Curling Iron
Vincents, B&B Supply House	Professional Silent Dryer
Disposable Medical Shaver-3M	Visions Wet Line
Perm Rods	KM1 Motor Clipper
Bikini Trimmer	Razor cutting blade
Professional Hair Clippers	Sterling Professional Clippers
DeFuzzer, fabric shaver	Horse Clipper
2 -Speed Heated Massager	Swedish Style, 2 speed heated massager
Hot Oil Massager	Sweet Dreams-Bed Massager

The 2002 torch has been burning brightly since Gregory S. Wahl became President and CEO. Greg is married to Elizabeth Butkus and they have 4 sons, Brian, Mike, Kevin and Dan. There was never a doubt in Jack's mind that Greg would be the next President. Most of the Senior Managers felt the same. The training process was automatically in motion by Jack passing on to Greg the responsibility to solve a problem or head up the responsibility for a project. Early on he was an active member of the Wahl senior management team and reported on the status of virtually all manufacturing/engineering projects. Wahl had a huge number of projects in progress over the years in which they were able to have sustained growth. Greg was directly responsible for product development and quality control as well as technology in the plastic, production, and assembly departments. He was overloaded but never turned down any assignments. Jack and Greg worked together and gradually separated out responsibilities. They divided the lists of projects, gradually Jack's list got shorter as Greg's got longer. Jack says he always knew that Greg would give him an honest answer, even though it often wasn't the answer he wanted.

Greg is an outdoor person, who loves nature, the forest and streams. He is an active collector of prairie seeds. Fly casting on his own stream is probably his main avocation today. Jack says he is happy to be able to say, he is the one responsible for Greg's outdoor interest. They spent a lot of time outdoors on long weekends at state parks in Wisconsin, snow skiing, water skiing, swimming, ice skating and fishing. Jack taught Greg how to tie the canoe or the speedboat on the top of the station wagon. When he would tie it Jack knew that it would stay there. Jack taught Greg and Greg taught Jack how to paddle a canoe through rapids and not break the paddle, pitch a tent, build a fire and cook over the campfire. Greg's sisters were not too interested, and his brother Mark was eleven years younger, so often Greg would bring a friend. He studied nature, he knew the technical name of most all of God's creatures. One time Greg picked up a stick about 3 or 4 inches long and asked Jack to hold it for him. A few minutes later it started to wiggle, "hey, it's alive," Jack was afraid he was going to get bit and Greg laughed. He said it is a harmless

Woodstick. A few years after Greg's employment at Wahl started, he asked Jack, "what's the best way to get ahead in the company?" Jack told him, "you should be open to take on new projects as they are offered. Be like a sponge and absorb as much as you can. See that you follow through with the completion of the job. In other words, you would become so valuable to the company as a problem solver, it would become impossible for them not to reward you."

Greg had been selected and Jack trained him as much as possible prior to his retirement in May of 2001. Greg has all of the qualifications necessary to be the new leader. His name is on the door, so Jack believes he needs to stay out of his way at the plant. Jack knows the task is difficult and Greg is doing it well. He knows the Board of Directors expect a performance that continues the growth path. As you can see, a flicker of the torch has marked the sales curve but the numbers have been quickly surpassed by the successive years.

A letter signed by Warren, Bob and Jack, to all employees on February 9, 1973, records a surprising $27,000 profit sharing contribution. The last 10 years over a million dollars each year has been contributed into profit sharing.

Jack says, "A dozen years ago" a $200 million sales goal was absolutely unthinkable, but look where we are now.

"We have stepped ahead with our march toward a successful Global operation. And so corporate history moves on."

Afterword.

This book should have told you why and how we put a major effort into making the right choice, but as in most family companies, it didn't always happen. We have had a couple of bloopers too painful to talk about, but we cut our losses and moved on.

"Obviously, I couldn't get everything I wanted in this book, my short-term memory at 78 years of age is sliding slightly, and I apologize if I have omitted anything that should be included. I also want to thank all the employees who worked with me over the $51^{1/2}$ years I was a full-time employee of the company. Our story is unique and I couldn't bear it if no one knew or remembered what the company had done. It wasn't just for the money."

END NOTES

CHAPTER 2

[1] Matthew Josephson, *Edison* (New York, 2003), p. 64. Much of the material on Edison in this chapter is from Josephson.

[2] Samuel Insull, *Memoirs of Samuel Insull*: An Autobiography, p. 69

[3] Josephson, p. 378

[4] *American Catholics*, Charles R. Morris (Time Books: 1997)

[5] Williams, "Few People had Much to Spend 30 Years Ago," *Gazette*, February 8, 1929.

[6] "Twenty Six Get Diplomas," *Sterling Evening Gazette*, June 7, 1912.

[7] "Young Men Must Have Initiative." *Sterling Daily Standard*, June 14, 1912.

[8] Ibid.

CHAPTER 3

[9] "Wahl Products Are World Wide In Distribution," Daily Gazette, May 6, 1931.

[10] "Merrill Benson Dies On Hospital Ship Off New York Harbor," *Daily Gazette*, October, 1918.

[11] Scott Williams, "Wahl Manufacturing Company Is Helping to Bob the Hair of the Nation," *Daily Gazette*, January 17, 1925.

[12] Ibid.

[13] "Announce Leo Wahl Chosen As Bank President," *Daily Gazette*, June 9, 1931.

[14] "Organize Company to Manufacture Wahl Vibrators," *Daily Gazette*, November 24, 1914.

[15]Mary Ellen Ducey and Erica Nordmeier, "World War I and the Rainbow Division," *Nebraska Library Association Quarterly*, Vol. 3, No. 4, Winter 2000, pp. 27-30.

[16]"Soldiers of the Rainbow: The First California Engineers During the Mexican Border Crisis and World War I, 1916-1919," www.militarymuseum.org/Rainbow.htm.

[17] "Merril Benson Dies," *op. cit.*

[18] "Captain Wahl Tells of his Work Overseas," *Daily Gazette*, May 10, 1919

[19] "History of Wahl Clipper Corporation, "December. 1967.

CHAPTER 4

[20] The way radical sociologist C. Wright Mills described organized labor in the past–World War II ear. America Since 1941, a History, James T. Patterson (Fort Worth: 1994), p.40.

CHAPTER 5

[21] "Family Business Hums," Cathy Rogers, Rockford Register Star, March 4, 1983.

[22] The material in this chapter and the preceding one comes from *Manufacturing in America: A Legacy of Excellence*, National Association of Manufacturers (_____:1996), pp. 127, 132.

[23] Ibid., p. 153.

[24] *Wahl Annual Report 1984*, p. 9.

[25] *Op. cit.* "Family Business Hums."

CHAPTER 6

[26] *"Union Sundown,"* Bob Dylan, Special Rider Music, 1983.

[27] The following paragraphs on the development of the European Union is taken from a trade journal article included in the 1989 Wahl Annual Report, which was issued a few months after the Iron Curtain crumbled. CHAPTER 7

[8] Maggie Rohwer, "Sauk Valley's Working World," *Sterling Daily Gazette*, April 25, 1992.

[29] Bob Dylan, *"Not Dark Yet,"* (Special Rider Music: 1997).

[30] *1994 Wahl Annual Report*

[31] Ibid.

[32] *"U. S. Manufacturing in Crisis,"* Industrial Maintenance & Plant Operation (IMPO) Newsletter, March 24, 2003.

[33] Bob Dylan, *"It's Alright Ma (I'm Only Bleeding),"* Special Rider Music, 1965, 1993.

[34] Merriam Webster's Collegiate Dictionary, *10th Edition*, (Springfield, MA: 1993), p. 1196.

[35] T. S. Eliot, *The Four Quartets*, from The Complete Poems of T. S. Eliot.

1987 Management Bonus Plan Participants
As of March 15, 1987

67¢ per share to all record holders as of March 15th

<u>TOP MANAGEMENT</u> @ 1,000 Shares
William Burke
Richard Harding
Robert Thurber
Gregory Wahl
James Wahl
Noel Wallen
Linda Clemens

<u>MIDDLE MANAGEMENT</u> @ 1,000 Shares
Rueben Bilbrey
Ed Benters
Harold Davis
Sandy DeWolf
William Grim
Marion Halley
Ruth Heflebower
Jerry Hutsell
Clifford Jording
David Kendall
John Morgan
Leon Neese
Carl Nelson
James Parrent
Jewelene Pratt
Roger Pratt
Timothy Stephens
Leonardo Staranko
Leo Wahl
David Wahl

<u>500 Shares</u>
Keith Dirks

Wahl Picture Gallery

Leo J. Wahl at about 12 to 14 years of age, 1904-1906.

Vera Glafka (Wahl),
Leo J. Wahl's mother, 1800's.

Leo J. Wahl around 36 years of age, 1928.

WAHL

Elizabeth Wahl Weyreuch and Verna Glafka Wahl

Leo's father, 1800's

Leo Wahl, six months

Henry Glafka family, on farm south of Walnut, Illinois, early 1900's.

Leo J. Wahl, about 16 years old, and his family, Feb. 22, 1908.
First Row: *Helen Leitz, Everett Wahl, Willard Kelsey, Clyde Wahl, Vera Wahl Francel,*
Marie Wahl (baby is probably Glenn Wahl or Lloyd Wahl).
Second Row: *Aunt Cass Leitz, probably Grandma Wahl's sister, Grandma and*
Grandpa Wahl, next two are probably Mr. and Mrs. William Wahl (Russell Wahl's parents)
Third Row: *Otto Leitz, William Wahl, Callie Leitz Mitchell, Mrs. Edward Wahl, R.W. E. Mitchell,*
Mr. Leitz, Mrs. Charles Wahl, Uncle Charles Wahl, and Uncle Edward Wahl (Dr. Wahl).
Fourth Row: *Leo Wahl, Aunt Cal Wahl, Fred Wahl, Gifford Wahl, Uncle Glenn Wahl,*
Aunt Helen Wahl, Uncle Frank Wahl, and Uncle Henry Wahl.

Leo J. Wahl, at lunch in the garden, University of De Poiters, Paris, 1919

Leo and Verna Wahl and family, January 11, 1926, on their way from Tampa, Florida to Miami, Florida.

Leo and Verna Wahl with another new car, white walls and wheel pants (ferder skirts) going for a drive, 1940.

WAHL PICTURE GALLERY

Leo and Verna Wahl with children, in laws, and grandchildren, 1954.
Standing L-R: *Warren, Mary, Margaret, and Jack.*
Seated in Chairs: *Bob holding David, Mary, Leo, Verna, Mary Jane, and Raymond.*
Seated on Floor: *Rosemary, Joan, Betsy, Lee, Teresa, Jim, and Greg*

Leo and Verna Wahl's children, early 1970s.
Standing L-R: *Warren and Bob.*
Sitting L-R: *MSGR. Ray, Mary Jane, and Jack.*

Gallery 227

Leo J. Wahl, in uniform during WW I, 1917.

Leo J. Wahl, on ship to France during WW I, 1917.

Robert Wahl, 1945.

Thursday, January 17, 1946

Wahl Assigned to Dangerous Task in Japanese Waters

According to a dispatch from Hiro Wan, Japan, John F. Wahl, Fl/c, son of Mr. and Mrs. Leo F. Wahl, is serving on a navy "guinea pig" vessel in one of the strangest and most dangerous missions growing out of the Pacific war.

Fl/c JOHN F. WAHL

Wahl is a member of the crew of the SS Joseph Holt, which is dedicated to deliberately seeking out and exploding a new type of mine that cannot be swept by ordinary methods. Each day a handful of volunteers take her through the waters of Japan's inland sea, cruising back and forth over the doubtful channels until satisfied that the routes are safe for shipping. The only way to determine whether time has neutralized these mines is to pass over them.

So far the Holt has not had an explosion.

Because she is such a large ship for her skeltaon crew of volunteers, she appears to be deserted as her ghost-like hulk moves over the dangerous waters. Empty passageways echo eerily to the sound of feet.

The Holt and two other ships assigned to the same work have been made as safe as possible for their crews. Engine room controls have been extended to her main deck so no one would be trapped below in event of an explosion. The men wear tank helmets for head protection. Overheads and some of the decks have been padded with mattresses to cushion shock and falls.

Wahl assigned to dangerous task in Japanese Waters, 1946.

Warren and Bob Wahl, upon Warren's graduation from flight school, 1944.

ROBERT WAHL

Private Robert Wahl, son of Mr. and Mrs. Leo Wahl, enlisted in the army April 29, and is now at Fargo, N. D., where he is taking specialized training. He is a graduate of Community high school and attended Notre Dame university one year prior to entering the service.

WARREN WAHL

Aviation Cadet Warren Wahl, son of Mr. and Mrs. Leo Wahl, is stationed at Murray, Ky. He entered the service April 12, 1943. He is a graduate of Community high school; he also attended St. Ambrose college, Davenport, Iowa, and Notre Dame university.

Bob and Warren in Sterling Daily Gazette,1945-46.

Leo, Verna, Jack, Mary Jane, and Ray boarding a flight to Denver, 1938

WAHL PICTURE GALLERY

1701 Locust St. home, built in 1926-27, Sterling, Illinois.

Margaret & Jack Wahl   *1952*   *Leo & Verna Wahl*

The first Wahl owned plan, built in 1923, located on 407 East Third St., Sterling, Illinois. The building has since been torn down and replaced by an accounting firm office of Lindgren, Callihan, Van Osdol & Co., Ltd.

Leo J. Wahl, around 1940.

*Jack, Warren, and Bob Wahl leaving the new factory
on North Locust St., Sterling, Illinois, 1957.*

Meeting of the Canadian partners at the Forrest Inn, Sterling, Illinois, 1965.
Seated L-R: *John F. Wahl, Warren P. Wahl, Bob Swenson, Tom Whitehead, Don Hennessey, Bob Wahl.* Standing L-R: *Reubin Bilbrey, Ray Meyers, Laymond Miller, Bruce Swanson, Leslie Black, Bob Kanaca, Jim Fox, Dave Garland, Cliff Jording, Vic Bein, Joe Rice, Ray Bable, Fred Goble, Dale Weinken, Carl Nelson, Jasper Dividell, 1965.*

Board of Directors, May 13, 1982.
Left to right: *James O. Wahl, John F. Wahl, Robert L. Wahl, William J. Gearns, and Wayne Wahl.*

WAHL

Warren Wahl

Wahl Clipper Corporation receives the coveted President "E" Award for Excellence in Exporting, 1989.

WAHL PICTURE GALLERY

Board of Directors, 1982.
L-R: *H. Barry Musgrove, John F. Wahl, Robert L. Wahl, Wayne F. Wahl, William J. Gearns*

1985 Management Team:
These highly qualified team players, are seated L-R:
Robert J. Thumber, Director of Consumer Sales; John F. Wahl, President; Richard L. Harding, Plant Mfg. Manager.;
Standing L-R: *Gregory S. Wahl, Vice-President, Engineering; Billy Joe Cornstubble, Director of Marketing; Noel Wallen, Vice-President, International Operations; William B. Burke, Treasurer and Controller.*

Wahl plant expansion company photo, 1985.
Note Bud Wahl and Mary front row.

Senior Management Team, 1986.
On table: *Brian Hollands.*
Seated L-R: *Pat Anello, Bill Barke, Jack Wahl, and Tony Kallock.*
Standing L-R: *Al Corrigan, Greg Wahl, and Dick Harding.*

Management Team, 1986.
Seated L-R: Billy Joe Cornstubble, John F. Wahl, Noel Wallen, Greg Wahl
Standing L-R: Richard L. Harding, William B. Burke, Robert J. Thurber, James O. Wahl

Senior Management Team, 1987.
Seated L-R: Greg Wahl, John F. Wahl, and Noel Wallen.
Standing L-R: Bill Burke, Dick Harding, Bob Thuber, and Jim Wahl.

Wahl Clipper Board of Directors, 1989.
L-R: James O. Wahl, John F. Wahl, Robert L. Wahl, Mary Jane Wahl Gearns,
and Wayne Wahl.

Ground Breaking for 41,000 sq ft addition, 1989.
L-R: William B. Burke, Pat Anello, Tony Kallock, Greg Wahl, Mary Jane Gearns,
Wayne Wahl (behind Jack), Jack Wahl (with shovel), Bob Wahl,
Bob Thurber, Dick Harding.

WAHL PICTURE GALLERY

The Group from Russia with Jack Wahl and Donna Rosenthall. Gordon Lankton (far left), Urs Pflugert (to right of Donna), and Arkady Drughilovsky, 1991.

Jack looking through a hole in the Berlin Wall, 1994.

WAHL

Members of Board, 1994.
Seated L-R: *Wayne Wahl, Mary Jane Gearns, Robert L. Wahl.*
Standing L-R: *James O. Wahl, Dan S. Blount, John F. Wahl.*

Senior Managers, 1994.
Seated L-R: *Pat Anello, Bill Burke, John F. Wahl, Tony Kallock.*
Standing L-R: *Brian Hollands, Alan Corrigan, Greg S. Wahl,*
Richard Harding, and James O. Wahl.

Members of the Board, 1995.
Seated L-R: *MSGR. Raymond Wahl, Robert L. Wahl, John F. Wahl,
Mary Jane Gearns.*
Standing L-R: *Ray Neifewinder, Dan S. Blount, James O. Wahl, and Wayne Wahl.*

Senior Management Team, 1997.
Seated L-R: *Jim Wahl, Greg Wahl, John F. Wahl, and Brian Hollands.*
Standing L-R: *Bill Burke, Don Matthews, Alan Corrigan, Dick Harding,
and Pat Anello.*

Board of Directors, 2003.
Seated L-R: David Lindsay, James O. Wahl, MSGR. Raymond Wahl, Leo T. Wahl, David Wahl, Ronal
Friedman. Standing L-R: Gregory S. Wahl, John F. Wahl, Mary Jane Gearns, and Theron Odlang.

Jack, second from left, and his sister Mary Jane Gearns received the award for their
father, Leo J. Wahl, who was inducted into Sterling High School's
Hall of Fame, Oct. 10, 2002.

Jack Wahl holding a chart showing the company's dramatic sales increase, 1986.

Employees at the new Chinese factory, "Topping," went all out to build FrenZee curling irons. Still, they could not meet the demand even with two shifts and full production. Companies must be very careful with production like this, where demand goes from 0 to half a million units and then back to 0. Only a strong company can survive this type of operation.

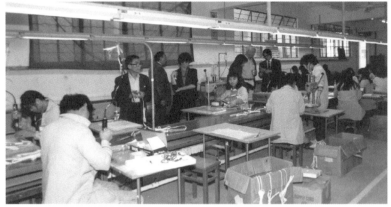

Work at the Topping factory, Sept. 1988.

Dinner at the Topping factory, Sept. 1988.

Topping Factory, 160 employees, Sept. 1988.

Xiaolon Sun, Sandy Conley, Jack Wahl, and Mr. Xia, in front of the first Wahl factory in China, 1994.

Sandy Conley and Jack Wahl at the Great Wall of China, 1994.

*Jack Wahl, William Xu Shi Yong, Gregory Wahl in
China, 1993-1994.*

Ariel view of the Sterling factory, 1990-91.

Wahl Clipper Corporation staff watches as the E flag is raised, to mark the company's award of the coveted Presidential "E Star" Award for Excellence in Exporting, 1994.

Jack Wahl and Paul Harvey shaking hands. and, on the right, the radio transcript, 1991.

HELLO AMERICANS, THIS IS PAUL HARVEY.

STAND BY FOR NEWS....

YOU CAN ASK ANY, *ANY* BARBER, BECAUSE FOR 77 YEARS, ALL OVER THE WORLD, ONE WORD HAS DESCRIBED THE FINEST PROFESSION AND NOW THAT ONE WORD "WAHL"....W A H L. (spelled out) DEFINES A NEW CUSTOM SHAVER, LIKE NONE OTHER.

YOU *NEVER* HAD SUCH A FAST SHAVE AS WITH THE WAHL. I'VE ALWAYS FINISHED SHAVING IN LESS THEN ONE MINUTE.   NONE OF THAT CIRCLING AROUND AND AROUND WHICH OTHER ELECTRICS REQUIRE.

EXTRA WIDE FOILS AND A POWERFUL MOTOR GIVE YOU A CLOSE SHAVE THE *FIRST TIME* AND THE WAHL COMES WITH THREE SEPARATE CUTTING HEADS SO THERE IS ONE JUST RIGHT FOR ANY BEARD, ANY TEXTURE, A PERFECT GIFT, BECAUSE ONE WAHL FITS *ALL.*

LET'S DO THIS, TRY ONE FOR 30 DAYS 0N ME. IF YOU ARE NOT CONVINCED WAHL HAS IT ALL SEND IT BACK FOR A FULL REFUND. NOW YOU CAN'T PUT IT OFF.

TO LOCATE YOUR NEAREST WAHL RETAILER TELEPHONE 1-800-48 SHAVE OR TRY SEARS OR SERVICE MERCHANDISE. (pause) 1-800 THEN 48 SHAVE. (END)

Ad for The Wahl Stubble Device, 1986, when Miami Vice star Don Johnson made a day-old beard the height of male fashion.

Jack Wahl's picture accompanying the Forbes magazine article, "Father Says Jump: Building a Brand with Third party Endorsement," 1995.

Jack Wahl Turns Over The Keys To The Family Clipper Business

Jack Wahl says retirement will give him a chance to enjoy such diversions as his vintage Olds convertible. However, Wahl will continue to consult the company's men's shaver strategy, for which he has played a lead role since introducing the shavers a decade ago.

STERLING, IL— Jack Wahl arrived at work at the Wahl Clipper headquarters here on a sunny late summer morning wearing a navy blue business suit.

It was only a gesture, a tribute perhaps to a career, indeed a life, in the family hair clipper business.

By 9:30 a.m., he was in a T-shirt, shorts and sneakers, all the more comfortable to drive in his '70 metallic green Olds 442 convertible— with the top down, of course— to his second home along the Rock River (Wahl's first home, the one in which he has lived since his birth in 1926, is just a couple miles away near downtown Sterling).

First, though, it was one more official walk through the Wahl Clipper doors in a suit, one more time as day-to-day CEO of the company his father, Leo J. Wahl, founded more than 80 years ago, a company now under the guidance of his eldest son, Greg.

"Now, I can throw it out," Wahl said about the navy blue suit.

Jack Wahl is retiring. The 74-year-old made the announcement at the company's spring board meeting. And now he appears ready, somewhat reluctantly, to pull away in his vintage Olds— leaving behind a legacy of 18 grandchildren

(future company execs, no doubt); and a legacy of growing Wahl from a $7.2 million company when he became president in 1977 into a global men's grooming leader with sales in excess of $160 million. And it was profitable each year, he proclaims.

In this exclusive interview with HOMEWORLD BUSINESS® Editor Peter Giannetti, Jack Wahl looks back at the key moments in his time at the helm of Wahl Clipper and his expectations for the future of a company that refuses to relinquish the spirit of family entrepreneurialism as it shapes itself into a more complex global manufacturing, sales and marketing enterprise.

Jack Wahl turns over the keys, 2001.

Gregory S. Wahl, President and CEO.

=WAHL= *1925*

These two articles are being used extensively in progressive beauty parlors—

Our New Model 88 Clipper

is the lightest and most perfectly constructed clipper on the market today. It weighs two ounces less than one pound and fits the hand perfectly. It runs quietly and smoothly, cutting the hair with practically no effort. It has plenty of power and requires no attention other than oiling the blades. The case is made entirely of durable aluminum and should last a lifetime. We guarantee this clipper to give satisfaction for one year.

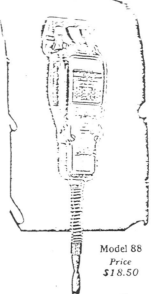

Model 88
Price
$18.50

Vibrators

Price $8.50

Quality rather than quantity is stressed in the manufacture of the Wall Vibrator. It is entirely dependable and safe to use. Because there is no motor, no oil is required and the machine is always clean and ready to use. It is a noiseless, high speed Vibrator that can be adjusted to any stroke, carrying a one-year guarantee.

America's Leading Clipper and Vibrator Manufacturers

Wahl Clipper Corporation : STERLING ILLINOIS

Sales sheet on Model 88 Clipper, 1925.

Wahl Clipper Corporation ad, Daily Gazette,
July 14-17, 1934, Sterling, Illinois.

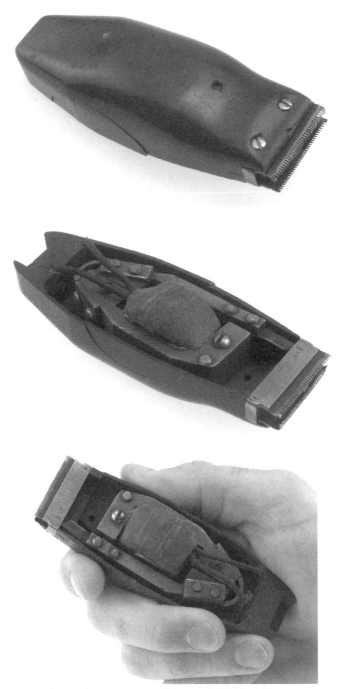

First electric shaver constructed by Leo J. Wahl, 1949 prototype.

At left, dryer, original hand-held aluminum dryer with wooden handle and with centrifugal fan, 1933.
At right, low-cost thermoplastic hand-held dryer with heating & stand, 1958.

Styler Dryer, 1965.

Sales sheet for Wahl electric shaver, 1958.

Sales sheet for Wahl Clip-pet ad, 1961.

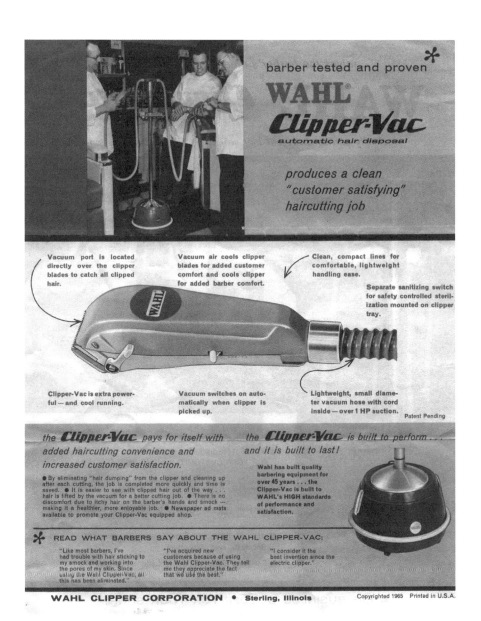

Sales sheet, Walh ClipperVac, 1965

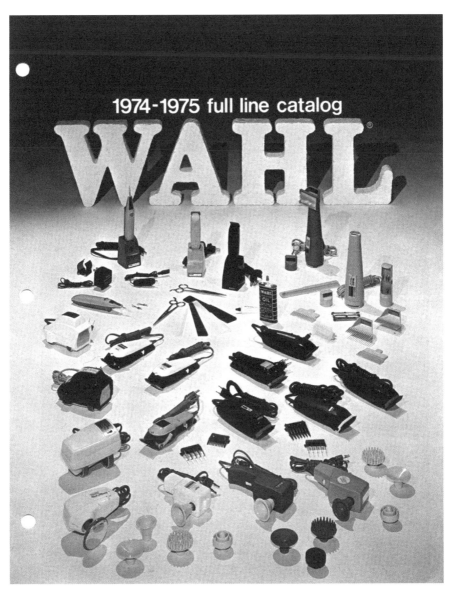

1974-75 Wahl full-line catalog

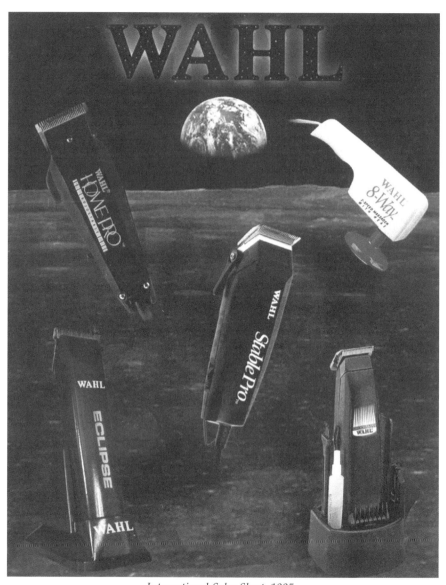

International Sales Sheet, 1995.

BIG PRODUCTS.

BIG PROMOTIONS.

BIG RESULTS. —

© 1997 Wahl Clipper Corporation

Wahl promotional ad featuring Richard Karns(from Tool Time), 1997.

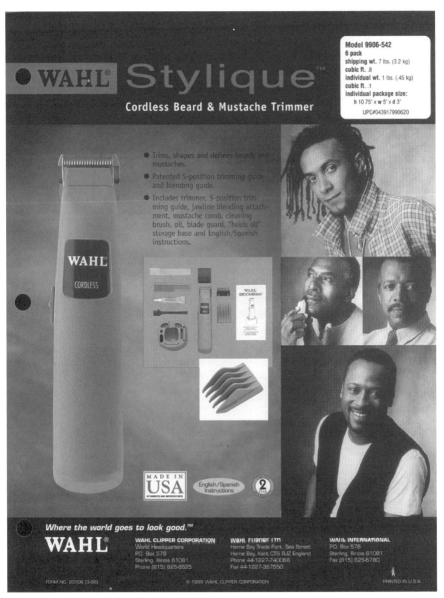

Sales sheet for Stylique cordless beard and mustache trimmer, 1995.

CORDLESS CONVENIENCE
FOR ELECTRONIC
AND ELECTRICAL WORK

Sales sheet for cordless soldering iron, 1974.

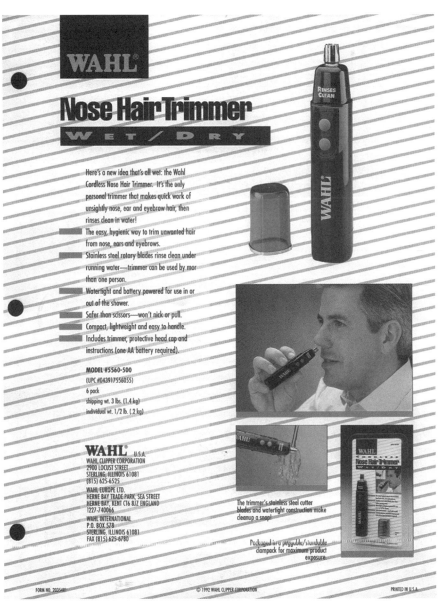

Sales sheet of Wet/Dry Nose Hair Trimmer, 1992.

Custom Shave System 4400, 1997.

Sales sheet for DynaFlex Custom Shave System, 2001.

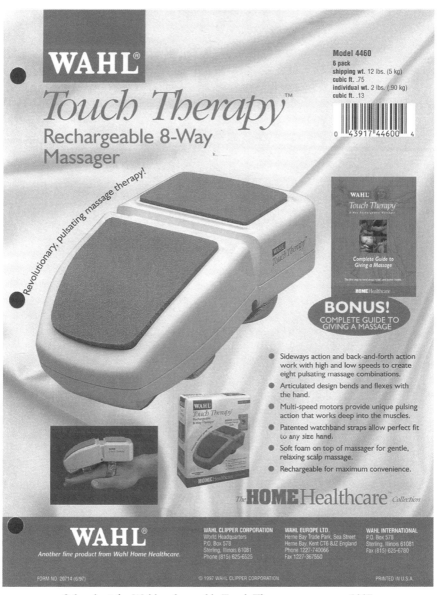

Sales sheet for Wahl rechargeable Touch Therapy massagers, 1997.

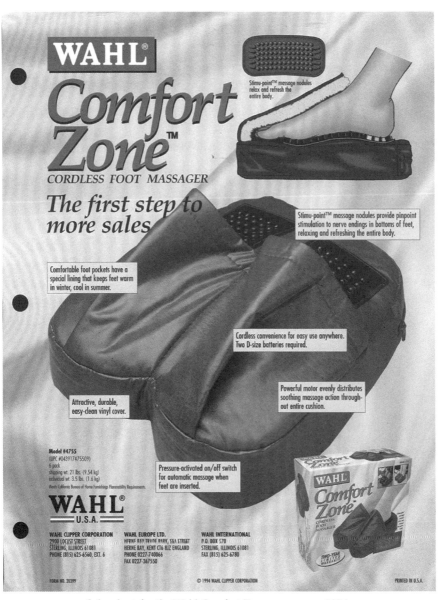

Sales sheet for the Wahl Comfort Zone massagers, 1994.

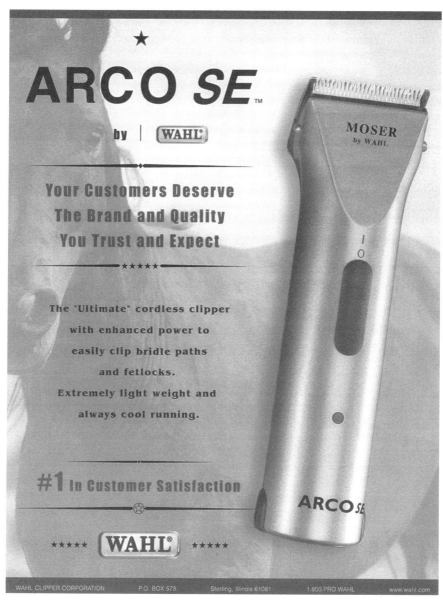

2000

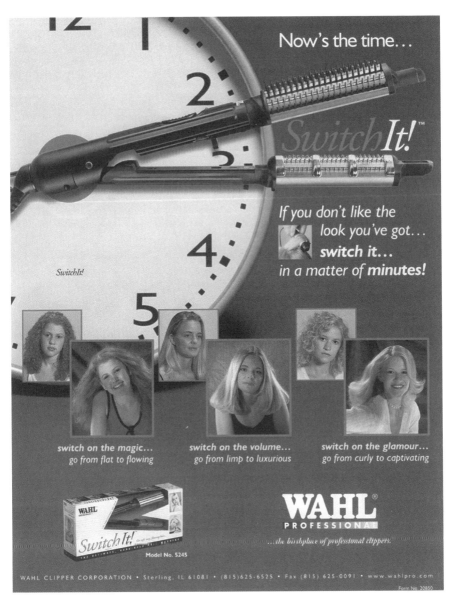

Sales sheet for Switch It! iron, 2000.

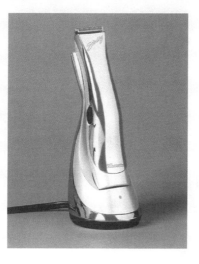

Sterling® Silhouette™

Super slender...super convenient...super powerful.

CORDLESS RECHARGEABLE TRIMMER
with Precision Easy-Change Blades

Powerful, premium quality, lightweight cordless trimmer.
Super slender styling for a perfect fit in your hand.
Single hole blades for super-easy changes.

Trimmer automatically recharges when placed in its stand
with LED indicator light.

Single hole high precision blades
for super-quick blade changes.

No. 8776 includes precision cordless
trimmer; automatic recharge stand; 4
cutting guides for lengths from 1/8"
to 1/2"; cleaning brush; oil; blade
guard and operating instructions.

*The red blade guard
guarantees it's pro-
fessional quality.*

Sterling® WAHL®

MADE IN THE USA

Form #20976-001

WAHL CLIPPER CORPORATION • 2900 Locust Street • Sterling, IL 61081 • (815) 625-6525 • Fax (815) 625-7073 • www.wahlpro.com

Sales sheet for Sterling Silhouette, cordless rechargeable trimmer, 2001.

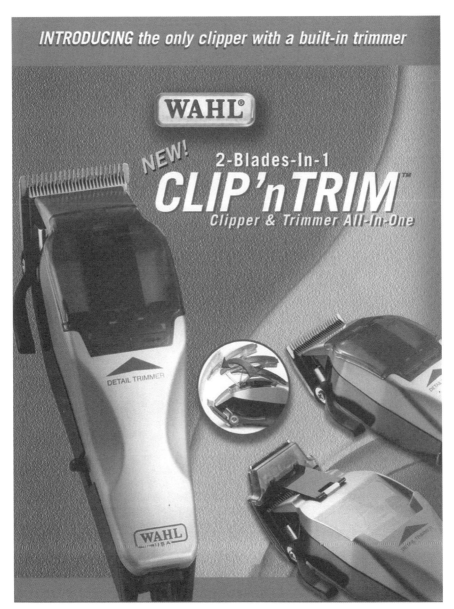

Sales sheet for Clip'nTrim, Clipper and Trimmer All In One, 2004.

Sales sheet for 25-piece haircutting kit with how-to-video, 2001.

LASER9747 & 9742

The Laser Clipper/Shear is the ultimate clipper! 170 watts of power is more than enough power to clip the dirtiest, wooliest sheep and llamas. The Laser can be converted from a fiber shear for sheep, goats, llamas and alpacas to a hair clipper for horses and cattle. The Laser is for the livestock owner who needs versatility.

blade included

2242 Fine Blade

also works with

Shear Head Option

STAR9741

Wahl Clipper's best selling and most versatile large animal clipper! The Star features a safety-reset switch to protect you and your clipper from overload. The Star is most commonly used for body clipping horses, heads and legs of show cattle and light sheep shearing when used with the Wizard Blade (Model #2246).

blade included

2242 Fine Blade

also works with

2246 Wizard Blade

for sheep, llamas, & goats

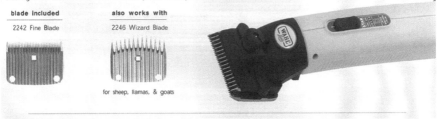

SHOWMAN9746

The Showman delivers raw clipping and shearing power wherever you need it! The powerful direct current motor operates from a hip-mounted power pack. If you need clipping power in the field or enjoy cordless operation, the Showman is for you. Our patented Wizard Blade allows the Showman to shear the wooliest sheep, goats, llamas and alpacas.

blade included

2242 Fine Blade

also works with

2246 Wizard Blade

for sheep, llamas, & goats

Wahl Lister Shearing Equipment is the longest established manufacturer of shearing and clipping equipment in the world. Our vast experience is second to none and over the years we have created a range of shears & clippers with patented features that ensure a wide user loyalty and professional, quality results. Wahl Lister shears & clippers are extremely adaptable, and with the correct choice of blades, a clipper can clip both cattle and horses or dagg out sheep and fully shear small numbers. All Lister clippers and Laser Shears come in a durable carry case complete with one set of blades or comb and cutter, accessories and a 1-year warranty.

WAHL®
Lister

Wahl Clipper Corporation   2900 N Locust St.   Sterling, IL 61081   800 PRO WAHL   www.wahl.com   #21053

Mid 1990's.

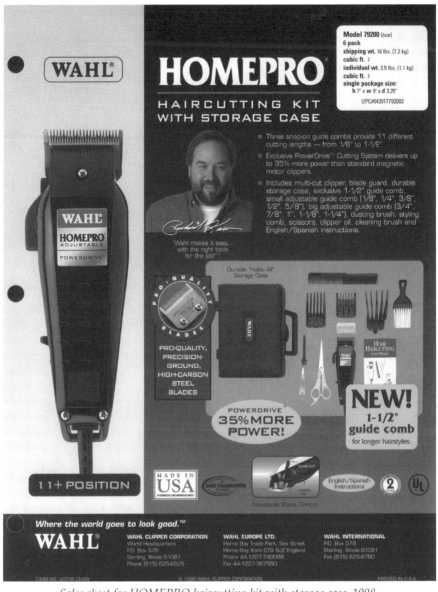

Sales sheet for HOMEPRO haircutting kit with storage case, 1998.

designed to solve the unique shaving problems of the black man

Men with very curly hair have special beard problems. Their whiskers are so curly they tend to grow back into the skin, causing ingrown hair and razor bumps.

Traditional razors, with slotted or mesh heads, often pass right over the whiskers without cutting them off. And safety razors often cut "too close" into ingrown hair bumps or leave a sharp, pointed end on the hair that can easily become ingrown.

The SHAVER/SHAPER is designed to end all that. Its open-tooth blade design actually picks up and straightens curly hair as it's cutting them off. And since the SHAVER/SHAPER's high speed cutting blades travel flat across the beard, the whisker is at a 90° angle to the skin when cut. This leaves the whiskers with blunt-cut ends which tend to be less likely to grow back into the skin.

great as an Afro-shaper, too

The precision cutting action of the SHAVER/SHAPER makes it ideal for use in touching up Afro hair styles, too. It can be used to maintain expensive hair styles as well as for defining parts, and for trimming around hairlines, necklines and ears.

Wahl shaver/shaper, an indispensable all-around grooming tool for today's black man

WAHL® CLIPPER CORPORATION • STERLING, ILLINOIS 61081 • (815) 625-6525

"World's Largest Manufacturer of Electric Hair Clippers"

Sales sheet for Wahl Shaver/Shaper for black men, 1980.

Home Pro XL Deluxe Haricutting Kit, 1995.

Sales Sheet for the updated Wahl Groomsman, 1995.

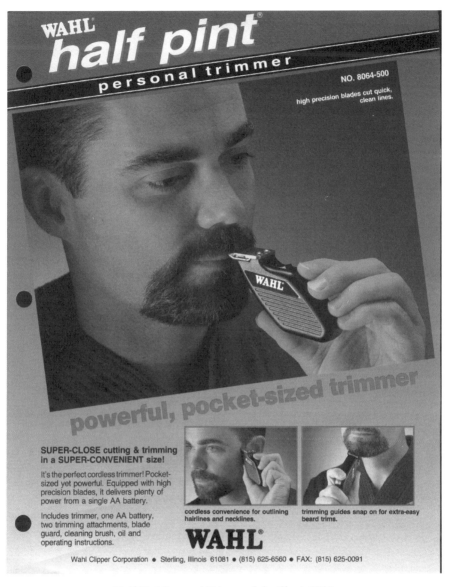

Half Pint Personal Trimmer Sales Sheet, 1994.

Sales sheet for a 12 piece kit, 1995.

A *clipper blade* that cuts like a razor!

The razor clipper blade snaps on the Sterling Eclipse clipper for razor-cut styles that are safer, easier, and a whole lot faster than a conventional razor.

Even if you've never used a razor to cut hair, you can achieve professional results the first time you use the new razor blade.

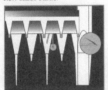

The razor blade can be used on the Sterling Eclipse clipper.

Every razor clipper blade comes with a **free** 25-minute video that shows you exactly how to use it.

The razor blade's revolutionary, high tech design cuts hairs at varying angles and lengths for maximum movement, texture and volume.

No. 2190 Razor Clipper Blade is available where professionals shop.

Short cutting teeth and a super-sharp razor blade cut individual hairs at varying angles and lengths.

(patent applied for)

WAHL CLIPPER CORPORATION
2900 Locust Street • Sterling, IL 61081
Ph:(815) 625-6525 • FAX: (815) 625-0091

A Clipper Blade that cuts like a Razor, 1997.

Rotary Motordriven cordless "Sterling Eslipse" Haircutting Clipper, 1996.

Bravo Sales Sheet, 1984.

The "Peanut" motordriven clipper, 1992.

Ningbo Wahl—Adds Second Factory

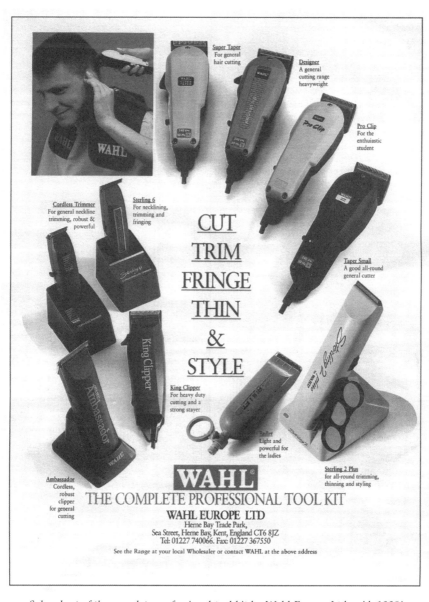

Sales sheet of the complete professional tool kit by Wahl Europe Ltd, mid. 1990's.

Legend 2 Professional cord/cordless Clipper, 1998.

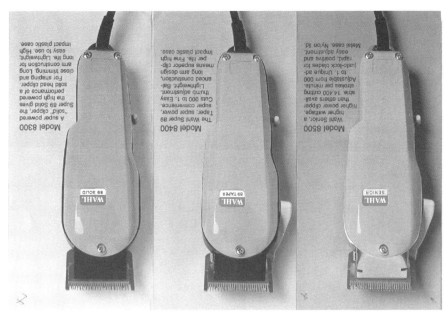

Wahl Senior 1

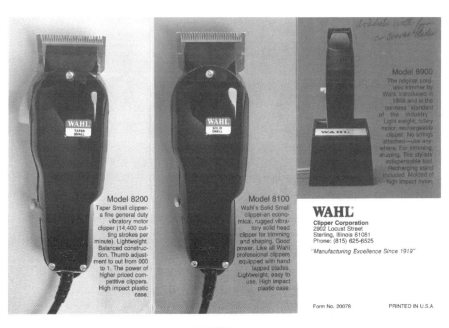

Wahl Taper 1

cordless
beard and
mustache
trimmer

THE GROOMSMAN

Model No. 9900

Shipping wt. 7 lbs.
Individual wt. 1 lb.
6-pack carton
Suggested Retail
$27.98
(Batteries included)

Consumer-Oriented Packaging

Right from the shelf, the Groomsman begins to
sell itself. Classy, dynamic 4-color packaging —
designed for maximum impact — helps to tell the
Groomsman's "benefit story" while providing the
consumer with enough information to make a
positive buying decision.

Groomsmen Shaver

WAHL®
Massagers and Personal Care Products...
FOR THE ACTIVE LIFE YOU LEAD!

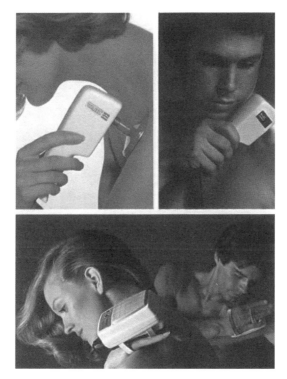

Massagers and Personal Care products

Msgr. Raymond Wahl

Wahl's Lady's Choice Custom Shaver